I0351561

C-1040 CAREER EXAMINATION SERIES

*This is your*
*PASSBOOK for...*

# Supervising Accountant

*Test Preparation Study Guide*
*Questions & Answers*

NLC®

NATIONAL LEARNING CORPORATION®

**National Learning Corporation**

212 Michael Drive, Syosset, NY 11791
(516) 921-8888 • www.passbooks.com
E-mail: info@passbooks.com

# PASSBOOK® SERIES

THE *PASSBOOK® SERIES* has been created to prepare applicants and candidates for the ultimate academic battlefield – the examination room.

At some time in our lives, each and every one of us may be required to take an examination – for validation, matriculation, admission, qualification, registration, certification, or licensure.

Based on the assumption that every applicant or candidate has met the basic formal educational standards, has taken the required number of courses, and read the necessary texts, the *PASSBOOK® SERIES* furnishes the one special preparation which may assure passing with confidence, instead of failing with insecurity. Examination questions – together with answers – are furnished as the basic vehicle for study so that the mysteries of the examination and its compounding difficulties may be eliminated or diminished by a sure method.

This book is meant to help you pass your examination provided that you qualify and are serious in your objective.

The entire field is reviewed through the huge store of content information which is succinctly presented through a provocative and challenging approach – the question-and-answer method.

A climate of success is established by furnishing the correct answers at the end of each test.

You soon learn to recognize types of questions, forms of questions, and patterns of questioning. You may even begin to anticipate expected outcomes.

You perceive that many questions are repeated or adapted so that you can gain acute insights, which may enable you to score many sure points.

You learn how to confront new questions, or types of questions, and to attack them confidently and work out the correct answers.

You note objectives and emphases, and recognize pitfalls and dangers, so that you may make positive educational adjustments.

Moreover, you are kept fully informed in relation to new concepts, methods, practices, and directions in the field.

You discover that you are actually taking the examination all the time: you are preparing for the examination by "taking" an examination, not by reading extraneous and/or supererogatory textbooks.

In short, this PASSBOOK®, used directedly, should be an important factor in helping you to pass your test.

# SUPERVISING ACCOUNTANT

## DUTIES AND RESPONSIBILITIES

Under general direction, with much latitude for independent action or decision, directs and administers the activities of an accounting division or equivalent organizational unit with an accounting or financial function; performs related work.

## EXAMPLES OF TYPICAL TASKS

Devises methods and procedures, plans, assigns, supervises, reviews and coordinates the work of the staff. Supervises and participates in the preparation of periodic budgetary reports, financial reports, and other related accounting reports of a complex nature. Develops audit procedures, forms, techniques and systems for the maintenance of fiscal controls and statistical records. Participates in preparation and revision of accounting manuals and instructions. Makes recommendations regarding departmental policy. Conducts or participates in conferences with all levels in or out of government relating to the functions of the division or unit.

## SUBJECT OF EXAMINATION

The written test will be of the multiple-choice type and may include questions on staff supervision and development; management principles and applications; auditing principles and procedures; accounting systems; cost accounting; partnership and corporate accounting; budgeting and fiscal practices; and other related areas .

# HOW TO TAKE A TEST

## I. YOU MUST PASS AN EXAMINATION

### *A. WHAT EVERY CANDIDATE SHOULD KNOW*

Examination applicants often ask us for help in preparing for the written test. What can I study in advance? What kinds of questions will be asked? How will the test be given? How will the papers be graded?

As an applicant for a civil service examination, you may be wondering about some of these things. Our purpose here is to suggest effective methods of advance study and to describe civil service examinations.

Your chances for success on this examination can be increased if you know how to prepare. Those "pre-examination jitters" can be reduced if you know what to expect. You can even experience an adventure in good citizenship if you know why civil service exams are given.

### *B. WHY ARE CIVIL SERVICE EXAMINATIONS GIVEN?*

Civil service examinations are important to you in two ways. As a citizen, you want public jobs filled by employees who know how to do their work. As a job seeker, you want a fair chance to compete for that job on an equal footing with other candidates. The best-known means of accomplishing this two-fold goal is the competitive examination.

Exams are widely publicized throughout the nation. They may be administered for jobs in federal, state, city, municipal, town or village governments or agencies.

Any citizen may apply, with some limitations, such as the age or residence of applicants. Your experience and education may be reviewed to see whether you meet the requirements for the particular examination. When these requirements exist, they are reasonable and applied consistently to all applicants. Thus, a competitive examination may cause you some uneasiness now, but it is your privilege and safeguard.

### *C. HOW ARE CIVIL SERVICE EXAMS DEVELOPED?*

Examinations are carefully written by trained technicians who are specialists in the field known as "psychological measurement," in consultation with recognized authorities in the field of work that the test will cover. These experts recommend the subject matter areas or skills to be tested; only those knowledges or skills important to your success on the job are included. The most reliable books and source materials available are used as references. Together, the experts and technicians judge the difficulty level of the questions.

Test technicians know how to phrase questions so that the problem is clearly stated. Their ethics do not permit "trick" or "catch" questions. Questions may have been tried out on sample groups, or subjected to statistical analysis, to determine their usefulness.

Written tests are often used in combination with performance tests, ratings of training and experience, and oral interviews. All of these measures combine to form the best-known means of finding the right person for the right job.

## II. HOW TO PASS THE WRITTEN TEST

### *A. NATURE OF THE EXAMINATION*

To prepare intelligently for civil service examinations, you should know how they differ from school examinations you have taken. In school you were assigned certain definite pages to read or subjects to cover. The examination questions were quite detailed and usually emphasized memory. Civil service exams, on the other hand, try to discover your present ability to perform the duties of a position, plus your potentiality to learn these duties. In other words, a civil service exam attempts to predict how successful you will be. Questions cover such a broad area that they cannot be as minute and detailed as school exam questions.

In the public service similar kinds of work, or positions, are grouped together in one "class." This process is known as *position-classification.* All the positions in a class are paid according to the salary range for that class. One class title covers all of these positions, and they are all tested by the same examination.

### *B. FOUR BASIC STEPS*

**1) Study the announcement**

How, then, can you know what subjects to study? Our best answer is: "Learn as much as possible about the class of positions for which you've applied." The exam will test the knowledge, skills and abilities needed to do the work.

Your most valuable source of information about the position you want is the official exam announcement. This announcement lists the training and experience qualifications. Check these standards and apply only if you come reasonably close to meeting them.

The brief description of the position in the examination announcement offers some clues to the subjects which will be tested. Think about the job itself. Review the duties in your mind. Can you perform them, or are there some in which you are rusty? Fill in the blank spots in your preparation.

Many jurisdictions preview the written test in the exam announcement by including a section called "Knowledge and Abilities Required," "Scope of the Examination," or some similar heading. Here you will find out specifically what fields will be tested.

**2) Review your own background**

Once you learn in general what the position is all about, and what you need to know to do the work, ask yourself which subjects you already know fairly well and which need improvement. You may wonder whether to concentrate on improving your strong areas or on building some background in your fields of weakness. When the announcement has specified "some knowledge" or "considerable knowledge," or has used adjectives like "beginning principles of..." or "advanced ... methods," you can get a clue as to the number and difficulty of questions to be asked in any given field. More questions, and hence broader coverage, would be included for those subjects which are more important in the work. Now weigh your strengths and weaknesses against the job requirements and prepare accordingly.

**3) Determine the level of the position**

Another way to tell how intensively you should prepare is to understand the level of the job for which you are applying. Is it the entering level? In other words, is this the position in which beginners in a field of work are hired? Or is it an intermediate or advanced level? Sometimes this is indicated by such words as "Junior" or "Senior" in the class title. Other jurisdictions use Roman numerals to designate the level – Clerk I, Clerk II, for example. The word "Supervisor" sometimes appears in the title. If the level is not indicated by the title, check the description of duties. Will you be working under very close supervision, or will you have responsibility for independent decisions in this work?

**4) Choose appropriate study materials**

Now that you know the subjects to be examined and the relative amount of each subject to be covered, you can choose suitable study materials. For beginning level jobs, or even advanced ones, if you have a pronounced weakness in some aspect of your training, read a modern, standard textbook in that field. Be sure it is up to date and has general coverage. Such books are normally available at your library, and the librarian will be glad to help you locate one. For entry-level positions, questions of appropriate difficulty are chosen – neither highly advanced questions, nor those too simple. Such questions require careful thought but not advanced training.

If the position for which you are applying is technical or advanced, you will read more advanced, specialized material. If you are already familiar with the basic principles of your field, elementary textbooks would waste your time. Concentrate on advanced textbooks and technical periodicals. Think through the concepts and review difficult problems in your field.

These are all general sources. You can get more ideas on your own initiative, following these leads. For example, training manuals and publications of the government agency which employs workers in your field can be useful, particularly for technical and professional positions. A letter or visit to the government department involved may result in more specific study suggestions, and certainly will provide you with a more definite idea of the exact nature of the position you are seeking.

III. KINDS OF TESTS

Tests are used for purposes other than measuring knowledge and ability to perform specified duties. For some positions, it is equally important to test ability to make adjustments to new situations or to profit from training. In others, basic mental abilities not dependent on information are essential. Questions which test these things may not appear as pertinent to the duties of the position as those which test for knowledge and information. Yet they are often highly important parts of a fair examination. For very general questions, it is almost impossible to help you direct your study efforts. What we can do is to point out some of the more common of these general abilities needed in public service positions and describe some typical questions.

1) General information

Broad, general information has been found useful for predicting job success in some kinds of work. This is tested in a variety of ways, from vocabulary lists to questions about current events. Basic background in some field of work, such as sociology or economics, may be sampled in a group of questions. Often these are principles which have become familiar to most persons through exposure rather than through formal training. It is difficult to advise you how to study for these questions; being alert to the world around you is our best suggestion.

2) Verbal ability

An example of an ability needed in many positions is verbal or language ability. Verbal ability is, in brief, the ability to use and understand words. Vocabulary and grammar tests are typical measures of this ability. Reading comprehension or paragraph interpretation questions are common in many kinds of civil service tests. You are given a paragraph of written material and asked to find its central meaning.

3) Numerical ability

Number skills can be tested by the familiar arithmetic problem, by checking paired lists of numbers to see which are alike and which are different, or by interpreting charts and graphs. In the latter test, a graph may be printed in the test booklet which you are asked to use as the basis for answering questions.

4) Observation

A popular test for law-enforcement positions is the observation test. A picture is shown to you for several minutes, then taken away. Questions about the picture test your ability to observe both details and larger elements.

5) Following directions

In many positions in the public service, the employee must be able to carry out written instructions dependably and accurately. You may be given a chart with several columns, each column listing a variety of information. The questions require you to carry out directions involving the information given in the chart.

6) Skills and aptitudes

Performance tests effectively measure some manual skills and aptitudes. When the skill is one in which you are trained, such as typing or shorthand, you can practice. These tests are often very much like those given in business school or high school courses. For many of the other skills and aptitudes, however, no short-time preparation can be made. Skills and abilities natural to you or that you have developed throughout your lifetime are being tested.

Many of the general questions just described provide all the data needed to answer the questions and ask you to use your reasoning ability to find the answers. Your best preparation for these tests, as well as for tests of facts and ideas, is to be at your physical and mental best. You, no doubt, have your own methods of getting into an exam-taking mood and keeping "in shape." The next section lists some ideas on this subject.

## IV. KINDS OF QUESTIONS

Only rarely is the "essay" question, which you answer in narrative form, used in civil service tests. Civil service tests are usually of the short-answer type. Full instructions for answering these questions will be given to you at the examination. But in case this is your first experience with short-answer questions and separate answer sheets, here is what you need to know:

**1) Multiple-choice Questions**

Most popular of the short-answer questions is the "multiple choice" or "best answer" question. It can be used, for example, to test for factual knowledge, ability to solve problems or judgment in meeting situations found at work.

A multiple-choice question is normally one of three types—

- It can begin with an incomplete statement followed by several possible endings. You are to find the one ending which *best* completes the statement, although some of the others may not be entirely wrong.
- It can also be a complete statement in the form of a question which is answered by choosing one of the statements listed.

- It can be in the form of a problem – again you select the best answer.

Here is an example of a multiple-choice question with a discussion which should give you some clues as to the method for choosing the right answer:

When an employee has a complaint about his assignment, the action which will *best* help him overcome his difficulty is to

A. discuss his difficulty with his coworkers
B. take the problem to the head of the organization
C. take the problem to the person who gave him the assignment
D. say nothing to anyone about his complaint

In answering this question, you should study each of the choices to find which is best. Consider choice "A" – Certainly an employee may discuss his complaint with fellow employees, but no change or improvement can result, and the complaint remains unresolved. Choice "B" is a poor choice since the head of the organization probably does not know what assignment you have been given, and taking your problem to him is known as "going over the head" of the supervisor. The supervisor, or person who made the assignment, is the person who can clarify it or correct any injustice. Choice "C" is, therefore, correct. To say nothing, as in choice "D," is unwise. Supervisors have and interest in knowing the problems employees are facing, and the employee is seeking a solution to his problem.

**2) True/False Questions**

The "true/false" or "right/wrong" form of question is sometimes used. Here a complete statement is given. Your job is to decide whether the statement is right or wrong.

SAMPLE: A roaming cell-phone call to a nearby city costs less than a non-roaming call to a distant city.

This statement is wrong, or false, since roaming calls are more expensive.

This is not a complete list of all possible question forms, although most of the others are variations of these common types. You will always get complete directions for answering questions. Be sure you understand *how* to mark your answers – ask questions until you do.

V. RECORDING YOUR ANSWERS

Computer terminals are used more and more today for many different kinds of exams.

For an examination with very few applicants, you may be told to record your answers in the test booklet itself. Separate answer sheets are much more common. If this separate answer sheet is to be scored by machine – and this is often the case – it is highly important that you mark your answers correctly in order to get credit.

An electronic scoring machine is often used in civil service offices because of the speed with which papers can be scored. Machine-scored answer sheets must be marked with a pencil, which will be given to you. This pencil has a high graphite content which responds to the electronic scoring machine. As a matter of fact, stray dots may register as answers, so do not let your pencil rest on the answer sheet while you are pondering the correct answer. Also, if your pencil lead breaks or is otherwise defective, ask for another.

Since the answer sheet will be dropped in a slot in the scoring machine, be careful not to bend the corners or get the paper crumpled.

The answer sheet normally has five vertical columns of numbers, with 30 numbers to a column. These numbers correspond to the question numbers in your test booklet. After each number, going across the page are four or five pairs of dotted lines. These short dotted lines have small letters or numbers above them. The first two pairs may also have a "T" or "F" above the letters. This indicates that the first two pairs only are to be used if the questions are of the true-false type. If the questions are multiple choice, disregard the "T" and "F" and pay attention only to the small letters or numbers.

Answer your questions in the manner of the sample that follows:

32. The largest city in the United States is
    A. Washington, D.C.
    B. New York City
    C. Chicago
    D. Detroit
    E. San Francisco

1) Choose the answer you think is best. (New York City is the largest, so "B" is correct.)
2) Find the row of dotted lines numbered the same as the question you are answering. (Find row number 32)
3) Find the pair of dotted lines corresponding to the answer. (Find the pair of lines under the mark "B.")
4) Make a solid black mark between the dotted lines.

## VI. BEFORE THE TEST

Common sense will help you find procedures to follow to get ready for an examination. Too many of us, however, overlook these sensible measures. Indeed, nervousness and fatigue have been found to be the most serious reasons why applicants fail to do their best on civil service tests. Here is a list of reminders:

- Begin your preparation early – Don't wait until the last minute to go scurrying around for books and materials or to find out what the position is all about.
- Prepare continuously – An hour a night for a week is better than an all-night cram session. This has been definitely established. What is more, a night a week for a month will return better dividends than crowding your study into a shorter period of time.
- Locate the place of the exam – You have been sent a notice telling you when and where to report for the examination. If the location is in a different town or otherwise unfamiliar to you, it would be well to inquire the best route and learn something about the building.
- Relax the night before the test – Allow your mind to rest. Do not study at all that night. Plan some mild recreation or diversion; then go to bed early and get a good night's sleep.
- Get up early enough to make a leisurely trip to the place for the test – This way unforeseen events, traffic snarls, unfamiliar buildings, etc. will not upset you.
- Dress comfortably – A written test is not a fashion show. You will be known by number and not by name, so wear something comfortable.

- Leave excess paraphernalia at home – Shopping bags and odd bundles will get in your way. You need bring only the items mentioned in the official notice you received; usually everything you need is provided. Do not bring reference books to the exam. They will only confuse those last minutes and be taken away from you when in the test room.
- Arrive somewhat ahead of time – If because of transportation schedules you must get there very early, bring a newspaper or magazine to take your mind off yourself while waiting.
- Locate the examination room – When you have found the proper room, you will be directed to the seat or part of the room where you will sit. Sometimes you are given a sheet of instructions to read while you are waiting. Do not fill out any forms until you are told to do so; just read them and be prepared.
- Relax and prepare to listen to the instructions
- If you have any physical problem that may keep you from doing your best, be sure to tell the test administrator. If you are sick or in poor health, you really cannot do your best on the exam. You can come back and take the test some other time.

## VII. AT THE TEST

The day of the test is here and you have the test booklet in your hand. The temptation to get going is very strong. Caution! There is more to success than knowing the right answers. You must know how to identify your papers and understand variations in the type of short-answer question used in this particular examination. Follow these suggestions for maximum results from your efforts:

**1) Cooperate with the monitor**

The test administrator has a duty to create a situation in which you can be as much at ease as possible. He will give instructions, tell you when to begin, check to see that you are marking your answer sheet correctly, and so on. He is not there to guard you, although he will see that your competitors do not take unfair advantage. He wants to help you do your best.

**2) Listen to all instructions**

Don't jump the gun! Wait until you understand all directions. In most civil service tests you get more time than you need to answer the questions. So don't be in a hurry. Read each word of instructions until you clearly understand the meaning. Study the examples, listen to all announcements and follow directions. Ask questions if you do not understand what to do.

**3) Identify your papers**

Civil service exams are usually identified by number only. You will be assigned a number; you must not put your name on your test papers. Be sure to copy your number correctly. Since more than one exam may be given, copy your exact examination title.

**4) Plan your time**

Unless you are told that a test is a "speed" or "rate of work" test, speed itself is usually not important. Time enough to answer all the questions will be provided, but this does not mean that you have all day. An overall time limit has been set. Divide the total time (in minutes) by the number of questions to determine the approximate time you have for each question.

**5) Do not linger over difficult questions**

If you come across a difficult question, mark it with a paper clip (useful to have along) and come back to it when you have been through the booklet. One caution if you do this – be sure to skip a number on your answer sheet as well. Check often to be sure that you have not lost your place and that you are marking in the row numbered the same as the question you are answering.

**6) Read the questions**

Be sure you know what the question asks! Many capable people are unsuccessful because they failed to *read* the questions correctly.

**7) Answer all questions**

Unless you have been instructed that a penalty will be deducted for incorrect answers, it is better to guess than to omit a question.

**8) Speed tests**

It is often better NOT to guess on speed tests. It has been found that on timed tests people are tempted to spend the last few seconds before time is called in marking answers at random – without even reading them – in the hope of picking up a few extra points. To discourage this practice, the instructions may warn you that your score will be "corrected" for guessing. That is, a penalty will be applied. The incorrect answers will be deducted from the correct ones, or some other penalty formula will be used.

**9) Review your answers**

If you finish before time is called, go back to the questions you guessed or omitted to give them further thought. Review other answers if you have time.

**10) Return your test materials**

If you are ready to leave before others have finished or time is called, take ALL your materials to the monitor and leave quietly. Never take any test material with you. The monitor can discover whose papers are not complete, and taking a test booklet may be grounds for disqualification.

## VIII. EXAMINATION TECHNIQUES

1) Read the general instructions carefully. These are usually printed on the first page of the exam booklet. As a rule, these instructions refer to the timing of the examination; the fact that you should not start work until the signal and must stop work at a signal, etc. If there are any *special* instructions, such as a choice of questions to be answered, make sure that you note this instruction carefully.

2) When you are ready to start work on the examination, that is as soon as the signal has been given, read the instructions to each question booklet, underline any key words or phrases, such as *least*, *best*, *outline*, *describe* and the like. In this way you will tend to answer as requested rather than discover on reviewing your paper that you *listed without describing*, that you selected the *worst* choice rather than the *best* choice, etc.

3) If the examination is of the objective or multiple-choice type – that is, each question will also give a series of possible answers: A, B, C or D, and you are called upon to select the best answer and write the letter next to that answer on your answer paper – it is advisable to start answering each question in turn. There may be anywhere from 50 to 100 such questions in the three or four hours allotted and you can see how much time would be taken if you read through all the questions before beginning to answer any. Furthermore, if you come across a question or group of questions which you know would be difficult to answer, it would undoubtedly affect your handling of all the other questions.

4) If the examination is of the essay type and contains but a few questions, it is a moot point as to whether you should read all the questions before starting to answer any one. Of course, if you are given a choice – say five out of seven and the like – then it is essential to read all the questions so you can eliminate the two that are most difficult. If, however, you are asked to answer all the questions, there may be danger in trying to answer the easiest one first because you may find that you will spend too much time on it. The best technique is to answer the first question, then proceed to the second, etc.

5) Time your answers. Before the exam begins, write down the time it started, then add the time allowed for the examination and write down the time it must be completed, then divide the time available somewhat as follows:
   - If 3-1/2 hours are allowed, that would be 210 minutes. If you have 80 objective-type questions, that would be an average of 2-1/2 minutes per question. Allow yourself no more than 2 minutes per question, or a total of 160 minutes, which will permit about 50 minutes to review.
   - If for the time allotment of 210 minutes there are 7 essay questions to answer, that would average about 30 minutes a question. Give yourself only 25 minutes per question so that you have about 35 minutes to review.

6) The most important instruction is to *read each question* and make sure you know what is wanted. The second most important instruction is to *time yourself properly* so that you answer every question. The third most important instruction is to *answer every question.* Guess if you have to but include something for each question. Remember that you will receive no credit for a blank and will probably receive some credit if you write something in answer to an essay question. If you guess a letter – say "B" for a multiple-choice question – you may have guessed right. If you leave a blank as an answer to a multiple-choice question, the examiners may respect your feelings but it will not add a point to your score. Some exams may penalize you for wrong answers, so in such cases *only*, you may not want to guess unless you have some basis for your answer.

7) Suggestions
   a. Objective-type questions
      1. Examine the question booklet for proper sequence of pages and questions
      2. Read all instructions carefully
      3. Skip any question which seems too difficult; return to it after all other questions have been answered
      4. Apportion your time properly; do not spend too much time on any single question or group of questions

5. Note and underline key words – *all, most, fewest, least, best, worst, same, opposite,* etc.
6. Pay particular attention to negatives
7. Note unusual option, e.g., unduly long, short, complex, different or similar in content to the body of the question
8. Observe the use of "hedging" words – *probably, may, most likely,* etc.
9. Make sure that your answer is put next to the same number as the question
10. Do not second-guess unless you have good reason to believe the second answer is definitely more correct
11. Cross out original answer if you decide another answer is more accurate; do not erase until you are ready to hand your paper in
12. Answer all questions; guess unless instructed otherwise
13. Leave time for review

b. Essay questions
1. Read each question carefully
2. Determine exactly what is wanted. Underline key words or phrases.
3. Decide on outline or paragraph answer
4. Include many different points and elements unless asked to develop any one or two points or elements
5. Show impartiality by giving pros and cons unless directed to select one side only
6. Make and write down any assumptions you find necessary to answer the questions
7. Watch your English, grammar, punctuation and choice of words
8. Time your answers; don't crowd material

8) Answering the essay question

Most essay questions can be answered by framing the specific response around several key words or ideas. Here are a few such key words or ideas:

M's: manpower, materials, methods, money, management
P's: purpose, program, policy, plan, procedure, practice, problems, pitfalls, personnel, public relations

a. Six basic steps in handling problems:
1. Preliminary plan and background development
2. Collect information, data and facts
3. Analyze and interpret information, data and facts
4. Analyze and develop solutions as well as make recommendations
5. Prepare report and sell recommendations
6. Install recommendations and follow up effectiveness

b. Pitfalls to avoid
1. *Taking things for granted* – A statement of the situation does not necessarily imply that each of the elements is necessarily true; for example, a complaint may be invalid and biased so that all that can be taken for granted is that a complaint has been registered

2. *Considering only one side of a situation* – Wherever possible, indicate several alternatives and then point out the reasons you selected the best one
3. *Failing to indicate follow up* – Whenever your answer indicates action on your part, make certain that you will take proper follow-up action to see how successful your recommendations, procedures or actions turn out to be
4. *Taking too long in answering any single question* – Remember to time your answers properly

## IX. AFTER THE TEST

Scoring procedures differ in detail among civil service jurisdictions although the general principles are the same. Whether the papers are hand-scored or graded by machine we have described, they are nearly always graded by number. That is, the person who marks the paper knows only the number – never the name – of the applicant. Not until all the papers have been graded will they be matched with names. If other tests, such as training and experience or oral interview ratings have been given, scores will be combined. Different parts of the examination usually have different weights. For example, the written test might count 60 percent of the final grade, and a rating of training and experience 40 percent. In many jurisdictions, veterans will have a certain number of points added to their grades.

After the final grade has been determined, the names are placed in grade order and an eligible list is established. There are various methods for resolving ties between those who get the same final grade – probably the most common is to place first the name of the person whose application was received first. Job offers are made from the eligible list in the order the names appear on it. You will be notified of your grade and your rank as soon as all these computations have been made. This will be done as rapidly as possible.

People who are found to meet the requirements in the announcement are called "eligibles." Their names are put on a list of eligible candidates. An eligible's chances of getting a job depend on how high he stands on this list and how fast agencies are filling jobs from the list.

When a job is to be filled from a list of eligibles, the agency asks for the names of people on the list of eligibles for that job. When the civil service commission receives this request, it sends to the agency the names of the three people highest on this list. Or, if the job to be filled has specialized requirements, the office sends the agency the names of the top three persons who meet these requirements from the general list.

The appointing officer makes a choice from among the three people whose names were sent to him. If the selected person accepts the appointment, the names of the others are put back on the list to be considered for future openings.

That is the rule in hiring from all kinds of eligible lists, whether they are for typist, carpenter, chemist, or something else. For every vacancy, the appointing officer has his choice of any one of the top three eligibles on the list. This explains why the person whose name is on top of the list sometimes does not get an appointment when some of the persons lower on the list do. If the appointing officer chooses the second or third eligible, the No. 1 eligible does not get a job at once, but stays on the list until he is appointed or the list is terminated.

## X. HOW TO PASS THE INTERVIEW TEST

The examination for which you applied requires an oral interview test. You have already taken the written test and you are now being called for the interview test – the final part of the formal examination.

You may think that it is not possible to prepare for an interview test and that there are no procedures to follow during an interview. Our purpose is to point out some things you can do in advance that will help you and some good rules to follow and pitfalls to avoid while you are being interviewed.

*What is an interview supposed to test?*

The written examination is designed to test the technical knowledge and competence of the candidate; the oral is designed to evaluate intangible qualities, not readily measured otherwise, and to establish a list showing the relative fitness of each candidate – as measured against his competitors – for the position sought. Scoring is not on the basis of "right" and "wrong," but on a sliding scale of values ranging from "not passable" to "outstanding." As a matter of fact, it is possible to achieve a relatively low score without a single "incorrect" answer because of evident weakness in the qualities being measured.

Occasionally, an examination may consist entirely of an oral test – either an individual or a group oral. In such cases, information is sought concerning the technical knowledges and abilities of the candidate, since there has been no written examination for this purpose. More commonly, however, an oral test is used to supplement a written examination.

*Who conducts interviews?*

The composition of oral boards varies among different jurisdictions. In nearly all, a representative of the personnel department serves as chairman. One of the members of the board may be a representative of the department in which the candidate would work. In some cases, "outside experts" are used, and, frequently, a businessman or some other representative of the general public is asked to serve. Labor and management or other special groups may be represented. The aim is to secure the services of experts in the appropriate field.

However the board is composed, it is a good idea (and not at all improper or unethical) to ascertain in advance of the interview who the members are and what groups they represent. When you are introduced to them, you will have some idea of their backgrounds and interests, and at least you will not stutter and stammer over their names.

*What should be done before the interview?*

While knowledge about the board members is useful and takes some of the surprise element out of the interview, there is other preparation which is more substantive. It *is* possible to prepare for an oral interview – in several ways:

**1) Keep a copy of your application and review it carefully before the interview**

This may be the only document before the oral board, and the starting point of the interview. Know what education and experience you have listed there, and the sequence and dates of all of it. Sometimes the board will ask you to review the highlights of your experience for them; you should not have to hem and haw doing it.

**2) Study the class specification and the examination announcement**

Usually, the oral board has one or both of these to guide them. The qualities, characteristics or knowledges required by the position sought are stated in these documents. They offer valuable clues as to the nature of the oral interview. For example, if the job involves supervisory responsibilities, the announcement will usually indicate that knowledge of modern supervisory methods and the qualifications of the candidate as a supervisor will be tested. If so, you can expect such questions, frequently in the form of a hypothetical situation which you are expected to solve. NEVER go into an oral without knowledge of the duties and responsibilities of the job you seek.

**3) Think through each qualification required**

Try to visualize the kind of questions you would ask if you were a board member. How well could you answer them? Try especially to appraise your own knowledge and background in each area, *measured against the job sought*, and identify any areas in which you are weak. Be critical and realistic – do not flatter yourself.

**4) Do some general reading in areas in which you feel you may be weak**

For example, if the job involves supervision and your past experience has NOT, some general reading in supervisory methods and practices, particularly in the field of human relations, might be useful. Do NOT study agency procedures or detailed manuals. The oral board will be testing your understanding and capacity, not your memory.

**5) Get a good night's sleep and watch your general health and mental attitude**

You will want a clear head at the interview. Take care of a cold or any other minor ailment, and of course, no hangovers.

*What should be done on the day of the interview?*

Now comes the day of the interview itself. Give yourself plenty of time to get there. Plan to arrive somewhat ahead of the scheduled time, particularly if your appointment is in the fore part of the day. If a previous candidate fails to appear, the board might be ready for you a bit early. By early afternoon an oral board is almost invariably behind schedule if there are many candidates, and you may have to wait. Take along a book or magazine to read, or your application to review, but leave any extraneous material in the waiting room when you go in for your interview. In any event, relax and compose yourself.

The matter of dress is important. The board is forming impressions about you – from your experience, your manners, your attitude, and your appearance. Give your personal appearance careful attention. Dress your best, but not your flashiest. Choose conservative, appropriate clothing, and be sure it is immaculate. This is a business interview, and your appearance should indicate that you regard it as such. Besides, being well groomed and properly dressed will help boost your confidence.

Sooner or later, someone will call your name and escort you into the interview room. *This is it.* From here on you are on your own. It is too late for any more preparation. But remember, you asked for this opportunity to prove your fitness, and you are here because your request was granted.

*What happens when you go in?*

The usual sequence of events will be as follows: The clerk (who is often the board stenographer) will introduce you to the chairman of the oral board, who will introduce you to the other members of the board. Acknowledge the introductions before you sit down. Do not be surprised if you find a microphone facing you or a stenotypist sitting by. Oral interviews are usually recorded in the event of an appeal or other review.

Usually the chairman of the board will open the interview by reviewing the highlights of your education and work experience from your application – primarily for the benefit of the other members of the board, as well as to get the material into the record. Do not interrupt or comment unless there is an error or significant misinterpretation; if that is the case, do not hesitate. But do not quibble about insignificant matters. Also, he will usually ask you some question about your education, experience or your present job – partly to get you to start talking and to establish the interviewing "rapport." He may start the actual questioning, or turn it over to one of the other members. Frequently, each member undertakes the questioning on a particular area, one in which he is perhaps most competent, so you can expect each member to participate in the examination. Because time is limited, you may also expect some rather abrupt switches in the direction the questioning takes, so do not be upset by it. Normally, a board member will not pursue a single line of questioning unless he discovers a particular strength or weakness.

After each member has participated, the chairman will usually ask whether any member has any further questions, then will ask you if you have anything you wish to add. Unless you are expecting this question, it may floor you. Worse, it may start you off on an extended, extemporaneous speech. The board is not usually seeking more information. The question is principally to offer you a last opportunity to present further qualifications or to indicate that you have nothing to add. So, if you feel that a significant qualification or characteristic has been overlooked, it is proper to point it out in a sentence or so. Do not compliment the board on the thoroughness of their examination – they have been sketchy, and you know it. If you wish, merely say, "No thank you, I have nothing further to add." This is a point where you can "talk yourself out" of a good impression or fail to present an important bit of information. Remember, *you close the interview yourself.*

The chairman will then say, "That is all, Mr. ______, thank you." Do not be startled; the interview is over, and quicker than you think. Thank him, gather your belongings and take your leave. Save your sigh of relief for the other side of the door.

*How to put your best foot forward*

Throughout this entire process, you may feel that the board individually and collectively is trying to pierce your defenses, seek out your hidden weaknesses and embarrass and confuse you. Actually, this is not true. They are obliged to make an appraisal of your qualifications for the job you are seeking, and they want to see you in your best light. Remember, they must interview all candidates and a non-cooperative candidate may become a failure in spite of their best efforts to bring out his qualifications. Here are 15 suggestions that will help you:

**1) Be natural – Keep your attitude confident, not cocky**

If you are not confident that you can do the job, do not expect the board to be. Do not apologize for your weaknesses, try to bring out your strong points. The board is interested in a positive, not negative, presentation. Cockiness will antagonize any board member and make him wonder if you are covering up a weakness by a false show of strength.

**2) Get comfortable, but don't lounge or sprawl**

Sit erectly but not stiffly. A careless posture may lead the board to conclude that you are careless in other things, or at least that you are not impressed by the importance of the occasion. Either conclusion is natural, even if incorrect. Do not fuss with your clothing, a pencil or an ashtray. Your hands may occasionally be useful to emphasize a point; do not let them become a point of distraction.

**3) Do not wisecrack or make small talk**

This is a serious situation, and your attitude should show that you consider it as such. Further, the time of the board is limited – they do not want to waste it, and neither should you.

**4) Do not exaggerate your experience or abilities**

In the first place, from information in the application or other interviews and sources, the board may know more about you than you think. Secondly, you probably will not get away with it. An experienced board is rather adept at spotting such a situation, so do not take the chance.

**5) If you know a board member, do not make a point of it, yet do not hide it**

Certainly you are not fooling him, and probably not the other members of the board. Do not try to take advantage of your acquaintanceship – it will probably do you little good.

**6) Do not dominate the interview**

Let the board do that. They will give you the clues – do not assume that you have to do all the talking. Realize that the board has a number of questions to ask you, and do not try to take up all the interview time by showing off your extensive knowledge of the answer to the first one.

**7) Be attentive**

You only have 20 minutes or so, and you should keep your attention at its sharpest throughout. When a member is addressing a problem or question to you, give him your undivided attention. Address your reply principally to him, but do not exclude the other board members.

**8) Do not interrupt**

A board member may be stating a problem for you to analyze. He will ask you a question when the time comes. Let him state the problem, and wait for the question.

**9) Make sure you understand the question**

Do not try to answer until you are sure what the question is. If it is not clear, restate it in your own words or ask the board member to clarify it for you. However, do not haggle about minor elements.

**10) Reply promptly but not hastily**

A common entry on oral board rating sheets is "candidate responded readily," or "candidate hesitated in replies." Respond as promptly and quickly as you can, but do not jump to a hasty, ill-considered answer.

**11) Do not be peremptory in your answers**

A brief answer is proper – but do not fire your answer back. That is a losing game from your point of view. The board member can probably ask questions much faster than you can answer them.

**12) Do not try to create the answer you think the board member wants**

He is interested in what kind of mind you have and how it works – not in playing games. Furthermore, he can usually spot this practice and will actually grade you down on it.

**13) Do not switch sides in your reply merely to agree with a board member**

Frequently, a member will take a contrary position merely to draw you out and to see if you are willing and able to defend your point of view. Do not start a debate, yet do not surrender a good position. If a position is worth taking, it is worth defending.

**14) Do not be afraid to admit an error in judgment if you are shown to be wrong**

The board knows that you are forced to reply without any opportunity for careful consideration. Your answer may be demonstrably wrong. If so, admit it and get on with the interview.

**15) Do not dwell at length on your present job**

The opening question may relate to your present assignment. Answer the question but do not go into an extended discussion. You are being examined for a *new* job, not your present one. As a matter of fact, try to phrase ALL your answers in terms of the job for which you are being examined.

*Basis of Rating*

Probably you will forget most of these "do's" and "don'ts" when you walk into the oral interview room. Even remembering them all will not ensure you a passing grade. Perhaps you did not have the qualifications in the first place. But remembering them will help you to put your best foot forward, without treading on the toes of the board members.

Rumor and popular opinion to the contrary notwithstanding, an oral board wants you to make the best appearance possible. They know you are under pressure – but they also want to see how you respond to it as a guide to what your reaction would be under the pressures of the job you seek. They will be influenced by the degree of poise you display, the personal traits you show and the manner in which you respond.

## ABOUT THIS BOOK

This book contains tests divided into Examination Sections. Go through each test, answering every question in the margin. We have also attached a sample answer sheet at the back of the book that can be removed and used. At the end of each test look at the answer key and check your answers. On the ones you got wrong, look at the right answer choice and learn. Do not fill in the answers first. Do not memorize the questions and answers, but understand the answer and principles involved. On your test, the questions will likely be different from the samples. Questions are changed and new ones added. If you understand these past questions you should have success with any changes that arise. Tests may consist of several types of questions. We have additional books on each subject should more study be advisable or necessary for you. Finally, the more you study, the better prepared you will be. This book is intended to be the last thing you study before you walk into the examination room. Prior study of relevant texts is also recommended. NLC publishes some of these in our Fundamental Series. Knowledge and good sense are important factors in passing your exam. Good luck also helps. So now study this Passbook, absorb the material contained within and take that knowledge into the examination. Then do your best to pass that exam.

# EXAMINATION SECTION

# EXAMINATION SECTION

## TEST 1

DIRECTIONS: Each question or incomplete statement is followed by several suggested answers or completions. Select the one that BEST answers the question or completes the statement. *PRINT THE LETTER OF THE CORRECT ANSWER IN THE SPACE AT THE RIGHT.*

1. The owner's equity in a business may derive from which of the following sources? 1.______
   I. Excess of revenue over expenses
   II. Investment by the owner
   III. Accounts payable

   A. I only
   B. II only
   C. III only
   D. I and II
   E. I, II and III

2. Entries made on the books at the end of a period to take care of changes occurring in accounts are called ______ entries. 2.______
   A. fiscal
   B. closing
   C. reversing
   D. correcting
   E. adjusting

3. In accounting, net income should be defined as an increase in 3.______
   A. assets
   B. cash
   C. merchandise
   D. sales
   E. capital

4. Treasury stock is CORRECTLY defined as 4.______
   A. a corporation's own stock that has been issued and then reacquired
   B. new issues of a corporation's stock before they are sold on the open market
   C. stock issued by the United States Office of the Treasury
   D. any stock that a corporation acquires and holds for more than 90 days
   E. any stock held by a corporation that receives dividends in excess of 5 percent of initial cost of the stock

5. The Accumulated Depreciation account should be shown in the financial statements as 5.______
    A. an operating expense
    B. an extraordinary loss
    C. a liability
    D. stockholders' equity
    E. a contra (deduction) to an asset account

6. If fixed expenses are $26,000 and variable expenses are 75 percent of sales, the net income that would result from $500,000 in sales is 6.______
    A. $75,000
    B. $99,000
    C. $200,000
    D. $375,000
    E. $401,000

7. Cost of goods sold is determined by which of the following? 7.______
    A. Beginning inventory plus net purchases minus ending inventory
    B. Beginning inventory plus purchases plus purchase returns minus ending inventory
    C. Beginning inventory minus net purchases plus ending inventory
    D. Purchases minus transportation-in plus beginning inventory minus ending inventory
    E. Net sales minus ending inventory

8. Company X produces chairs of a single type, it has a plant capacity of 50,000 chairs per year and total fixed expenses of $100,000 per year. Variable costs per chair are $2.00 and the current selling price is $5.00 per chair. At the beginning of 2016, the company purchases a specialized machine that costs $10,000, lasts one year, and reduces variable costs to $1.50 per chair. If the company produces and sells at 90 percent of capacity, what is the net income for 2016? 8.______
    A. $8,750
    B. $23,000
    C. $47,500
    D. $50,000
    E. $83,000

9. All of the following T-accounts contain the correct sides that would be used for increasing and decreasing an account EXCEPT 9.______

A.

| Revenue | |
|---|---|
| Decrease | Increase |

B.

| Assets | |
|---|---|
| Increase | Decrease |

C.

| Expenses | |
|---|---|
| Increase | Decrease |

D.

| Owner's Equity | |
|---|---|
| Increase | Decrease |

E.

| Liabilities | |
|---|---|
| Decrease | Increase |

10. Green Corporation with assets of $5,000,000 and liabilities of $2,000,000 has 6,000 shares of capital stock outstanding (par value $300). What is the book value per share? 10.______

A. $200 B. $300
C. $500 D. $833
E. None of the above

11. Of the following, the BEST description of a controlling account is that it is a 11.______

A. schedule of accounts payable
B. purchase form that itemizes merchandise bought
C. ledger that contains a single type of account
D. statement that lists the individual account balances in the creditors' ledger
E. general ledger account that summarizes the balance in the accounts of a subsidiary ledger

12. At the end of the fiscal year, a company estimates that $4,300 of Accounts Receivable will be uncollectible. If, prior to adjustment, the company's Allowance for Bad Debts account has a credit balance of $1,600, what is the APPROPRIATE adjusting entry? 12.______

| | Debit | Credit | Amount |
|---|---|---|---|
| A. | Allowance for Bad Debts | Bad Debts Expense | $4,300 |
| B. | Allowance for Bad Debts | Accounts Receivable | $4,300 |
| C. | Accounts Receivable | Allowance for Bad Debts | $1,600 |
| D. | Bad Debts Expense | Allowance for Bad Debts | $2,700 |
| E. | Bad Debts Expense | Accounts Receivable | $2,700 |

13. A fast-moving widget stamping machine was purchased for cash. The list price was $4,000 with an applicable trade discount of 20 percent and a cash discount allowable of 2/10, n/30. Payment was made within the discount period. Freight costs of $100, F.O.B. origin, were paid. In order to install the machine properly, a platform was built and wiring installed for a total cost of $200. The trial run costs were $300 for labor and $50 for materials. The cost of the machine would be recorded as 13.______

A. $3,626 B. $3,628
C. $3,786 D. $3,828
E. $4,178

14. All of the following expenditures should be charged to an asset account rather than an expense account of the current period EXCEPT the cost of 14.______

A. overhauling a delivery truck, which extends its useful life by two years
B. purchasing a new component for a machine, which serves to increase the machine's productive capacity
C. constructing a parking lot for a leased building
D. installing a new piece of equipment
E. replacing worn-out tires on a delivery truck

15. In a period of rising prices, which of the following inventory methods results in the HIGHEST cost of goods sold? 15.____
   A. FIFO
   B. LIFO
   C. Average cost
   D. Periodic inventory
   E. Perpetual inventory

16. A company forecasts that during the next year it will be able to sell 80,000 units of its special product at a competitive selling price of $10 per unit. The company has the capacity to produce 120,000 units per year. Its total fixed costs are $528,000. Its variable costs are estimated at $3 per unit. The company has the opportunity to sell 10,000 additional units during the same year at a special contract price of $50,000. This special contract will not affect the regular sales volume or price. 16.____
   Acceptance of the contract will cause the year's net income to
   A. increase by $20,000
   B. increase by $26,000
   C. increase by $50,000
   D. decrease by $50,000
   E. decrease by $24,000

17. Which of the following standard cost variances provides information about the extent to which the manufacturing plant of a company was used at normal capacity? 17.____
   A. Materials quantity (usage) variance
   B. Labor efficiency (time) variance
   C. Labor rate variance
   D. Overhead spending (controllable) variance
   E. Overhead volume variance

18. The following information refers to the purchase of merchandise by L Company. List price of merchandise, $1,050; trade discount 20 percent, 2/10, n/30; F.O.B. shipping point; freight cost prepaid by seller and added to the invoice, $100. What is the net amount to be paid to the vendor, within the discount period, for the merchandise? 18.____
   A. $819.00
   B. $901.60
   C. $919.00
   D. $921.20
   E. $923.20

19. X Corporation declares and issues a 5 percent stock dividend on common stock, payable in common stock, shortly after the close of the year. All of the following statements about the nature and effect of the dividend are true EXCEPT: 19.____
   A. total stockholders' equity in the corporation is not changed
   B. dividend does not constitute income to the stockholders
   C. book value per share of common stock is not changed
   D. amount of retained earnings is reduced
   E. amount of total assets is not changed

20. The financial statement prepared to report the financing and investing activities of a business entity for a period of time is called the 20.______
    A. Income Statement
    B. Statement of Retained Earnings
    C. Balance Sheet
    D. Statement of Changes in Owners' Equity
    E. Statement of Changed in Financial Position

21. A feature of the process cost system that is NOT a feature of the job order cost system is 21.______
    A. computation of the equivalent units of production
    B. compilation of the costs of each batch or job produced
    C. use of the Raw Materials Inventory account
    D. preparation of a Cost of Goods Manufactured statement for each accounting period
    E. application of manufacturing overhead on a predetermined basis

22. Net purchases for the year amounted to $80,000. The merchandise inventory at the beginning of the year was $19,000. On sales of $120,000, a 30 percent gross profit on the selling price was realized. The inventory at the end of the year was 22.______
    A. $13,000
    B. $15,000
    C. $17,000
    D. $25,000
    E. $63,000

23. The balance sheet of Harold Company shows current assets of $200,000 and current liabilities of $100,000. The company uses cash to acquire merchandise inventory. As a result of this transaction, which of the following is TRUE of working capital and the current ratio? 23.______
    A. Both are unchanged
    B. Working capital is unchanged; the current ratio increases
    C. Both decrease
    D. Working capital decreases; the current ratio increases
    E. Working capital decreases; the current ratio is unchanged

24. *In determining net income from business operations, the costs involved in generating revenue should be charged against that revenue.* The statement above BEST describes the ______ principle. 24.______
    A. cost
    B. going-concern
    C. profit
    D. matching
    E. business entity

25. Which of the following is the BEST explanation of the amount reported on the balance sheet as accumulated depreciation? 25.____
    A. Self-insurance fund to protect against losses of the related assets from fire or other casualty
    B. Decrease in market value of the related assets
    C. Cash accumulated to purchase replacements as the related assets wear out
    D. Cost of the related assets which has been allocated to operations
    E. Estimated amount needed to replace the related assets as they wear out

---

## KEY (CORRECT ANSWERS)

| | | |
|---|---|---|
| 1. D | 11. E | 21. A |
| 2. E | 12. D | 22. B |
| 3. E | 13. C | 23. A |
| 4. A | 14. E | 24. D |
| 5. E | 15. B | 25. D |
| 6. B | 16. A | |
| 7. A | 17. E | |
| 8. C | 18. E | |
| 9. D | 19. C | |
| 10. C | 20. E | |

---

# TEST 2

DIRECTIONS: Each question or incomplete statement is followed by several suggested answers or completions. Select the one that BEST answers the question or completes the statement. *PRINT THE LETTER OF THE CORRECT ANSWER IN THE SPACE AT THE RIGHT.*

1. What is the number of days' inventory on hand for a firm with cost of goods sold of $750,000 and average ending inventory of $150,000? 1.______
   A. 5
   B. 10
   C. 20
   D. 50
   E. 73

2. During the current year, accounts receivable increased from $27,000 to $41,000, and sales were $225,000. Based on this information, how much cash did the company collect from its customers during the year? 2.______
   A. $211,000
   B. $225,000
   C. $239,000
   D. $252,000
   E. $266,000

3. Accounts receivable turnover helps determine 3.______
   A. the balance of accounts payable
   B. customers who have recently paid their bills
   C. how quickly a firm collects cash on its credit sales
   D. when to write off delinquent accounts
   E. credit sales

4. The income statement is designed to measure 4.______
   A. whether a firm is able to pay its bills
   B. how solvent a company has been
   C. how much cash flow a firm is likely to generate
   D. the financial position of a firm
   E. the results of business operations

5. A company prepares a bank reconciliation in order to 5.______
   A. determine the correct amount of the cash balance
   B. satisfy banking regulations
   C. determine deposits not yet recorded by the bank
   D. double-check the amount of petty cash
   E. record all check disbursements

6. An inventory valuation method usually affects 6.______
   A. the cost of goods sold but not the balance sheet
   B. the balance sheet but not the cost of goods sold
   C. both the income statement and the balance sheet
   D. neither the income statement nor the balance sheet
   E. the cost of goods sold, but not the income statement

7. A liability for dividends is recorded on the __________ date. 7.____
   A. declaration
   B. record
   C. payment
   D. collection
   E. statement

8. Assets are classified as intangible under which of the following conditions? 8.____
   A. They are converted into cash within one year
   B. They have no physical substance
   C. They are acquired in a merger
   D. They are long term and used in operations
   E. They are short term and used in operations

9. Return on assets helps users of financial statements evaluate which of the following? 9.____
   A. Profitability
   B. Liquidity
   C. Solvency
   D. Cash flow
   E. Reliability

10. The accounting concept that emphasizes the existence of a business firm separate and apart from its owners is ordinarily termed the ____ concept. 10.____
    A. business separation
    B. consistency
    C. going-concern
    D. business materiality
    E. business entity

11. Equity investors are most interested in which aspect(s) of a company? 11.____
    I. Book value
    II. Profitability
    III. Cash flow

    A. I only
    B. II only
    C. III only
    D. I and II only
    E. II and III only

12. One disadvantage of the corporation as compared to other types of business organizations is that 12.____
    A. greater legal liability is assigned to stockholders
    B. greater ethical responsibility is expected of officers and employees
    C. greater profit is required by owners
    D. shares of stock can be sold and transferred to new owners
    E. greater tax burden is levied on the entity

13. Land held for future use and not intended for operations should be classified as 13.______
    A. property, plant and equipment
    B. an intangible asset
    C. inventory
    D. an investment
    E. a current asset

14. If an individual borrows $95,000 on July 1 from Community Bank by signing a $95,000, 9 percent, one-year note, what is the accrued interest as of December 31? 14.______
    A. $0
    B. $2,138
    C. $4,275
    D. $6,413
    E. $8,550

15. In the preparation of the Statement of Cash Flows, which of the following transactions will NOT be reported as a financing activity? 15.______
    A. Sale of common stock
    B. Sale of bonds
    C. Issuance of long-term note to bank
    D. Issuance of 30-day note to trade creditor
    E. Purchase of treasury stock

16. A company bought a patent at a cost of $180,000. The patent had an original legal life of 17 years. The remaining legal life is 10 years, but the company expects its useful life will only be six years. When should the cost of the patent be charged to expenses? 16.______
    A. Immediately
    B. Over the next six years
    C. Over the next 10 years
    D. Over the next 17 years
    E. Over the next 40 years

17. How is treasury stock reported on the balance sheet? 17.______
    A. As an increase in liabilities
    B. As an increase in assets
    C. As a decrease in assets
    D. As an increase in stockholders' equity
    E. As a decrease in stockholders' equity

18. The selected accounts below are from TJ Supply's balance sheet. What is TJ Supply's working capital? 18.____

| | |
|---|---|
| Cash: | $40,000 |
| Accounts receivable: | $120,000 |
| Inventory: | $300,000 |
| Prepaid rent: | $2,000 |
| Accounts payable: | $150,000 |
| Salaries payable: | $7,000 |
| Long-term bonds payable: | $200,000 |

A. $40,000
B. $105,000
C. $160,000
D. $305,000
E. $462,000

19. A machine with a useful life of eight years was purchased for $600,000 on January 1. The estimated salvage value is $50,000. 19.____
What is the first year's depreciation by using the double-declining-balance method?

A. $50,000
B. $68,000
C. $75,000
D. $137,500
E. $150,000

20. Newman Corporation uses the allowance method of accounting for its accounts receivable. The company currently has a $100,000 balance in accounts receivable and a $5,000 balance in its allowance for uncollectible accounts. The company decides to write off $4,000 of its accounts receivable. What would be the balance in its net accounts receivable before and after the write-off? 20.____

| | Before | After |
|---|---|---|
| A. | $95,000 | $91,000 |
| B. | $95,000 | $95,000 |
| C. | $100,000 | $96,000 |
| D. | $105,000 | $101,000 |
| E. | $105,000 | $105,000 |

21. Trading securities must be reported on the balance sheet at 21.____

A. historical cost
B. cost plus earnings minus dividends
C. book value
D. fair market value
E. net present value

22. An accrued expense results in 22.______
    A. an accrued liability
    B. an accrued revenue
    C. a prepaid expense
    D. an unearned revenue
    E. a contra owner's equity account

23. The L Company purchased new machinery and incurred the following costs: 23.______

| | |
|---|---|
| Invoice price | $30,000 |
| Freight (F.O.B. shipping point) | $2,000 |
| Foundation for machinery | $1,000 |
| Installation costs | $900 |
| Annual maintenance of machinery | $600 |

The total cost of the machinery is
    A. $30,000
    B. $31,900
    C. $32,000
    D. $33,900
    E. $34,500

24. Which of the following is true of annual depreciation expense? 24.______
    A. It represents the amount required for annual maintenance of a long-term asset
    B. It represents the annual revenue earned by an asset
    C. It allocates the cost of use of a long-term asset to the revenue that it generates
    D. It is required to fulfill the economic entity assumption
    E. It reduces cash

25. The matching concept matches 25.______
    A. customers with businesses
    B. expenses with revenues
    C. assets with liabilities
    D. creditors with businesses
    E. debits with credits

## KEY (CORRECT ANSWERS)

| | | |
|---|---|---|
| 1. E | 11. E | 21. D |
| 2. A | 12. E | 22. A |
| 3. C | 13. D | 23. D |
| 4. E | 14. C | 24. C |
| 5. A | 15. D | 25. B |
| 6. C | 16. B | |
| 7. A | 17. E | |
| 8. B | 18. D | |
| 9. A | 19. E | |
| 10. E | 20. B | |

# EXAMINATION SECTION

## TEST 1

DIRECTIONS: Each question or incomplete statement is followed by several suggested answers or completions. Select the one that BEST answers the question or completes the statement. *PRINT THE LETTER OF THE CORRECT ANSWER IN THE SPACE AT THE RIGHT.*

1. Gross income of an individual for Federal income tax purposes does NOT include 1.____
   A. interest credited to a bank savings account
   B. gain from the sale of sewer authority bonds
   C. back pay received as a result of job reinstatement
   D. interest received from State Dormitory Authority bonds

2. A cash-basis, calendar-year taxpayer purchased an annuity policy at a total cost of $20,000. Starting on January 1 of 2022, he began to receive annual payments of $1,500. His life expectancy as of that date was 16 years. 2.____
   The amount of annuity income to be included in his gross income for the taxable year 2022 is
   A. none B. $250 C. $1,250 D. $1,500

3. The transactions related to a municipal police retirement system should be included in a(n) _____ fund. 3.____
   A. intra-governmental service
   B. trust
   C. general
   D. special revenue

4. The budget for a given cost during a given period was $100,000. The actual cost for the period was $90,000. 4.____
   Based upon these facts, one should say that the responsible manager has done a better than expected job in controlling the cost if the cost is _____ budgeted production.
   A. variable and actual production equaled
   B. a discretionary fixed cost and actual production equaled
   C. variable and actual production was 90% of
   D. variable and actual production was 80% of

5. In the conduct of an audit, the MOST practical method by which an accountant can satisfy himself as to the physical existence of inventory is to 5.____
   A. be present and observe personally the audited firm's physical inventory being taken
   B. independently verify an adequate proportion of all inventory operations performed by the audited firm
   C. mail confirmation requests to vendors of merchandise sold to the audited firm within the inventory year
   D. review beforehand the adequacy of the audited firm's plan for inventory taking, and during the actual inventory-taking states, verify that this plan is being followed

Questions 6-7.

DIRECTIONS: Questions 6 and 7 are to be answered on the basis of the following information.

For the month of March, the ABC Manufacturing Corporation's estimated factory overhead for an expected volume of 15,000 lbs. of a product was as follows:

| | Amount | Overhead Rate Per Unit |
|---|---|---|
| Fixed Overhead | $3,000 | $.20 |
| Variable Overhead | $9,000 | $.60 |

Actual volume was 10,000 lbs. and actual overhead expense was $7,700.

6. The Spending (Budget) Variance was _____ (Favorable). 6.____
   A. $1,300 B. $6,000 C. $7,700 D. $9,000

7. The Idle Capacity Variance was 7.____
   A. $300 (Favorable) B. $1,000 (Unfavorable)
   C. $1,300 (Favorable) D. $8,000 (Unfavorable)

Questions 8-11.

DIRECTIONS: Questions 8 through 11 are to be answered on the basis of the following information.

A bookkeeper, who was not familiar with proper accounting procedures, prepared the following financial report for Largor Corporation as of December 31, 2021. In addition to the errors in presentation, additional data below was not considered in the preparation of the report. Restate this balance sheet in proper form, giving recognition to the additional data, so that you will be able to determine the required information to answer Questions 8 through 11.

LARGOR CORPORATION
December 31, 2021

| | | | |
|---|---|---|---|
| Current Assets | | | |
| Cash | | $110,000 | |
| Marketable Securities | | 53,000 | |
| Accounts Receivable | $261,400 | | |
| Accounts Payable | 125,000 | 136,400 | |
| Inventories | | 274,000 | |
| Prepaid Expenses | | 24,000 | |
| Treasury Stock | | 20,000 | |
| Cash Surrender Value of Officers' Life Insurance Policies | | 105,000 | $722,400 |
| Plant Assets | | | |
| Equipment | | 350,000 | |
| Building | 200,000 | | |
| Reserve for Plant Expansion | 75,000 | 125,000 | |
| Land | | 47,500 | |
| TOTAL ASSETS | | | $1,244,900 |

| | | | |
|---|---|---|---|
| Liabilities | | | |
| Salaries Payable | | 16,500 | |
| Cash Dividend Payable | | 50,000 | |
| Stock Dividend Payable | | 70,000 | |
| Bonds Payable | 200,000 | | |
| Less Sinking Fund | 90,000 | 110,000 | |
| TOTAL LIABILITIES | | | $246,500 |
| | | | |
| Stockholders' Equity: | | | |
| Paid In Capital | | | |
| Common Stock | | 350,000 | |
| | | | |
| Retained Earnings and Reserves | | | |
| Reserve for Income Taxes | 90,000 | | |
| Reserve for Doubtful Accounts | 6,500 | | |
| Reserve for Treasury Stock | 20,000 | | |
| Reserve for Depreciation Equipment | 70,000 | | |
| Reserve for Depreciation Building | 80,000 | | |
| Premium on Common Stock | 15,000 | | |
| Retained Earnings | 366,900 | 648,400 | 998,400 |
| | | | |
| TOTAL LIABILITIES & EQUITY | | | 1,244,900 |

Additional Data

A. Bond Payable will mature eight (8) years from Balance Sheet date.
B. The Stock Dividend Payable was declared on December 31, 2021.
C. The Reserve for Income Taxes represents the balance due on the estimated liability for taxes on income for the year ended December 31.
D. Advances from Customers at the Balance Sheet date totaled $13,600. This total is still credited against Accounts Receivable.
E. Prepaid Expenses include Unamortized Mortgage Costs of $15,000.
F. Marketable Securities were recorded at cost. Their market value at December 31, 2021 was $50,800.

8. After restatement of the balance sheet in proper form and giving recognition to the additional data, the Total Current Assets should be 8.____
A. $597,400 B. $702,400 C. $712,300 D. $827,300

9. After restatement of the balance sheet in proper form and giving recognition to the additional data, the Total Current Liabilities should be 9.____
A. $261,500 B. $281,500 C. $295,100 D. $370,100

10. After restatement of the balance sheet in proper form and giving recognition to the additional data, the net book value of plant and equipment should be 10.____
A. $400,000 B. $447,500 C. $550,000 D. $597,500

11. After restatement of the balance sheet in proper form and giving recognition to the additional data, the Stockholders Equity should be 11.____
A. $320,000 B. $335,000 C. $764,700 D. $874,700

12. When preparing the financial statement, dividends in arrears on preferred stock should be treated as a 12.____
    A. contingent liability
    B. deduction from capital
    C. parenthetical remark
    D. valuation reserve

13. The IPC Corporation has an intangible asset which it values at $1,000,000 and has a life expectancy of 60 years. 13.____
    The appropriate span of write-off, as determined by good accounting practice, should be _____ years.
    A. 17
    B. 34
    C. 40
    D. 60

14. The following information was used in costing inventory on October 31: 14.____

| | | | | |
|---|---|---|---|---|
| October | 1 - | Beginning inventory | 800 units | @ $1.20 |
| | 4 - | Received | 200 units | @ $1.40 |
| | 16 - | Issued | 400 units | |
| | 24 - | Received | 200 units | @ $1.60 |
| | 27 - | Issued | 500 units | |

    Using the LIFO method of inventory evaluation (end-of-month method), the total dollar value of the inventory at October 31 was
    A. $360
    B. $460
    C. $600
    D. $1,200

15. If a $400,000 par value bond issue paying 8%, with interest dates of June 30 and December 31, is sold in November 1 for par plus accrued interest, the cash proceeds received by the issuer on November 1 should be APPROXIMATELY 15.____
    A. $405,000
    B. $408,000
    C. $411,000
    D. $416,000

16. The TOTAL interest cost to the issuer of a bond issue sold for more than its face value is the periodic interest payment _____ amortization. 16.____
    A. plus the discount
    B. plus the premium
    C. minus the discount
    D. minus the premium

17. If shareholders donate shares of stock back to the company, such stock received by the company is properly classified as 17.____
    A. Treasury stock
    B. Unissued stock
    C. Other assets – investment
    D. Current assets - investment

18. Assume the following transactions have occurred: 18.____
    1. 10,000 shares of capital stock of Omer Corp., par value $50, have been sold and issued on initial sale @ $55 per share during the month of June
    2. 2,000 shares of previously issued stock were purchased from shareholders during the month of September @ $58 per share.

    As of September 30, the stockholders' equity section TOTAL should be
    A. $434,000
    B. $450,000
    C. $480,000
    D. $550,000

19. Mr. Diak, a calendar-year taxpayer in the construction business, agrees to construct a building for the Supermat Corporation to cost a total of $500,000 and to require about two years to complete. By December 31, 2021, he has expended $150,000 in costs, and it was determined that the building was 35% completed. 19.____
If Mr. Diak is reporting income under the completed contract method, the amount of gross income he will report for 2021 is
A. none B. $25,000 C. $175,000 D. $350,000

20. When the Board of Directors of a firm uses the present-value technique to aid in deciding whether or not to buy a new plant asset, it needs to have information reflecting 20.____
A. the cost of the new asset only
B. the increased production from use of new asset only
C. an estimated rate of return
D. the book value of the asset

# KEY (CORRECT ANSWERS)

| | | | |
|---|---|---|---|
| 1. | D | 11. | D |
| 2. | B | 12. | C |
| 3. | B | 13. | C |
| 4. | A | 14. | A |
| 5. | D | 15. | C |
| 6. | A | 16. | D |
| 7. | B | 17. | A |
| 8. | C | 18. | A |
| 9. | C | 19. | A |
| 10. | B | 20. | C |

# TEST 2

DIRECTIONS: Each question or incomplete statement is followed by several suggested answers or completions. Select the one that BEST answers the question or completes the statement. *PRINT THE LETTER OF THE CORRECT ANSWER IN THE SPACE AT THE RIGHT.*

Questions 1-3.

DIRECTIONS: Questions 1 through 3 are to be answered on the basis of the following information.

During your audit of the Avon Company, you find the following errors in the records of the company:

1. Incorrect exclusion from the final inventory of items costing $3,000 for which the purchase was not recorded.
2. Inclusion in the final inventory of goods costing $5,000, although a purchase was not recorded. The goods in question were being held on consignment from Reldrey Company.
3. Incorrect exclusion of $2,000 from the inventory count at the end of the period. The goods were in transit (F.O.B. shipping point); the invoice had been received and the purchase recorded.
4. Inclusion of items on the receiving dock that were being held for return to the vendor because of damage. In counting the goods in the receiving department, these items were incorrectly included. With respect to these goods, a purchase of $4,000 had been recorded.

The records (uncorrected) showed the following amounts:
1. Purchases, $170,000
2. Pretax income, $15,000
3. Accounts payable, $20,000; and
4. Inventory at the end of the period, $40,000.

1. The CORRECTED inventory is 1.____
A. $36,000 B. $42,000 C. $43,000 D. $44,000

2. The CORRECTED income for the year is 2.____
A. $12,000 B. $15,000 C. $17,000 D. $18,000

3. The CORRECT accounts payable liabilities are 3.____
A. $16,000 B. $17,000 C. $19,000 D. $23,000

4. An auditing procedure that is MOST likely to reveal the existence of a contingent liability is 4.____
A. a review of vouchers paid during the month following the year end
B. confirmation of accounts payable
C. an inquiry directed to legal counsel
D. confirmation of mortgage notes

Questions 5-6.

DIRECTIONS: Questions 5 and 6 are to be answered on the basis of the following information.

Mr. Zelev operates a business as a sole proprietor and uses the cash basis for reporting income for income tax purposes. His bank account during 2021 for the business shows receipts totaling $285,000 and cash payments totaling $240,000. Included in the cash payments were payments for three-year business insurance policies whose premiums totaled $1,575. It was determined that the expired premiums for this year were $475. Further examination of the accounts and discussion with Mr. Zelev revealed the fact that included in the receipts were the following items, as well as the proceeds received from customers:

$15,000 which Mr. Zelev took from his savings account and deposited in the business account.

$20,000 which Mr. Zelev received from the bank as a loan which will be repaid next year.

Included in the cash payments were $10,000, which Mr. Zelev took on a weekly basis from the business receipts to use for his personal expenses.

5. The amount of net income to be reported for income tax purposes for calendar year 2022 for Mr. Zelev is 5.____
   A. $21,100 B. $26,100 C. $31,100 D. $46,100

6. Assuming the same facts as those reported above, Mr. Zelev would be required to pay a self-employment tax for 2022 of 6.____
   $895.05 B. $1,208.70 C. $1,234.35 D. $1,666.90

7. For the year ended December 2021, you are given the following information relative to the income and expense statements for the Sungam Manufacturers, Inc.: 7.____

| | |
|---|---|
| Sales | $1,000.000 |
| Sales Returns | 95,000 |

<u>Cost of Sales</u>

| | |
|---|---|
| Opening Inventories | $200,000 |
| Purchases During the Year | 567,000 |
| Direct Labor Costs | 240,000 |
| Factory Overhead | 24,400 |
| Inventories End of Year | 235,000 |

On June 5, 2021, a fire destroyed the plant and all of the inventories then on hand. You are given the following information and asked to ascertain the amount of the estimated inventory loss.

| | |
|---|---|
| Sales up to June 15 | $545,000 |
| Purchased to June 15 | 254,500 |
| Direct Labor | 233,000 |
| Overhead | 14,550 |
| Salvaged Inventory | 95,000 |

The ESTIMATED inventory loss is
A. $96,000 B. $162,450 C. $189,450 D. $257,450

8. Losses and excessive costs with regard to inventory can occur in any one of several operating functions of an organization.
The operating function which bears the GREATEST responsibility for the failure to give proper consideration to transportation costs of material acquisitions is
A. accounting B. purchasing C. receiving D. shipping 8.____

Questions 9-17.

DIRECTIONS: Questions 9 through 17 are to be answered on the basis of the following information.

You are conducting an audit of the PAP Company, which has a contract to supply the municipal hospitals with specialty refrigerators on a cost-plus basis. The following information is available:

| | |
|---|---|
| Materials Purchased | $1,946,700 |
| | |
| Inventories, January 1 | |
| Materials | 268,000 |
| Finished Goods (100 units) | 43,000 |
| Direct Labor | 2,125,800 |
| Factory Overhead (40% variable) | 764,000 |
| Marketing Expenses (all fixed) | 516,000 |
| Administrative Expenses (all fixed) | 461,000 |
| Sales (12,400 units) | 6,634,000 |
| | |
| Inventories, March 31 | |
| Materials | 167,000 |
| Finished Goods (200 units) | (omitted) |
| No Work in Process | |

9. The NET INCOME for the period is
A. $755,500 B. $1,237,500 C. $1,732,500 D. $4,980,500 9.____

10. The number of units manufactured is
A. 12,400 B. 12,500 C. 12,600 D. 12,700 10.____

11. The unit cost of refrigerators manufactured is MOST NEARLY
A. $389.00 B. $395.00 C. $398.00 D. $400.00 11.____

12. The TOTAL variable costs are
A. $305,600 B. $464,000 C. $4,479,100 D. $4,937,500 12.____

13. The TOTAL fixed costs are
A. $458,400 B. $1,435,400 C. $1,471,800 D. $1,741,000 13.____

While you are conducting your audit, the PAP Company advises you that they have changed their inventory costing from FIFO to LIFO. You are interested in pursuing the matter further because this change will affect the cost of the refrigerators. An examination of material part 2-317 inventory card shows the following activity:

May 2 – Received 100 units @ $5.40 per unit
May 8 – Received 30 units @ $8.00 per unit
May 15 – Issued 50 units
May 22 – Received 120 units @ $9.00 per unit
May 29 – Issued 100 units

14. Using the FIFO method under a perpetual inventory control system, the TOTAL cost of the units issued in May is 14.____
    A. $690 B. $960 C. $1,590 D. $1,860

15. Using the FIFO method under a perpetual inventory control system, the VALUE of the closing inventory is 15.____
    A. $780 B. $900 C. $1,080 D. $1,590

16. Using the LIFO method under a perpetual inventory control system, the TOTAL cost of the units issued in May is 16.____
    A. $1,248 B. $1,428 C. $1,720 D. $1,860

17. Using the LIFO method under a perpetual inventory control system, the value of the closing inventory is 17.____
    A. $612 B. $380 C. $1,512 D. $1,680

Questions 18-20.

DIRECTIONS: For Questions 18 through 20, consider that the EEF Corporation has a fully integrated cost accounting system.

18. Unit cost of manufacturing dresses was $7.00. Spoiled dresses numbered 400 with a sales value of $800. 18.____
    When it is not customary to have a Spoiled Work account, the MOST appropriate account to be credited is
    A. Work in Process B. Cost of Sales
    C. Manufacturing Overhead D. Finished Goods

19. Overtime premium for factory workers (direct labor) totaled $400 for the payroll period. This was due to inadequate plant capacity. 19.____
    The account to be DEBITED is
    A. Work in Process B. Cost of Sales
    C. Manufacturing Overhead D. Finished Goods

20. A month-end physical inventory of stores shows a shortage of $175. The account to be DEBITED to correct this shortage is 20.____
    A. Stores
    B. Work in Process
    C. Cost of Sales
    D. Manufacturing Overhead

## KEY (CORRECT ANSWERS)

| | | | |
|---|---|---|---|
| 1. | A | 11. | B |
| 2. | A | 12. | C |
| 3. | C | 13. | B |
| 4. | C | 14. | B |
| 5. | A | 15. | B |
| 6. | D | 16. | A |
| 7. | B | 17. | A |
| 8. | B | 18. | A |
| 9. | A | 19. | C |
| 10. | B | 20. | C |

# EXAMINATION SECTION
# TEST 1

DIRECTIONS: Each question or incomplete statement is followed by several suggested answers or completions. Select the one that BEST answers the question or completes the statement. *PRINT THE LETTER OF THE CORRECT ANSWER IN THE SPACE AT THE RIGHT.*

Questions 1-5.

DIRECTIONS: Questions 1 through 5 are to be answered on the basis of the following information.

Assume that you are working in an agency and that you are requested to verify certain financial data with respect to the various business entities described below. This information is required to verify that tax returns and/or other financial reports submitted to your agency are correct.

In an auditing review of the income statements of several business firms (Companies X, Y, and Z), you find the financial information given below. Based upon the account balances shown, select the correct answer for the statement information requested.

1. Company X 1._____

| | |
|---|---|
| Sales | $ 160,000 |
| Opening inventory | $ 70,000 |
| Purchases | $ 80,000 |
| Purchase returns | $ 1,200 |
| Cost of goods sold | $ 127,000 |

The ending inventory based upon the above data is

A. $21,800 B. $23,000 C. $24,200 D. $33,000

2. Company Y 2._____

| | |
|---|---|
| Opening inventory | $ 50,000 |
| Purchases | $ 145,000 |
| Ending inventory | $ 28,500 |
| Gross profit | $ 56,000 |
| Sales and administrative expenses | $ 64,000 |

Sales for the period based upon the above data are

A. $110,500 B. $166,500 C. $222,500 D. $286,500

3. Company Z 3._____

| | |
|---|---|
| Sales for the period | $ 200,000 |
| Net profit | 7% of sales |
| Purchases | $ 180,000 |
| Ending inventory | $ 70,000 |
| Gross profit | $ 60,000 |

Cost of goods sold for Company Z is

A. $110,000 B. $140,000 C. $180,000 D. $250,000

4. The opening inventory of Company Z would be 4.____

A. $10,000 B. $20,000 C. $30,000 D. $80,000

5. The operating expenses for Company Z would be 5.____

A. $10,000 B. $14,000 C. $20,000 D. $46,000

Questions 6-8.

DIRECTIONS: Questions 6 through 8 are to be answered on the basis of the following information, which is taken from the books and records of a business firm.

| | |
|---|---|
| Sales for the calendar year | $52,000 |
| Based upon FIFO Inventory: | |
| Goods available for sale | $46,900 |
| Inventory at December 31 | $12,700 |
| Based upon LIFO Inventory: | |
| Goods available for sale | $46,900 |
| Inventory at December 31 | $10,400 |

6. If FIFO Inventory valuation is used, the gross profit will be 6.____

A. $5,100 B. $15,500 C. $17,800 D. $34,200

7. If LIFO Inventory valuation method is used, the gross profit will be 7.____

A. $2,300 B. $15,500 C. $17,800 D. $36,500

8. If LIFO Inventory method is used, compared with the FIFO method, the cost of goods sold will be 8.____

A. more by $2,300
B. less by $2,300
C. more by $10,400
D. less by $12,700

9. Which one of the following would NOT properly be classified as an asset on the balance sheet of a business firm? 9.____

A. Investment in stock of another firm
B. Premium cost of a three-year fire insurance policy
C. Cash surrender value of life insurance on life of corporate officer; policy is owned by the company and the company is the beneficiary
D. Amounts owing to employees for services rendered

10. Which one of the following would NOT properly be classified as a current asset? 10.____

A. Travel advances to salespeople
B. Postage in a postage meter
C. Cash surrender value of life insurance policy on an officer which policy names the corporation as the beneficiary
D. Installment notes receivable due over 18 months in accordance with normal trade practice

11. Able, Baker, and Carr formed a partnership. Able contributed $10,000; Baker contributed $5,000; and Carr contributed an automobile with a fair market value of $5,000. They have no partnership agreement. The first year, the partnership earned $18,000. The partners will share the profits as follows: Able, ______; Baker, ______; Carr, ______. 11.____

A. $9,000; $4,500; $4,500
B. $6,000; $6,000; $6,000
C. $12,000; $6,000; no share
D. $8,000; $5,000; $5,000

Questions 12-13.

DIRECTIONS: Questions 12 and 13 are to be answered on the basis of the information below.

The XYZ partnership had the following balance sheet as of December 31:

| | |
|---|---|
| Cash | $ 5,000 |
| Other assets | 40,000 |
| Total | $45,000 |
| Liabilities | $12,000 |
| X Capital | 20,000 |
| Y Capital | 10,000 |
| Z Capital | 3,000 |
| Total | $45,000 |

The partners shared profits equally. They decided to liquidate the partnership at December 31.

12. If the other assets were sold for $52,000, each partner will be entitled to a final cash distribution of: 12.____
X, ______; Y, ______; Z, ______.

A. $15,000; $15,000; $15,000
B. $24,000; $14,000; $7,000
C. $20,000; $10,000; $3,000
D. $23,000; $13,000; $6,000

13. If the other assets were sold for $31,000, each partner will be entitled to a final cash distribution of: 13.____
X, ______; Y, ______; Z, ______.

A. $14,000; $5,000; $5,000
B. $8,000; $8,000; $8,000
C. $15,000; $15,000; $15,000
D. $17,000; $7,000; no cash share

14. Items selling for $40 for which there were 10% selling costs were purchased for inventory at $20 each. Selling prices and costs remained steady, but at the date of the financial statement the market price had dropped to $16. The inventory remaining from the original purchase was written down to $16. 14.____
Of the following, it is CORRECT to state that the ______ overstated.

A. cost of sales of the subsequent year will be
B. current year's income is
C. income of the following year will be
D. closing inventory of the current year is

15. Dividends in arrears on a cumulative preferred stock should be reported on the balance sheet as 15.____

A. an accrued liability
B. restricted retained earnings
C. an explanatory note
D. a deduction from preferred stock

16. The effect of recording the payment of a 10% dividend paid in stock would be to 16.____

A. *increase* the current ratio
B. *decrease* the amount of working capital
C. *increase* the total stockholder equity
D. *decrease* the book value per share of stock outstanding

17. The owner of a truck which originally had cost $12,000 but now has a book value of $1,500 was offered $3,000 for it by a used truck dealer. However, the owner traded it in for a new truck listed at $19,000 and received a trade-in allowance of $4,000. 17.____
The cost basis for the new truck following the Federal income tax rules properly amounts to

A. $15,000 B. $16,000 C. $16,500 D. $17,500

18. In planning for purchases to be made during the next month, the following information is to be used: 18.____

| | | |
|---|---|---|
| Budgeted sales for the month | 73,000 | units |
| Inventory at beginning of the month | 19,000 | units |
| Planned inventory at end of the month | 14,000 | units |

From the above information, the amount of units to be purchased is ______ units.

A. 40,000 B. 59,000 C. 68,000 D. 78,000

19. A branch office of a company has the following plan: 19.____

| | |
|---|---|
| Cash balance at beginning of the month | $ 10,000 |
| Planned cash balance at end of the month | $ 15,000 |
| Expected receipts for the month | $ 180,000 |
| Expected disbursements for the month | $ 205,000 |

In order to comply with this plan, the accountant should recommend that the branch obtain an additional allocation of

A. $20,000 B. $25,000 C. $30,000 D. $50,000

20. A company uses the reserve method of bad debt expense and sets up a bad debt account at 2% of sales. The sales were $500,000. The company wrote off $7,500 in accounts receivable. 20.____
The effect of these entries on net income for the period is a(n)

A. $2,500 increase
B. $7,500 decrease
C. $8,000 decrease
D. $10,000 decrease

21. The Daled Corporation has applied to their bank for a $50,000 loan which they will need for 90 days. The bank grants the loan, which will be discounted at 7% interest (use a 360-day year). 21.____
The Daled Corporation will receive credit in their account at the bank for

A. $46,500 B. $49,125 C. $50,000 D. $50,875

Questions 22-25.

DIRECTIONS: Questions 22 through 25 are to be answered on the basis of the information below.

Assume that you are reviewing some accounts of a company and find the following: the Machinery Account and the Accumulated Depreciation - Machinery Account.

Machinery

| | | | | | | | |
|---|---|---|---|---|---|---|---|
| Jan. | 1, | 2014 | Machine | #1 | 20,000 | July 1, 2015 | 6,000 |
| Jan. | 1, | 2015 | Machine | #2 | 16,000 | | |
| July. | 1, | 2015 | Machine | #3 | 12,000 | | |
| Jan. | 1, | 2017 | Machine | #4 | 20,000 | | |

Accumulated Depreciation - Machinery

| | | |
|---|---|---|
| | Dec. 31, 2014 | 5,000 |
| | Dec. 31, 2015 | 10,500 |

Machines are depreciated based upon a four-year life and using the straight-line method. Assume no salvage values.

On July 1, 2015 Machine #1, purchased on January 1, 2014, was sold for $6,000 cash. The bookkeeper debited Cash and credited Machinery for $6,000.

On January 1, 2017, Machine #2 was traded in for a newer model. The new machine had a list price of $34,000. A trade-in value of $10,000 was granted. $20,000 was paid in cash, and the bookkeeper debited Machinery and credited Cash for $20,000. Income tax rules should have been applied making this entry.

If any errors were made in recording the machine values or depreciation, you are asked to correct them and determine the corrected asset values and proper accumulated depreciation.

22. As of December 31, 2014, you determine that these two accounts 22.____

A. are correct
B. are incorrect
C. overstate asset book values
D. understate asset book values

23. As of December 31, 2015, you determine that to correct the Machinery Account balance you should leave it 23.____

A. unchanged
B. increased by $6,000
C. decreased by $14,000
D. decreased by $5,500

24. As of December 31, 2015, you determine that, to reflect the proper balance, the Accumulated Depreciation -Machinery account should 24.____

A. remain unchanged
B. be increased by $10,000
C. be decreased by $10,000
D. be decreased by $5,500

25. After the January 1, 2017 entry, you determine that the Machinery Account should properly 25.____

A. remain unchanged
B. reflect a corrected balance of $52,000
C. reflect a corrected balance of $40,000
D. reflect a corrected balance of $56,000

Questions 26-29.

DIRECTIONS: Questions 26 through 29 are to be answered on the basis of the information below.

Assume that you are assigned to prepare an Audit Report Summary on the L Company. The L Company uses the accrual method and has an accounting year ending December 31. The bookkeeper of the company has made the following errors:

1. A $1,500 collection from a customer was received on December 29, 2016, but not recorded until the date of its deposit in the bank, January 4, 2017.
2. A supplier's $1,900 invoice for inventory items received December 2016 was not recorded until January 2017. (Inventories at December 31, 2016 and 2017 were stated correctly, based on physical count.)
3. Depreciation for 2016 was understated by $700.
4. In September 2016, a $350 invoice for office supplies was charged to the Utilities Expense account. Office supplies are expensed as purchased.
5. December 31, 2016, sales on account of $2,500 were recorded in January 2017, although the merchandise had been shipped and was not in the inventory.

Assume that no other errors have occurred and that no correcting entries have been made. Ignore all income taxes.

26. After correcting the errors reported above, the corrected Net Income for 2016 was 26.____

A. overstated by $100
B. understated by $800
C. understated by $1,800
D. neither understated nor overstated

27. Working Capital on December 31, 2016 was 27.____

A. understated by $600
B. understated by $2,300
C. understated by $1,200
D. neither understated nor overstated

28. Total Assets on December 31, 2017 were 28.____

A. overstated by $1,100
B. overstated by $1,800
C. understated by $850
D. neither understated nor overstated

29. The cash balance was 29.____

A. correct as stated originally
B. overstated by $1,500
C. understated by $2,500
D. understated by $1,500

30. Currently preferred terminology for statements to be presented limits the use of the term *reserve* to 30.____

A. an actual liability of a known amount
B. estimated liabilities
C. appropriations of retained earnings
D. valuation (contra) accounts

# KEY (CORRECT ANSWERS)

| | | | | | |
|---|---|---|---|---|---|
| 1. | A | 11. | B | 21. | B |
| 2. | C | 12. | B | 22. | A |
| 3. | B | 13. | D | 23. | C |
| 4. | C | 14. | C | 24. | C |
| 5. | D | 15. | C | 25. | C |
| 6. | C | 16. | D | 26. | A |
| 7. | B | 17. | C | 27. | A |
| 8. | A | 18. | C | 28. | B |
| 9. | D | 19. | C | 29. | D |
| 10. | C | 20. | D | 30. | C |

# TEST 2

DIRECTIONS: Each question or incomplete statement is followed by several suggested answers or completions. Select the one that BEST answers the question or completes the statement. *PRINT THE LETTER OF THE CORRECT ANSWER IN THE SPACE AT THE RIGHT.*

Questions 1-4.

DIRECTIONS: Questions 1 through 4 are to be answered on the basis of the information below.

Salary expense was listed as a total of $27,600 for the month of June 2017. Withholding taxes were determined to be $7,250 for income taxes and $1,170 for FICA taxes withheld from employees. Payroll deductions for employee pension fund contribution amounted to $2,500.

Assume the employer's FICA tax share is equal to the employees' and that the employer's share of pension costs is double that of the employees and the employer also pays a 3% Unemployment Insurance Tax based upon $20,000 of the wages paid. The employer pays $1,500 for health insurance plans.

1. The amount of cash that must be obtained to meet this net payroll to pay employees is 1.____
   A. $16,680 B. $19,180 C. $20,350 D. $27,600

2. The total payroll tax expense for this payroll period is 2.____
   A. $1,170 B. $1,760 C. $2,340 D. $2,940

3. The total liability for withholding and payroll taxes payable is 3.____
   A. $2,340 B. $7,250 C. $8,420 D. $10,190

4. The expense of the employer for pension and health care fringe benefits is 4.____
   A. $1,500 B. $2,500 C. $5,000 D. $6,500

Questions 5-6.

DIRECTIONS: Questions 5 and 6 are to be answered on the basis of the following.

The Victory Corporation provides an incentive plan whereby its president receives a bonus equal to 10% of the corporate income in excess of $150,000. The bonus is based upon income before income taxes but after calculating the bonus.

5. If the income for the calendar year 2016, before income taxes and before the bonus, were $480,000 and the effective tax rate is 40%, the amount of the bonus would be 5.____
   A. $15,000 B. $30,000 C. $33,000 D. $48,000

6. The income tax expense for calendar year 2016 would be 6.____
   A. $60,000 B. $132,000 C. $180,000 D. $192,000

Questions 7-8.

DIRECTIONS: Questions 7 and 8 are to be answered on the basis of the information below.

A contract has been awarded to the low bidder. This contractor will then commence construction of a building for the total contract price of $30,000,000. The expected cost of construction is $27,510,000. You are given the additional facts:

| | 2017 | 2018 | 2019 |
|---|---|---|---|
| Contract Price as above | $30,000,000 | $30,000,000 | $30,000,000 |
| Actual Cost to Date | 9,170,000 | 13,755,000 | 27,510,000 |
| Estimated Cost to Complete | 18,340,000 | 13,755,000 | --- |
| Estimated Total Cost | $27,510,000 | $27,510,000 | $27,510,000 |
| Estimated Total Income Billings | 2,490,000 | | |
| | $ 9,000,000 | $ 9,000,000 | $ 9,000,000 |

7. For 2017, the income to be recognized on a percentage of completion basis would be 7.____

A. $830,000
B. $2,490,000
C. $3,000,000
D. $9,000,000

8. For 2018, the income to be recognized by the contractor on a percentage of completion basis would be 8.____

A. $415,000
B. $424,500
C. $830,000
D. $1,245,000

9. If the city borrows the $9,000,000 to pay the first billing for the contract above at 10% interest for two years, and the second $9,000,000 at 7% interest for one year, then the interest costs related to this building are approximately 9.____

A. $630,000
B. $1,800,000
C. $2,430,000
D. $3,000,000

10. The books of the Monmouth Corporation show the following: 10.____

| | 2016 | 2015 | 2014 |
|---|---|---|---|
| Average earnings for prior 3 years | $70,000 | $75,000 | $78,000 |
| Net tangible assets | $40,000 | $42,000 | $50,000 |

If it is expected that 15% would be normal earnings on net tangible assets, then the average excess earnings are

A. $7,120
B. $8,333
C. $9,800
D. $10,800

Questions 11-15.

DIRECTIONS: Questions 11 through 15 are to be answered on the basis of the information below.

When balance sheets are analyzed, working capital always receives close attention. Adequate working capital enables a company to carry sufficient inventories, meet current debts, take advantage of cash discounts, and extend favorable terms to customers. A company that is deficient in working capital and unable to do these things is in a poor competitive position.

Below is a Trial Balance as of June 30, 2017, in alphabetical order, of the Worth Corporation.

| | DEBITS | CREDITS |
|---|---|---|
| Accounts Payable | | $ 50,000 |
| Accounts Receivable | $ 40,000 | |
| Accrued Expenses Payable | | 10,000 |
| Capital Stock | | 10,000 |
| Cash | 20,000 | |
| Depreciation Expense | 5,000 | |
| Inventory | 60,000 | |
| Plant & Equipment (net) | 30,000 | |
| Retained Earnings | | 20,000 |
| Salary Expense | 35,000 | |
| Sales | | 100,000 |
| | $190,000 | $190,000 |

11. The Worth Corporation's Working Capital, based on the data above, is 11.___

A. $50,000 B. $55,000 C. $60,000 D. $65,000

12. Which one of the following transactions *increases* Working Capital? 12.___

A. Collecting outstanding accounts receivable
B. Borrowing money from the bank based upon a 90-day interest-bearing note payable
C. Paying off a 60-day note payable to the bank
D. Selling merchandise at a profit

13. The Worth Corporation's Current Ratio, based on the data above, is 13.___

A. 1.7 to 1 B. 2 to 1 C. 2.5 to 1 D. 4 to 3

14. Which one of the following transactions *decreases* the Current Ratio? 14.___

A. Collecting an accounts receivable
B. Borrowing money from the bank giving a 90-day interest-bearing note payable
C. Paying off a 60-day note payable to the bank
D. Selling merchandise at a profit

15. The payment of a current liability, such as Payroll Taxes Payable, will 15.____

A. *increase* the Current Ratio but have no effect on the Working Capital
B. *increase* the Working Capital, but have no effect on the Current Ratio
C. *decrease* both the Current Ratio and Working Capital
D. *increase* both the Current Ratio and Working Capital

16. During the year 2016, the Camp Equipment Co. made sales to customers totaling $100,000 that were subject to sales taxes of $8,000. Net cash collections totaled $92,000. Discounts of $3,000 were allowed. During the year 2016, uncollectible accounts in the sum of $2,000 were written off the books. 16.____
The net change in accounts receivable during the year 2016 was

A. $10,500 B. $11,000 C. $13,000 D. $13,500

17. The Cable Co. received a $6,000, 8%, 60-day note dated May 1, 2016 from a customer. On May 16, 2016, the Cable Co. discounted the note at 6% at the bank. The net proceeds from the discounting of the note amounted to 17.____

A. $5,954.40 B. $6,034.40 C. $6,064.80 D. $6,080.00

18. In reviewing the customers' accounts in the Accounts Receivable ledger for the entire year 2016, the following errors are discovered: 18.____
1. A sale in the amount of $500 to the J. Brown Co. was erroneously posted to the K. Brown Co.
2. A sales return of $100 from the Gale Co. was debited to their account.
3. A check was received from a customer, M. White and Co. in payment of a sale of $500 less 2% discount. The check was entered properly in the cash receipts book but was posted to the M. White and Co. account in the amount of $490.

The difference between the controlling account and its related accounts receivable schedule amounts to

A. $90 B. $110 C. $190 D. $210

19. Assume that you are called upon to audit a cash fund. You find in the cash drawer postage stamps and I.O.U.'s signed by employees, totaling together $425. In preparing a financial report, the $425 should be reported as 19.____

A. petty cash
B. investments
C. supplies and receivables
D. cash

20. On December 31, 2016, before adjustment, Accounts Receivable had a debit balance of $60,000 and the Allowance for Uncollectible Accounts had a debit balance of $1,000. If credit losses are estimated at 5% of Accounts Receivable and the estimated method of reporting bad debts is used, then bad debts expense for the year 2016 would be reported as 20.____

A. $1,000 B. $2,000 C. $3,000 D. $4,000

Questions 21-22.

DIRECTIONS: Questions 21 and 22 are to be answered on the basis of the information below.

Accrued salaries payable on $7,500 had not been recorded on December 31, 2015. Office supplies on hand of $2,500 at December 31, 2016 were erroneously treated as expense instead of inventory. Neither of these errors was discovered or corrected.

21. These two errors would cause the income for 2016 to be 21.____

A. understated by $5,000
B. overstated by $5,000
C. understated by $10,000
D. overstated by $10,000

22. The effect of these errors on the retained earnings at December 31, 2016 would be 22.____

A. understated by $2,500
B. overstated by $2,500
C. understated by $5,000
D. overstated by $5,000

Questions 23-24.

DIRECTIONS: Questions 23 and 24 are to be answered on the basis of the information below.

Arnold, Berg, and Cole operate a retail store under the trade name of ABC. Their partnership agreement provides for equally sharing profits and losses after salaries of $5,000 to Arnold, $10,000 to Berg, and $15,000 to Cole.

23. If the net income of the partnership (prior to salaries to partners) is $21,000, then Arnold's share of the profits, considering all aspects of the agreement, is determined to be 23.____

A. $2,000 B. $3,000 C. $5,000 D. $7,000

24. The share of the profits that apply to Berg, similarly, is determined to be 24.____

A. $2,000 B. $3,000 C. $5,000 D. $7,000

Questions 25-27.

DIRECTIONS: Questions 25 through 27 are to be answered on the basis of the following information.

The Kay Company currently uses FIFO for inventory valuation. Their records for the year ended June 30, 2017 reflect the following:

| | |
|---|---|
| July 1, 2016 inventory | 100,000 units @ $7.50 |
| Purchases during year | 400,000 units @ $8.00 |
| Sales during year | 350,000 units @ $15.00 |
| Expenses exclusive of income taxes | $1,290,000 |
| Cash balance on June 30, 2016 | $250,000 |
| Income tax rate | 45% |

Assume the July 1, 2016 inventory will be the LIFO base inventory.

25. If the company should change to the LIFO as of June 30, 2017, then their income before taxes for the year ended June 30, 2017, as compared with the income FIFO method, will be 25.____

A. *increased* by $50,000
B. *decreased* by $50,000
C. *increased* by $100,000
D. *decreased* by $100,000

26. Assuming the given tax rate (45%), the use of the LIFO method will result in an approximate tax expense for fiscal 2017 of 26.____

A. $45,000
B. $50,000
C. $72,000
D. $94,500

27. Assuming the given tax rate (45%), the use of the LIFO inventory method, compared with the FIFO method, will result in a change in the approximate income tax expense for fiscal 2017 as follows: 27.____

A. *increase* of $22,500
B. *decrease* of $22,500
C. *increase* of $45,000
D. *decrease* of $45,000

28. An accountant in an agency, in addition to his regular duties, has been assigned to train you, a newly appointed assistant accountant. He is not giving you the training you believe you need in order to perform your duties. Accordingly, the most appropriate first step that you, an assistant accountant, should take in order to secure the needed training is to 28.____

A. register for the appropriate courses at the local college as soon as possible
B. advise the accountant in a formal memo that his apparent lack of interest in your training is impeding your progress
C. discuss the matter with the accountant privately and try to discover what seems to be the problem
D. secure such training informally from more sympathetic accountants in the agency

29. You, an assistant accountant, have worked very hard and successfully helped complete a difficult audit of a large corporation doing business in the city. Your supervisor gives you a brief nod of approval when you expected a more substantial degree of recognition. You are angry and feel unappreciated. 29.____
Of the following, the most appropriate course of action for you to take would be to

A. voice your displeasure to your fellow workers at being taken for granted by an unappreciative supervisor
B. say nothing now and assume that your supervisor's nod of approval may be his customary acknowledgement of efforts well done
C. let your supervisor know that he owes you something by repeatedly stressing the outstanding job you've done
D. ease off on your work quality and productivity until your efforts are finally appreciated

30. You, an assistant accountant, have been assisting in an audit of the books and records of businesses as a member of a team. The accountant in charge of your group tells you to start preliminary work independently on a new audit. This audit is to take place at the offices of the business. The business officers have been duly notified of the audit date. Upon arrival at their offices, you find that their records and files are in disarray and that their personnel are antagonistic and uncooperative. Of the following, the MOST desirable action for you to take is to 30.___

A. advise the business officers that serious consequences may follow unless immediate cooperation is secured
B. accept whatever may be shown or told you on the grounds that it would be unwise to further antagonize uncooperative personnel
C. inform your supervisor of the situation and request instructions
D. leave immediately and return later in the expectation of encountering a more cooperative attitude

# KEY (CORRECT ANSWERS)

| | | | | | |
|---|---|---|---|---|---|
| 1. | A | 11. | C | 21. | C |
| 2. | B | 12. | D | 22. | A |
| 3. | D | 13. | B | 23. | A |
| 4. | D | 14. | B | 24. | D |
| 5. | B | 15. | A | 25. | B |
| 6. | C | 16. | B | 26. | C |
| 7. | A | 17. | B | 27. | B |
| 8. | A | 18. | D | 28. | C |
| 9. | C | 19. | C | 29. | B |
| 10. | B | 20. | D | 30. | C |

# EXAMINATION SECTION
# TEST 1

DIRECTIONS: Each question or incomplete statement is followed by several suggested answers or completions.Select the one that BEST answers the question or completes the statement. *PRINT THE LETTER OF THE CORRECT ANSWER IN THE SPACE AT THE RIGHT.*

1. With regard to the requirement of the auditing standard that sufficient and competent evidential matter be obtained, the term competent PRIMARILY refers to the evidence. 1._____
   A. consistency
   B. relevance
   C. measurability
   D. dependability

2. Audit working papers should NOT 2._____
   A. include any client-prepared papers or documents other than those prepared by the auditor
   B. be kept by the auditor after review and completion of the audit except for items required for the income tax return
   C. be submitted to the client to support the financial statements and to provide evidence of the audit work performed
   D. by themselves be expected to provide sufficient support for the auditor's operation

3. Mr. Jason Stone operates a small drugstore as an individual proprietor. During the past year, his books were not properly kept. He asks you, as a CPA, to give him some advice concerning the earnings of his business during the calendar year 2011. A review of his bank accounts and a diary of financial data reveal the information presented below: 3._____
   Deposits made during 2018 per bank statements totaled $226,000. Deposits include investments made by Mr. Shea as well as a loan he obtained from the bank for $25,000.
   Disbursements during 2018 per bank statement totaled $185,000. Included are personal withdrawals of $15,000 and payments on debt of $10,000.
   Net equity of Jason Stone at January 1, 2018 was determined to be $45,000.
   Net equity of Jason Stone at December 31, 2018 was determined to be $75,000.
   During 2018, funds invested by Jason Stone in the business amounted to $6,500.
   Based upon the *net worth* method, net income for the year ended December, 2018 was
   A. $35,000
   B. $38,500
   C. $40,000
   D. $42,000

4. Because of past association, a senior accountant is convinced of the competence and honesty of those who prepared the financial information which he is auditing. He consequently concludes that certain verification procedures are unnecessary. This conclusion by the senior accountant is ill-advised for the proper performance of his present audit MAINLY because the 4._____
   A. members of the staff often lack the specialized skills and training without which verification in an audit cannot proceed
   B. verification procedures depend upon the materiality of the subject matter under examination and not upon the personal characteristics of the individuals involved
   C. nature of opinion expressed in the report issued by the senior accountant, at the end of his audit, is grounded on personal considerations
   D. quality of the senior accountant's independence and his objective examination of the information under review is impaired

5. Of the following statement ratios, the one that represents *a growth ratio is* 5.____
   A. working capital ratio
   B. acid-test ratio
   C. long-term debt to total capitalization
   D. dollar earnings per share

Questions-6-8.

DIRECTIONS: Questions 6 through 8 are to be answered on the basis of the information given below.

During the course of an examinations of the financial statements of a wholesale establishment, the following facts were revealed for the year ended December 3, 2018:

I. Although merchandise: inventory costing $3,000 was on hand and.was-included in the inventory count on December 31, 2018, title had passed and it was billed to the customer on December 31, 2018 at a sale price of $4,500.
II. Merchandise had been billed to the customer on December 31, 2018 in the amount of $5,200 but had not been shipped to him. This merchandise which cost $3,500, was not included in the inventory at the end of the year. The goods were shipped and title passed on January 15, 2019.
III. Merchandise costing $6,000 was recorded as a purchase on December 31, 2018 but was Not included in the inventory at that date.
IV. Merchandise costing $5,000 was received on January 3, 2019, but was recorded on the books as of December 31,2018, and included in inventory as of December 31, 2018. The goods were shipped on December 30, 2018 by the vendor F.O.B. shipping point.
V. An examination of receiving records indicated that merchandise costing $7,000 was received on December 31, 2018. It was included in inventory as of that date but not recorded as a purchase.

6. Adjustments to correct the inventory figure will reflect a net adjustment so as to 6.____
   A. reduce it by $6,500
   B. increase it by $6,500
   C. reduce it by $8,000
   D. increase it by $8,000

7. Adjustments to correct the sales figure will result in a net adjustment to sales of a (n) 7.____
   A. increase by $5,200
   B. decrease by $5,200
   C. increase by $6,300
   D. decrease by $6,300

8. The net adjustment to purchases for the period ending December 31, 2018 will result in a(n) 8.____
   A. increase of $4,000
   B. decrease of $7,000
   C. increase of $7,000
   D. decrease of $4,000

Questions 9-10.

DIRECTIONS: Questions 9 and 10 are to be answered on the basis of the information given below.

A company worth $500,000 of common capital stock, par value $100 per share with retained earnings of $100,000, decides to change its capitalization from a par to a no-par basis. It, therefore, called in its 5,000 shares of par value stock and issued in place thereof 10,000 shares of no-par value stock.

9. The balance in the capital stock account after the change is 9.______
   A. $1,000,000 B. $500,000
   C. $,400,000 D. $200,000

10. The balance in the retained earnings account after the change is 10.______
    A. $90,000 B. $100,000 C. $125,000 D. $250,000

11. Among the assets on the December 31, 2018 balance sheet of the Wolf Corporation was the following: 11.______
    Investment in Sheep Company
    1,000 shares @ $90 bought January 1, 2018 $90,000
    The net worth section of the balance sheet of the Sheep Company on the same date was as follows:

| NET WORTH | | |
|---|---|---|
| Capital Stock, 1,000 shares | | $100,000 |
| Deficit January 1, 2018 | $20,000 | |
| Less Operating Profit 2018 | 15,000 | |
| Deficit December 31, 2018 | | 5,000 |
| Total Net worth | | $ 95,000 |

    The net debit or credit to Consolidated Surplus arising from consolidation of the Sheep Company with the parent Wolf Corporation is
    A. $3,000 credit B. $5,000 credit
    C. $7,000 debit D. $10,000 credit

Questions 12-15.

DIRECTIONS: Questions 12 through 15 are to be answered on the basis of the Trial Balances and the Notes below.

CLIMAX CORPORATION - Trial Balances (000 Omitted)

| | December 31, 2018 | | December 31, 2017 | |
|---|---|---|---|---|
| | Debit | Credit | Debit | Credit |
| Cash | $ 178 | | $ 84 | |
| Accounts Receivable | 300 | | 240 | |
| Allowance for Bad Debts | | $ 13 | | $ 10 |
| Merchandise Inventory | 370 | | 400 | |
| Building & Equipment | 420 | | 360 | |
| Allowance for Depreciation | | 180 | | 190 |
| Accounts Payable | | 220 | | 210 |
| Mortgage Bonds | | 300 | | 300 |
| Unamortized Bond Discount | 18 | | | 21 |
| Capital Stock | | 357 | | 270 |
| Retained Earnings | | 125 | | 90 |
| Net Sales | | $4,200 | | $4,000 |
| Cost of Goods Sold | $2,300 | | $2,100 | |
| Salaries & Wages | 1,500 | | 1,400 | |
| Heat & Utilities | 110 | | 100 | |
| Depreciation | 20 | | 20 | |
| Taxes & Insurance | 10 | | 10 | |
| Interest | 16 | | 15 | |
| Bad Debts | 20 | | 20 | |
| Losso on Equipment Sales (Note 1) | 6 | | — | |
| Dividends Paid (Note 2) | 127 | | 300 | |
| | $5,395 | $5,395 | $5,070 | $5,070 |

NOTES: (1) In 2018 equipment costing $40,000 and having a net bookvalue of $10,000 was sold for $4,000.
(2) Dividends paid in 2018 include a stock dividend of $27,000.

12. The net change in working capital from 2017 to 2018 is 12.______
A. $111,000 B. $130,000 C. $260,000 D. $333,000

13. The amount of funds provided from net income for the year ended December 31, 2018 is 13.______
A. $214,000 B. $244,000 C. $254,000 D. $284,000

14. The amount of funds applied to dividends during the year 2018 is 14.______
A. $100,000 B. $125,000 C. $175,000 D. $202,350

15. The amount of funds applied to building and equipment during the year 2018 is 15.______
A. $100,000 B. $70,000 C. $50,000 D. $30,000

Questions 16-17.

DIRECTIONS: Questions 16 and 17 are to be answered on the basis of the information given below.

The Natural Sales Company issues gift certificates in denominations of $5, $10 and $25. They are redeemable in merchandise having a markup of 30% of Selling Price.

During December, $35,000 of gift certificates was sold and $20,000 was redeemed. It is estimated that 5% of the certificates issued will never be redeemed.

16. The PROPER entry to reflect the current liability with respect to these certificates is 16.______
A. $13,250 B. $14,250 C. $15,250 D. $16,250

17. The cost of the merchandise issued to meet the redeemed certificates is 17.______
A. $11,000 B. $13,000 C. $14,000 D. $17,000

Questions 18-19.

DIRECTIONS: Questions 18 and 19 are to be answered on the basis of the information given below.

Arthur Evans commenced business in 2017 but did not maintain a complete set of proper records. He relied on the bank statements in order to compute his income. All his receipts Are deposited, and all his expenditures are made by check.

His bank statements and other records reflected the following:

| | |
|---|---|
| Bank balance per bank 12/31/2017 | $ 14,735 |
| Bank balance per bank 12/31/2018 | 18,380 |
| Deposits for 2018 per bank statement | 209,450 |
| Deposits in transit 12/31/2017 | 3,590 |
| Deposits in transit 12/31/2018 | 4,150 |

Checks returned with the January 2018 bank statement showed a total of $4,770 checks issued in 2018.

2018 checks not returned by the bank at December 31, 2018 amounted to $5,150.

$6,430 of checks were issued in 2018 in payment of purchases made in 2017.

$9,425 of deposits was made by Mr. Evans in 2018 representing 2017 sales.

Unpaid bills for 2018 amounted to $2,150 on December 31, 2018.

Accounts Receivable for 2018 on December 31, 2018 were $10,930.
Merchandise inventory figures on the following dates were:

| | |
|---|---|
| December 31, 2017 | $13,000 |
| December 31, 2018 | 17,580 |

On July 1, 2018, machinery costing $8,000 was purchased. The estimated life was 5 years with a salvage value of $500.

18. The balance of the cash in the bank according to the books on December 31, 2018 was 18._____
    A. $18,380 B. $17,380 C. $16,380 D. $15,380

19. The Sales Revenue for 2018 was 19._____
    A. $211,515 B. $209,515 C. $208,515 D. $207,515

Questions 20-21.

DIRECTIONS: Questions 20 and 21 are to be answered on the basis of the information given below.

In the examination of an imprest petty cash fund of $600, you were presented with the following fund composition shown below. The date of examining the petty cash fund was the balance sheet date.

| | |
|---|---|
| Currency - bills | $310.00 |
| Cash - coins | 3.15 |
| Postage stamps | 50.00 |
| Sales returns memos for cash refunded to customers | 15.50 |
| Check of one employee dated one month in advance | 75.00 |
| Vouchers for miscellaneous office expenses | 100.85 |
| Sales slip of an employee who purchased company merchandise; the money in payment was taken from the fund, entered as cash sale, and the sales slip inserted in the fund | 45.50 |

20. The corrected balance of petty cash for balance sheet purposes is 20._____
    A. $313.15 B. $319.32 C. $347.53 D. $409.27

21. A correcting journal entry to establish the correct fund balance would increase expenses by 21._____
    A. $100.85 B. $212.31 C. $28.28 D. $139.50

22. The PRIMARY objective of an audit, as generally understood in accounting practice, is to 22._____
    A. assert a series of claims for management as to the financial condition of the company
    B. establish the reliability or unreliability as to the financial statements and supporting accounting records of the company
    C. install special procedures involved in the periodic closing of the accounts prior to the preparation of financial statements of the company
    D. summarize accounts and financial transactions to determine the costs of processes or units of production for the company

Questions 23-25.

DIRECTIONS: Questions 23 through 25 are to be answered on the basis of the information given below.

The following data related to the business operations for the calendar years 2016, 2017, and 2018 of the Wholly Corporation.

| | 2016 | 2017 | 2018 |
|---|---|---|---|
| Net income per books | $170,000 | $190,000 | $140,000 |
| Dividends | 15,000 | 20,000 | 10,000 |
| Purchases made in year 2017 recorded as purchased in 2018 but recorded in inventory in 2017 | | 25,000 | |
| Inventory value December 31, 2018 underestimated | | | 5,000 |
| Depreciation omitted - | | | |
| applicable to 2016 | 3,000 | | |
| applicable to 2017 | | 4,500 | |
| applicable to 2018 | | | 6,000 |
| Overstatement of prepaid advertising as of January 1, 2017 | | 1,500 | |
| Salaries - earned during 2016 paid during 2017 - no accruals | 18,000 | | |
| Payroll taxes on salarie | 1,440 | | |

23. The net profit for 2016 after adjusting for the facts given above is 23.____
A. $146,060 B. $150,050 C. $164,200 D. $192,835

24. The net profit for 2017 after adjusting for facts given 24.____
A. $152,400 B. $165,700 C. $173,145 D. $181,440

25. If the balance of the retained earnings account was $265,000 on January1, 2016, the balance of the retainedearnings account on December 31, 2018 after corrections is 25.____
A. $711,500 B. $525,000 C. $424,360 D. $307,420

Questions 26-30.

DIRECTIONS: Each question numbered 26 through 30 consists of a description of a transaction that indicates a two fold change on the balance sheet. Each of these transactions may be classified under one of the following categories. Examine each question carefully. In the correspondingly numbered space at the right, mark the appropriate space for the letter preceding the category below which BEST represents the charges that should be made on the balance sheet, as of December 31, 2017.

A. Current Assets are *overstated* and Retained Earnings are *overstated*
B. Current Assets are *understated* and Retained Earnings are *understated*
C. Current Liabilities are *overstated* and Retained Earnings are *overstated*
D. Current Liabilities are *understated* and Retained Earnings are *overstated*

26. Goods shipped on consignment out were not included in the final inventory although the entries were properly madefor such consignments. 26.____

27. A number of cash sales made subsequent to the balance sheet date were recorded as sales in the prior periodbefore the balance sheet date. The merchandise was included in inventories. 27.____

28. A cash dividend declared December 21, 2017, payable on January 15, 2018 to stockholders of record as of December 28, 2017, had not been recorded as of December 31, 2017. 28.____

29. The provision for the allowance for doubtful accounts receivable for the current period that should have been made had not been recorded. 29.____

30. Merchandise received by December 31, 2017, and properly included in inventory on that date, was not entered as a purchase until January 2018. 30.____

Questions 31-33.

DIRECTIONS: Questions 31 through 33 are to be answered on the basis of the information given below.

Ten men work as a group on a particular manufacturing operation. When the weekly production of the group exceeds a standard number of pieces per hour, each man in the group is paid a bonus for the excess production; the bonus is in addition to his wages at the hourly rate. The amount of the bonus is computed by first determining the percentage by which the groups production exceeds the standard. One-half of this percentage is then applied to a wage rate of $1.25 to determine an hourly bonus rate. Each man in the group is paid, as a bonus, the bonus rate applied to his total hours worked during the week. The standard rate of production before a bonus can be earned is two hundred pieces per hour.

The production record for a given week was: Hours Worked Production

| Days | Hours worked | Production |
|---|---|---|
| Monday | 72 | 17,680 |
| Tuesday | 72 | 17,348 |
| Wednesday | 72 | 18,800 |
| Thuresday | 72 | 18,560 |
| Friday | 71.5 | 17,888 |
| Saturday | 40 | 9,600 |
| | 399.5 | 99,076 |

31. The rate of the bonus for the week is_____ %. 31.____
    A. 24  B. 20  C. 18  D. 12

32. The bonus paid to the ten-man group for the week is 32.____
    A. $59.93  B. $69.39  C. $95.00  D. $225.00

33. The total wages of one employee who worked 40 hours at a base rate of $1.00 per hour are 33.____
    A. $46  B. $50  C. $54  D. $58

34. A junior accountant reported to his senior that he had performed the operations listed below. 34.____
Which one of the following statements about these operations CORRECTLY describes the operation?
   A. Vouchered the amount of petty cash
   B. Vouchered.the receivables ledger accounts with the sales register
   C. Analyzed the fixed assets account
   D. Checked all entries in the general journal to original evidence

35. Sales during July 2018 for the Major Company were $267,500, of which $170,000 was on account. The sales figure presented to you includes the total sales tax charged to retail customers (assume a sales tax rate of 7%). 35.____
The sales tax liability that should be shown at the end of July 2018 is
   A. $8,300 B. $9,400
   C. $17,500 D. $18,750

Questions 36-37.

DIRECTIONS: Questions 36 and 37 are to be answered on the basis of the information given below.

During the audit of records of the Short Corporation for the year ended December 31, 2018, the auditor was presented with the following information:

The finished goods inventory consisted of 22,000 units carried at a cost of $17,600 at December 31, 2018. The finished goods inventory at the beginning of the year (January 1, 2018) consisted of 24,000 units, priced at a cost of $16,800. During the year, 4,000 units were manufactured at a cost of$3,600 and 6,000 units were sold.

36. To PROPERLY reflect the cost of the finished goods inventory at December 31, 2018, if the FIFO method was used, assuming there was no work-in-process inventory, would require an adjustment of 36.____
   A. $1,400 credit B. $1,400 debit C.$1,600 credit D. $1,600 debit

37. To PROPERLY reflect the cost of the finished goods inventory at December 31, 2018 if the LIFO method was used, assuming there was no work-in-process Inventory, would require an adjustment of 37.____
   A. $2,200 debit B. $2,200 credit C. $4,200 credit D. $4,200 debit

38. Within the general field of auditing, there are internal auditors and independent auditors who differ significantly one from the other in that the latter group: 38.____
   A. is responsible for a more complete, detailed examination of accounting data
   B. conduct standard audits established by custom and usage for a particular trade or industry
   C. direct their investigations primarily to matters of fraud and criminal'misrepresentation
   D. issue reports for the benefit of other interests, such as shareholders and creditors

39. Moreland Corporation sells merchandise at a gross profit of 25% of sales. Fire on the premises of this Corporation on July 16, 2018 resulted in the destruction of the merchandise. The Corporation's merchandise is insured against fire by a $150,000 insurance policy with an 80% co-insurance clause. The Corporation's records show the following: 39.______

| | |
|---|---|
| Sales -- January 1, 2018 to July 16, 2018 | $400,000 |
| Inventory -- January 1, 2018 | $ 65,000 |
| Purchases -- January 1, 2018 to July16, 2018 | $460,000 |
| Merchandise salvaged | $ 25,000 |

The amount of inventory destroyed by fire is
A. $150,000 B. $200,000 C. $225,000 D. $300,000

40. Below are the totals of the cash receipts and disbursement books of the Small Corporation for the calendar year 2018 40.______

Receipts $392,369.72
Disbursements $331,477.87

The bank balance on January 1, 2018 was $38,610.21. The bank balance on December 31, 2018 was $101,918.34. No checks were outstanding on January 1, 2018. Checks out standing on December 31, 2018 amounted to $5,416.28. Undeposited checks on hand December 31, 2018 were $3,000 which are included in the December cash receipts. Bank deposits for the year total $387,643.72.
The total SHORTAGE in cash is
A. $1,726 B. $2,416.28 C. $3,000 D. $3,452

41. A state corporation, all of whose business is done within the city, showed the following for 2018: 41.______

| | |
|---|---|
| Entire net income | $ 1,000 |
| Salaries to Officers deducted in determining entire net income | $ 40,000 |
| Average capital | $ 450,000 |

The corporation's city business tax payable (assuming a 7% rate on income and a .001 rate on capital) is
A. $546 B. $450 C. $70 D. $25

42. Sales revenue serves as the basis for determining taxes. 42.______
A. estate B. excise C. payroll D. property.

43. ABC Corporation operates in the city and would besubjected to the following taxes: 43.______
I. Federal Corporation Income Tax – Surtax 26% and Normal Tax 22%
II. State Franchise Tax - 72%

If income before taxes for 2018 was $370,000 per the federal tax return (after establishing estimate), assuming the rates as noted above, the tax liabilities that should be set up are Federal and State.
A. $180,000; $25,800 B. $177,600; $29,700
C. $165,500; $20,000 D. $171,100; $30,000

44. In the examination of a manufacturing company where inventory values are of a material amount, the client has restricted the extent of the independent CPA's audit examination of his records by not permitting the CPA to observe the taking of inventory at the close of the company's fiscal year. In such a case, which of the following opinions with regard to the audit report would be APPROPRIATE?______opinion. 44.______
 A. Unqualified B. Qualified
 C. Adverse D. Disclaimer of

45. Accounting data are subject to error from a variety of sources and for a variety of reasons. Of the following, the MOST efficient way to lessen this problem is to 45.______
 A. identify'and classify errors as to type and kind as soon as they are detected
 B. provide for machine calculation of accounting datawherever possible
 C. confirm accounting data by independent third parties
 D. designate an individual to be responsible for the accuracy of accounting data

46. Normally, an auditor does NOT rely upon his study and testing of a system of internal control to 46.______
 A. evaluate the reliability of the system
 B. uncover embezzlements of the client's system
 C. help determine the scope of other auditing procedures to be followed
 D. gain support for his opinion as to the accuracy and fairness of the financial statements

Questions 47-50.

DIRECTIONS: Questions 47 through 50 are to be answered on the basis of the information given below.

An office clerk who was not familiar with proper accounting procedures prepared the following financial report for the Dunrite Corporation as of June 30, 2018. In addition to the errors in presentation, additional data below were not considered in the preparationof the report. Restate this balance sheet in proper form, giving recognition to the additional data so that you will be able to determine the required information to answer these questions.

DUNRITE CORPORATION
June 30, 2018

| | | | |
|---|---|---|---|
| CURRENT ASSETS | | | |
| Cash | | | $155,000 |
| Marketable securities | | | 82,400 |
| Investment in affiliated company. | | | 175,000 |
| Treasury stock | | $ 25,500 | |
| Less reserve for trea | | 25,500 | |
| Accounts receivable | | $ 277,800 | |
| Accounts payable | | 135,000 | 142,800 |
| Total current assets | | | $555,200 |
| PLANT ASSETS | | | |
| Equipment | | $ 450,000 | |
| Building | $400,000 | | |
| Reserve for plant expansion | 100,000 | 300,000 | |
| Land. | | 50,000 | |
| Goodwill | | 35,000 | |
| Prepaid expenses | | 12,000 | 847,000 |
| Total Assets | | | $1,402,200 |

| | | | |
|---|---|---|---|
| LIABILITIES | | | |
| Cash dividend payable | | $ 25,000 | |
| Stock dividend payable | | 15,000 | |
| Accrued liabilities | | 15,700 | |
| Bonds payable | $400,000 | | |
| Sinking fund | 325,000 | 75,000 | |
| Total Current Liabilities | | | $ 130,700 |
| | | | |
| STOCKHOLDERS' EQUITY | | | |
| Paid-in capital | | | |
| Common stock | | $550,000 | |
| Retained earnings and reserves | | | |
| Premium common stock | $ 74,000 | | |
| Reserve - doubtful accounts | 7,500 | | |
| Reserve - depreciation of equipment | 140,000 | | |
| Reserve - depreciation building | 170,000 | | |
| Reserve - income-taxes | 50,000 | | |
| Retained earnings | 280,000 | $721,500 | |
| Total Liabilities and Equity | | | $1,402,200 |

ADDITIONAL DATA:

A. The reserve for income taxes represents the balance due on the estimated liability for taxes on income of the current fiscal year.
B. Marketable securities are recorded at cost and have a market value at June 30, 2018 of $81,000. They represent temporary investments.
C. The investment in the affiliated company is a minority interest carried at cost.
D. Bonds payable are due 10 years from the balance-sheet date.
E. The stock dividend payable was declared on June 30, 2018.

47. After restatement of the balance sheet in proper form, and giving recognition to The additional data, the Total Current Assets would be 47.______
A. $509,200 B. $519,700 C. $610,000 D. $735,000

48. After restatement of the balance sheet in proper form, and giving recognition to the Additional data, the Total Current Liabilities would be 48.______
A. $225,700 B. $325,200 C. $352,700 D. $480,000

49. After restatement of the balance sheet in proper form, and giving recognition to the additional data, the Stockholders' Equity shows a total of 49.______
A. $730,100 B. $819,000 C. $910,000 D. $1,019,000

50. After restatement of the balance sheet in proper form, and giving recognition to the additional data, the net book value of the total plant equipment would be 50.______
A. $440,000 B. $590,000 C. $750,000 D. $850,000

# KEY (CORRECT ANSWERS)

1. D
2. C
3. B
4. D
5. D
6. B
7. B
8. C
9. B
10. B
11. D
12. A
13. B
14. A
15. A
16. A
17. C
18. B
19. A
20. A
21. A
22. B
23. A
24. D
25. A
26. B
27. A
28. D
29. A
30. D
31. D
32. A
33. A
34. C
35. C
36. A
37. B
38. D
39. B
40. A
41. A
42. B
43. D
44. D
45. C
46. B
47. B
48. A
49. D
50. B

# TEST 2

DIRECTIONS: Each question or incomplete statement is followed by several suggested answers or completions.Select the one that BEST answers the question or completes the statement. *PRINT THE LETTER OF THE CORRECT ANSWER IN THE SPACE AT THE RIGHT.*

Question 1.

DIRECTIONS: Question 1 is based on the following portion of an income tax withholding table. In answering this question, assume that this table was in effect for the full year.

If the payroll period with respect to an employee is daily:

| And the wages are | | And the number of witholding exemptions claimed is | | | | |
|---|---|---|---|---|---|---|
| At least | But less than | 0 | 1 | 2 | 3 | 4 |
| | | The amount of income tax to be withheld shall be | | | | |
| $172 | $176 | $24.40 | $20.80 | $17.20 | $13.60 | $10.00 |
| 176 | 180 | 24.90 | 21.30 | 17.70 | 14.20 | 10.60 |
| 180 | 184 | 25.50 | 18.30 | 18.30 | 14.70 | 11.10 |

1. K received a daily wage of $176.40 the first 7 pay periods and $182.50 the last 19 pay periods. He claimed 3 exemptions the first 9 pay periods and 4 the rest of the year. Total income tax withheld during the year was 1.______
   A. $288.10
   B. $295.30
   C. $316.50
   D. $317.50
   E. none of the above

2. A voucher contained the following items: 2.______

| | | |
|---|---|---|
| 6 desks @89.20 | | $525.20 |
| 8 chairs @32.50 | | 260.00 |
| | Total | 885.20 |

The terms were given on the voucher as 3%, 10 days; net, 30 days. Verify the computations, which may be incorrect, and calculate the correct amount to be paid. If payment is made within the discount period, the amount to be paid is
   A. $761.64
   B. $771.34
   C. $795.20
   D. $858.64
   E. none of the above

3. Under the income tax law in effect for last year, an individual who is blind on the last day of the taxable year is entitled to claim an exemption of $600 because of such blindness, in addition to any other exemptions to which he may be entitled. 3.______
Richard Roe, who files his income tax returns on the calendar year basis, became permanently blind on December 15 of last year.
In filing his income tax return for last year, Mr. Roe may claim an exemption for blindness of
   A. $300
   B. $550
   C. $574
   D. $600
   E. none of the above

4. The Jones Company had a merchandise inventory of $24,625 on January 1 of last year. During that year, purchases made by the company amounted to $60,000, sales to $85,065, and cost of goo ds sold to $28,060. 4.____
The inventory on December 31 of last year was
   A. $25,065
   B. $28,500
   C. $49,690
   D. $57,005
   E. none of the above

---

# KEY (CORRECT ANSWERS)

1. D
2. B
3. D
4. E

---

# ACCOUNTING

# EXAMINATION SECTION

# TEST 1

DIRECTIONS: Each question or incomplete statement is followed by several suggested answers or completions. Select the one that BEST answers the question or completes the statement. *PRINT THE LETTER OF THE CORRECT ANSWER IN THE SPACE AT THE RIGHT.*

Questions 1-5.

DIRECTIONS: Questions 1 through 5 are to be answered on the basis of the following information.

When balance sheets are analyzed, working capital always receives close attention. Adequate working capital enables a company to carry sufficient inventories, meet current debts, take advantage of cash discounts and extend favorable terms to customers. A company that is deficient in working capital and unable to do these things is in a poor competitive position.

Below is a Trial Balance as of June 30, 2021, in alphabetical order, of the Worth Corporation.

| | Debits | Credits |
|---|---|---|
| Accounts Payable | | $50,000 |
| Accounts Receivable | $40,000 | |
| Accrued Expenses Payable | | 10,000 |
| Capital Stock | | 10,000 |
| Cash | 20,000 | |
| Depreciation Expense | 5,000 | |
| Inventory | 60,000 | |
| Plant & Equipment (net) | 30,000 | |
| Retained Earnings | | 20,000 |
| Salary Expense | 35,000 | |
| Sales | | 100,000 |
| | $190,000 | $190,000 |

1. The Worth Corporation's Working Capital, based on the data above, is 1.____
   A. $50,000 B. $55,000 C. $60,000 D. $65,000

2. Which one of the following transactions increases Working Capital? 2.____
   A. Collecting outstanding accounts receivable
   B. Borrowing money from the bank based upon a 90-day interest-bearing note payable
   C. Paying off a 60-day note payable to the bank
   D. Selling merchandise at a profit

3. The Worth Corporation's Current Ratio, based on the above data, is 3.____
A. 1.7 to 1 B. 2 to 1 C. 2.5 to 1 D. 4 to 3

4. Which one of the following transactions decreases the Current Ratio? 4.____
A. Collecting an account receivable
B. Borrowing money from the bank giving a 90-day interest-bearing note payable
C. Paying off a 60-day note payable to the bank
D. Selling merchandise at a profit

5. The payment of a current liability, such as Payroll Taxes Payable, will 5.____
A. *increase* the current ratio but have no effect on the working capital
B. *increase* the Working Capital, but have no effect on the current ratio
C. *decrease* both the current ratio and working capital
D. *increase* both the current ratio and working capital

6. During the year 2021, the Ramp Equipment Co. made sales to customers totaling $100,000 that were subject to sales taxes of $8,000. Net cash collections totaled $92,000. Discounts of $3,000 were allowed. During the year 2021, uncollectible accounts in the sum of $2,000 were written off the books. 6.____
The net change in accounts receivable during the year 2021 was
A. $10,500 B. $11,000 C. $13,000 D. $13,500

7. The Grable Co. received a $6,000, 8%, 60-day note dated May 1, 2021 from a customer. On May 16, 2021, the Grable Co. discounted the note at 6% at the bank. 7.____
The net proceeds from the discounting of the note amounted to
A. $5,954.40 B. $6,034.40 C. $6,064.80 D. $6,080.00

8. In reviewing the customers' accounts in the Accounts Receivable Ledger for the entire year 2020, the following errors are discovered. 8.____
- A sale in the amount of $500 to the J. Brown Co. was erroneously posted to the K. Brown Co.
- A sales return of $100 from the Gale Co. was debited to their account.
- A check was received from a customer, M. White and Co. in payment of a sale of $500 less 2% discount. The check was entered properly in the cash receipts book but was posted to the M. White and Co. account in the amount of $490.

The difference between the controlling account and its related accounts receivable schedule amounts to
A. $90 B. $110 C. $190 D. $210

9. Assume that you are called upon to audit a cash fund. You find in the cash drawer postage stamps and I.O.U.'s signed by employees, totaling together $425. 9.____
In preparing a financial report, the $425 should be reported as
A. petty cash B. investments
C. supplies and receivables D. cash

10. On December 31, 2020, before adjustment, Accounts Receivable had a debit balance of $60,000 and the Allowance for Uncollectible Accounts had a debit balance of $1,000. 10.____
If credit losses are estimated at 5% of Accounts Receivable and the estimated method of reporting bad debts is used, then bad debts expense for the year 2020 would be reported as
A. $1,000 B. $2,000 C. $3,000 D. $4,000

Questions 11-12.

DIRECTIONS: Questions 11 and 12 are to be answered on the basis of the following information.

Accrued salaries payable on $7,500 had not been recorded on December 31, 2021. Office supplies on hand of $2,500 at December 32, 2021 were erroneously treated as expense instead of inventory. Neither of these errors was discovered or corrected.

11. These two errors would cause the income for 4021 to be 11.____
A. *understated* by $5,000 B. *overstated* by $5,000
C. *understated* by $10,000 D. *overstated* by $10,000

12. The effect of these errors on the retained earnings at December 31, 2021 would be 12.____
A. *understated* by $2,500 B. *overstated* by $2,500
C. *understated* by $5,000 D. *overstated* by $5,000

Questions 13-14.

DIRECTIONS: Questions 13 and 14 are to be answered on the basis of the following information.

Albano, Borrone, and Colluci operate a retail store under the trade name of ABC. Their partnership agreement provides for equaling sharing profits and losses after salaries of $5,000 to Albano, $10,000 to Borrone, and $15,000 to Colluci.

13. If the net income of the partnership (prior to salaries to partners) is $21,000, then Albano's share of the profits, considering all aspects of the agreement, is determined to be 13.____
A. $2,000 B. $3,000 C. $5,000 D. $7,000

14. The share of the profits that apply to Borrone, similarly, is determined to be 14.____
A. $2,000 B. $3,000 C. $5,000 D. $7,000

Questions 15-17.

DIRECTIONS: Questions 15 through 17 are to be answered on the basis of the following information.

The Kay Company currently uses FIFO for inventory valuation. Their records for the year ended June 30, 2021 reflect the following:

| | |
|---|---|
| July 1, 2021 inventory | 100,000 units @ 7.50 |
| Purchases during year | 400,000 units @ $8.00 |
| Sales during year | 350,000 units @ $15.00 |
| Expenses exclusive of income taxes | $1,290,000 |
| Cash balance on June 30, 2021 | $250,000 |
| Income tax rate | 34% |

Assume the July 1, 2021 inventory will be the LIFO Base Inventory.

15. If the company should change to the LIFO as of June 30, 2021, then their income before taxes for the year-ended June 30, 2021, as compared with the income FIFO method, will be 15.____
    A. *increased* by $50,000
    B. *decreased* by $50,000
    C. *increased* by $100,000
    D. *decreased* by $100,000

16. Assuming the given tax rate (45%), the use of the LIFO method will result in an approximate tax expense for fiscal 2021 of 16.____
    A. $45,000
    B. $50,000
    C. $72,000
    D. $94,500

17. Assuming the given tax rate (45%), the use of the LIFO inventory method compared with the FIFO method, will result in a change in the approximate income tax expense for fiscal year 2021 as follows: 17.____
    A. *Increase* of $22,500
    B. *Decrease* of $22,500
    C. *Increase* of $45,000
    D. *Decrease* of $45,000

18. An accountant in an agency, in addition to his regular duties, has been assigned to train a newly appointed assistant accountant. The latter believes that he is not being given the training that he needs in order to perform his duties. Accordingly, the MOST appropriate FIRST step for the assistant accountant to take in order to secure the needed training is to 18.____
    A. register for the appropriate courses at the local college as soon as possible
    B. advise the accountant in a formal memo that his apparent lack of interest in the training is impeding his progress
    C. discuss the matter with the accountant privately and try to discover what seems to be the problem
    D. secure such training informally from more sympathetic accountants in the agency

19. You have worked very hard and successfully helped complete a difficult audit of a large corporation doing business with your agency. Your supervisor gives you a brief nod of approval when you expected a more substantial degree of recognition. You are angry and feel unappreciated. 19.____

Of the following, the MOST appropriate course of action for you to take would be to
   A. voice your displeasure to your fellow workers at being taken for granted by an unappreciative supervisor
   B. say nothing now and assume that your supervisor's nod of approval may be his customary acknowledgment of efforts well done
   C. let your supervisor know that he owes you something by repeatedly stressing the outstanding job you've done
   D. ease off on your work quality and productivity until your efforts are finally appreciated

20. You have been assisting in an audit of the books and records of businesses as a member of a team. The accountant in charge of your group tells you to start preliminary work independently on a new audit. This audit is to take place at the offices of the business. The business officers have been duly notified of the audit date. Upon arrival at their offices, you find that their records and files are in disarray and that their personnel are antagonistic and uncooperative. 20.____
Of the following, the MOST desirable action for you to take is to
   A. advise the business officers that serious consequences may follow unless immediate cooperation is secured
   B. accept whatever may be shown or told you on the grounds that it would be unwise to further antagonize uncooperative personnel
   C. inform your supervisor of the situation and request instructions
   D. leave immediately and return later in the expectation of encountering a more cooperative attitude

# KEY (CORRECT ANSWERS)

| | | | |
|---|---|---|---|
| 1. | C | 11. | C |
| 2. | D | 12. | A |
| 3. | B | 13. | A |
| 4. | B | 14. | D |
| 5. | A | 15. | B |
| 6. | B | 16. | C |
| 7. | B | 17. | B |
| 8. | D | 18. | C |
| 9. | C | 19. | B |
| 10. | D | 20. | C |

# TEST 2

DIRECTIONS: Each question or incomplete statement is followed by several suggested answers or completions. Select the one that BEST answers the question or completes the statement. *PRINT THE LETTER OF THE CORRECT ANSWER IN THE SPACE AT THE RIGHT.*

Questions 1-3.

DIRECTIONS: Questions 1 through 3 are to be answered on the basis of the following information.

The city is planning to borrow money with a 5-year, 7% bond issue totaling $10,000,000 on principle when other municipal issues are paying 8%.

Present value of $1 – 8% - 5 years -68057

Present value of annual interest payments – annuity 8% - 5 years – 3.99271

1. The funds obtained from this bond issue (ignoring any costs relating to issuance) would be, approximately, 1.____
   A. $9,515,390 B. $10,000,000 C. $10,484,620 D. $10,800,000

2. At the date of maturity, the bonds will be redeemed at 2.____
   A. $9,515,390 B. $10,000,000 C. $10,484,610 D. $10,800,000

3. As a result of this issue, the ACTUAL interest costs each year as related to the 7% interest payments will 3.____
   A. be the same as paid ($700,000)
   B. be more than $700,000
   C. be less than $700,000
   D. fluctuate depending on the market conditions

4. Following the usual governmental accounting concepts, the activities of a municipal employee retirement plan, which is financed by equal employer and employee contributions, should be accounted for in a(n) 4.____
   A. agency fund
   B. intragovernmental service fund
   C. special assessment fund
   D. trust fund

Questions 5-7.

DIRECTIONS: Questions 5 through 7 are to be answered on the basis of the following information.

The Balance Sheet of the JLA Corp. is as follows:

| | | | |
|---|---|---|---|
| Current Assets | $50,000 | Current Liabilities | $20,000 |
| Other Assets | 75,000 | Common Stock | 75,000 |
| Total | $125,000 | Retained Earnings | 30,000 |
| | | Total | $125,000 |

5. The working capital of the JLA Corp. is 5.____
A. $30,000 B. $50,000 C. $105,000 D. $125,000

6. The operating ratio of the JLA Corp. is 6.____
A. 2 to 1 B. 2½ to 1 C. 1 to 2 D. 1 to 2½

7. The stockholders' equity is 7.____
A. $30,000 B. $75,000 C. $105,000 D. $125,000

8. This question is based on the following figures taken from a set of books for the year ending June 30, 2021. 8.____

| | Trial Balance Before Adjustments | Trial Balance After Adjustments |
|---|---|---|
| Commissions Payable | cr... | cr $1,550 |
| Office Salaries | dr $9,500 | dr $10,680 |
| Rental Income | cr $4,300 | cr $4,900 |
| Accumulated Depreciation | cr $7,000 | cr $9,700 |
| Supplies Expense | dr $1,760 | dr $1,200 |

As a result of the adjustments reflected in the adjusted trial balance, the net income of the company before taxes will be
A. *increased* by $4,270 B. *decreased* by $4,270
C. *increased* by $5,430 D. *decreased* by $5,430

9. This question is based on the following facts concerning the operations of a manufacturer of office desks. 9.____

| | | | |
|---|---|---|---|
| Jan. 1, 2021 | Goods in Process Inventory | 4,260 units | 40% complete |
| Dec. 31, 2021 | Goods in Process Inventory | 3,776 units | 25% complete |
| Jan. 1, 2021 | Finished Goods Inventory | 2,630 units | |
| Dec. 31, 2021 | Finished Goods Inventory | 3,180 units | |

Sales consummated during the year: 127,460 units

Assuming that all the desks are the same style, the number of equivalent complete units, manufactured during the year 2021 is
A. 127,250 B. 127,460 C. 128,010 D. 131,510

Questions 10-11.

DIRECTIONS: Questions 10 and 11 are to be answered on the basis of the following information.

On January 1, 2021, the Lenox Corporation was organized with a cash investment of $50,000 by the shareholders. Some of the corporate records were destroyed. However, you were able to discover the following facts from various sources.

| | |
|---|---|
| Accounts Payable at December 31, 2021 (arising from merchandise purchased) | $16,000 |
| Accounts Receivable at December 31, 2021 (arising from the sales of merchandise) | $18,000 |
| Sales for the calendar year 2021 | $94,000 |
| Inventory, December 31, 2021 | 20,000 |
| Cost of Goods Sold is 60% of the selling price | |
| Bank loan outstanding – December 31, 2021 | 15,000 |
| Expenses paid in cash during the year | 35,000 |
| Expenses incurred but unpaid as of December 31, 2021 | 4,000 |
| Dividend paid | 25,000 |

10. The CORRECT cash balance is 10.____
    A. $5,600 B. $20,600 C. $38,600 D. $40,600

11. The stockholders' equity on December 31, 2021 is 11.____
    A. $23,600 B. Deficit of $26,400
    C. $27,600 D. $42,400

Questions 12-13.

DIRECTIONS: Questions 12 and 13 are to be answered on the basis of the following facts developed from the records of a company that sells its merchandise on the installment plan.

| Sales | Calendar Year 2020 | Calendar Year 2021 |
|---|---|---|
| Total volume of sales | $80,000 | $100,000 |
| Cost of Goods Sold | 60,000 | 40,000 |
| Gross Profit | $20,000 | $60,000 |
| Cash Collections | | |
| From 2020 Sales | $18,000 | $36,000 |
| From 2021 Sales | | 22,000 |
| Total Cash Collections | $18,000 | $58,000 |

12. Using the deferred profit method of determining thee income from installment sales, the gross profit on sales for the calendar year 2020 was 12.____
    A. $4,500 B. $18,000 C. $20,000 D. None

13. Using the deferred profit method of determining the income from installment sales, the gross profit on sales for the calendar year 2021 was 13.____
    A. $22,000 B. $22,200 C. $60,000 D. None

Questions 14-15.

DIRECTIONS: Questions 14 and 15 are to be answered on the basis of the data developed from an examination of the records of Ralston, Inc. for the month of April 2021.

Beginning Inventory: 10,000 units @ $4.00 each

| | Purchases | | Sales |
|---|---|---|---|
| April 10 | 20,000 units @ $5 each | April 13 | 15,000 units @ $8 each |
| 17 | 60,000 units @ $6 each | 21 | 50,000 units @ $9 each |
| 26 | 40,000 units @ $7 each | 27 | 50,000 units @ $10 each |

14. The gross profit on sales for the month of April, 2021, assuming that inventory is priced on the FIFO basis, is 14.____
    A. $330,000 B. $355,000 C. $395,000 D. $435,000

15. The gross profit on sales for the month of April 2021, assuming that inventory is priced on the LIFO basis is 15.____
    A. $330,000 B. $355,000 C. $395,000 D. $435,000

16. This question is to be answered on the basis of the data presented for June 30, 2021. 16.____

| | |
|---|---|
| Balance per Bank Statement | $24,019.00 |
| Balance per General Ledger | 20,592.64 |
| Proceeds of note collected by the bank which had not been recorded in the Cash account | 4,000.00 |
| Interest on note collected by the bank (no book entries made0 | 39.40 |
| Debit memo for Bank charges for the month of May | 23.50 |
| Deposit in Transit (June 30, 2021) | 2,144.00 |
| Customer's check returned by the bank due to lack of funds | 150.00 |
| Outstanding checks – June 30, 2021 | 1,631.46 |
| Error in recording check made by our bookkeeper – check cleared in the amount of $463.00 but entered in the bank book for $436.00 | |

If we wish to reconcile the bank and book balance so that the bank balance and the book balance are reconciled to a corrected balance, the corrected balance should be
    A. $20,592.64 B. $24,019.00 C. $24,531.54 D. $26,163.00

17. The Ateb Company has issued a $500,000 bond issue on January 2, 2021 at 8% interest, payable semi-annually, sold at par, with interest payable on June 30 and December 31. 17.____
    On September 30, 2021, at the close of the fiscal year of the Ateb Company, the interest expense accrual should reflect interest payable of, approximately,
    A. $10,000 B. $20,000 C. $40,000 D. $50,000

18. Assume that a new procedure requires that a particular and unvarying sequence of steps be followed in order to yield the desired data. You are assigned to be in charge of subordinates working with this procedure. 18.____

Which one of the following is MOST likely to impress subordinates with the importance of following the sequence of steps exactly as given?

A. Explain the consequences of error if the procedure is not followed.
B. Suggest how rewarding would be the feeling of finding errors before the supervisor catches them.
C. Indicate that independent verification of their work will be done by other staff members
D. Advise that upward career mobility usually results from following instructions exactly

19. It is essential for an experienced accountant to know approximately how long it will take him to complete a particular assignment because 19.____

A. his supervisors will need to obtain this information only from someone planning to perform the assignment
B. he must arrange his schedule to insure proper completion of the assignment consistent with agency objectives
C. he must measure whether he is keeping pace with others performing similar assignments
D. he must determine what assignments are essential and have the greatest priority within his agency

20. There are circumstances which call for special and emergency efforts by employees. You must assign your staff to make this type of effort. 20.____
Of the following, this special type of assignment is MOST likely to succeed if the

A. time schedule required to complete the assignment is precisely stated but is not adhered to
B. employees are individually free to determine the work schedule
C. assignment is clearly defined
D. employees are individually free to use any procedure or method available to them

# KEY (CORRECT ANSWERS)

| | | | |
|---|---|---|---|
| 1. | A | 11. | A |
| 2. | B | 12. | A |
| 3. | B | 13. | B |
| 4. | D | 14. | C |
| 5. | A | 15. | B |
| 6. | B | 16. | C |
| 7. | C | 17. | A |
| 8. | B | 18. | A |
| 9. | A | 19. | B |
| 10. | B | 20. | C |

# EXAMINATION SECTION
# TEST 1

DIRECTIONS: Each question or incomplete statement is followed by several suggested answers or completions. Select the one that BEST answers the question or completes the statement. *PRINT THE LETTER OF THE CORRECT ANSWER IN THE SPACE AT THE RIGHT.*

1. The allowance for doubtful accounts represents the 1.____

   A. difference between the gross value of accounts receivable and the net realizable value of accounts receivable
   B. amount of uncollectible accounts written off to date
   C. difference between total credit sales and collection on credit sales
   D. cash set aside to compensate for bad debt losses

2. What is the term for the interest deducted from the face amount of a note payable? 2.____

   A. Discount
   B. Fee
   C. Levy
   D. Contingency

3. The Yardman purchases a mower from an equipment dealer on February 1 for $7,200. The dealer has guaranteed the mower to have a useful life of 10 years. Assuming adjusting entries are prepared monthly, the book value of the mower on June 30 is 3.____

   A. $300
   B. $6480
   C. $6900
   D. $7,200

4. Gullstart, Inc. had operating cash flows of $240,000, total cash flows of $1 million, and average total assets of $5 million. Its cash flow on total assets ratio is 4.____

   A. 3.6%
   B. 4.8%
   C. 5.0%
   D. 12.4%

5. Which of the following assets would NOT be depreciated? 5.____

   A. Buildings
   B. Servers/information systems
   C. Land
   D. Store fixtures

Questions 6-8 refer to the following information: On January 1, five years ago, Winkler and Dunnebier Machinery purchased an envelope machine for $1.5 million. The machine was given a useful life of 5 years or 40,000 hours. During the machine's 5-year life span, its hourly usage was, respectively, 4000; 8000; 16,000,; 10,000; and 2000 hours.

6. Using the double-declining balance method, calculate the depreciation expense for the FIRST year. 6.____

   A. $135,000
   B. $360,000
   C. $540,000
   D. $600,000

7. Using the units-of-production method, calculate the depreciation expense for the THIRD year. 7.____

   A. $129,600
   B. $216,000
   C. $337,500
   D. $540,000

8. Using the straight-line method, calculate the depreciation expense for the FIFTH year. 8.____

   A. $44,400
   B. $67,500
   C. $270,000
   D. $360,000

9. The ______ principle requires expenses to be reported in the same period as the revenues the were earned as a result of the expenses. 9.____

   A. realization
   B. cost
   C. matching
   D. going-concern

10. To recognize insurance expired during an accounting period, the adjusting entry will affect the ______ account. 10.____

    I. asset
    II. expense
    III. liability
    IV. revenue

    A. I and II
    B. II and III
    C. III and IV
    D. I, II, III and IV

11. Adjusting entries for annual financial statements are generally made 11.____

    A. at the beginning of the year
    B. after every transaction
    C. periodically throughout the year
    D. at the end of the year

12. In a ledger, debit entries 12.____

    A. decrease assets
    B. increase owners' equity

C. decrease liabilities
D. decrease profitability

13. What is the term for a person who signs a note receivable and promises to pay the principal and interest? 13.____

A. Payee
B. Holder
C. Maker
D. Recipient

14. Trusty, Inc. had net credit sales for the year of $120,000. Accounts receivable at year's end are $40,000, and there is a $200 credit in allowance for doubtful accounts. If Trusty estimates bad debt losses based on an aging of accounts receivable as $2400, the expense for the year is 14.____

A. $200
B. $2200
C. $2400
D. $2600

15. When bonds are issued at a discount, the discount 15.____

A. appears on the balance sheet as a contra liability
B. reduces the overall cost of borrowing
C. appears on the income statement as other income
D. appears on the income statement as an expense

16. Dividends become a liability on the date that 16.____

A. the dividend is declared by the board of directors
B. the dividend is recorded
C. cumulative preferred stock dividends are declared in arrears
D. payment of the dividends is made

17. The financial statement of a large corporation is MOST likely to include 17.____

A. book value per share
B. earnings per share
C. the current ratio
D. return on assets

18. ______ are long-term notes issued with a pledge of specified property, plant, and equipment for the loan. 18.____

A. sinking-fund bonds
B. mortgage notes payable
C. bonds payable
D. foreclosures

19. Empire Waste sold a truck that originally cost $200,000 for $ 120,000. The accumulated depreciation on the truck was $80,000. Empire Waste should record a 19.____

A. $40,000 loss
B. $40,000 gain
C. $80,000 loss
D. break-even transaction

20. The "chart of accounts" refers to a 20.____

A. complete listing of the account titles to be used
B. collection of all a company's accounts
C. system of recording debit and credit entries for each transaction
D. statement that shows the name and balance of all ledger accounts

21. If net credit sales for a given year are $800,000 and the average accounts receivable are $40,000, the accounts receivable turnover is 21.____

A. 20
B. 50
C. 80
D. 100

22. During a period of steadily rising prices, the ______ method of inventory valuation is likely to result in the lowest cost of goods sold. 22.____

A. gross profit
B. last in, first out (LIFO)
C. first in, first out (FIFO)
D. specific identification

23. On an income statement, each of the following would appear below income from continuing operations, EXCEPT 23.____

A. discontinued operations
B. net income
C. extraordinary items
D. cumulative effect of accounting changes related to previous years

24. During the month of December, the liabilities of Duckworth increased $26,000 and the owners' equity decreased $6000. The assets of Duckworth ______ during December. 24.____

A. increased $20,000
B. increased $22,000
C. decreased $20,000
D. decreased $32,000

25. At year's end, Lavender, Inc. is estimating its ending inventory. The following information is available: 25.____

| | |
|---|---|
| Inventory as of October 1 | $ 12,500 |
| Net fourth-quarter sales | $40,000 |
| Net fourth-quarter purchases | $27,500 |

Lavender typically achieves a gross profit of around 15%. Using the gross profit method, calculate Lavender's ending inventory.

A. $4000
B. $6000
C. $10,000
D. $16,000

# KEY (CORRECT ANSWERS)

1. A
2. A
3. C
4. B
5. C
6. D
7. D
8. C
9. C
10. A
11. D
12. C
13. C
14. B
15. A
16. A
17. B
18. B
19. D
20. A
21. A
22. C
23. D
24. A
25. B

# TEST 2

DIRECTIONS: Each question or incomplete statement is followed by several suggested answers or completions. Select the one that BEST answers the question or completes the statement. *PRINT THE LETTER OF THE CORRECT ANSWER IN THE SPACE AT THE RIGHT.*

1. Which of the following is a balance sheet item that represents the portion of stockholders' equity resulting form profitable business operation? 1.____

   A. Retained earnings
   B. Cash
   C. Accounts receivable
   D. Capital stock

2. Which of the following is sued to compare revenues and expenses for a period of time in order to determine net income or loss? 2.____

   A. Balance sheet
   B. Owners' equity statement
   C. Statement of cash flows
   D. Income statement

3. Accounting transactions are first recorded in the 3.____

   A. ledger
   B. trial balance
   C. journal
   D. T-account

4. If net credit sales for a given year are $1.2 million and the average accounts receivable is $120,000, the average days to collect receivables is 4.____

   A. 10
   B. 30
   C. 36.5
   D. 71

5. Each of the following is included in an end-of-period worksheet, EXCEPT 5.____

   A. financial statement information
   B. closing entries
   C. trial balance
   D. information for adjusting entries

6. Generally accepted accounting principles suggest that a company's balance sheet show assets as the 6.____

   A. market value of the asset received in all cases
   B. cash equivalent value of what was given up or the asset received, whichever is more evident
   C. objective cost of external users
   D. cash outlay only, even if part of the consideration given was something other than cash

7. At the end of the accounting period, Tripod Industries failed to make an adjusting entry to record depreciation. The effect of this omission will be an 7.____

   A. understatement of expenses
   B. understatement of assets
   C. overstatement of liabilities
   D. overstatement of revenues

8. On October 1, Agitpro paid three months' rent for office space. The payment was originally recorded in prepaid rent. Agitpro's adjusting entry on October 31 would include a 8.____

   A. debit to rent payable
   B. credit to rent expense
   C. debit to prepaid rent
   D. credit to prepaid rent

9. Beulah's Salon purchased a hair dryer on January 1 for $5,400. The dryer has a useful life of 10 years and a salvage value of $400. Using the double-declining balance method, calculate the depreciation expense for the second year of the dryer's useful life. 9.____

   A. $628
   B. $800
   C. $864
   D. $1026

10. The face amount of a bond, plus the unamortized premium, is referred to as its ______ value. 10.____

    A. carrying
    B. discounted
    C. par
    D. adjusted

11. Metabolon has a $10,000 credit balance in its allowance for doubtful accounts. During October it wrote off $4000 as uncollectible from a bankrupt customer. This entry will 11.____

    A. reduce owners' equity
    B. not affect the net income for the period
    C. increase total assets
    D. reduce total assets

12. A company uses a perpetual inventory system. When goods sold have been returned, the company should record the return with a 12.____

    A. debit to sales returns and allowances
    B. credit to inventory
    C. debit to cost of goods sold
    D. credit to sales returns and allowances

13. The objectives of financial reporting are met largely by each of the following, EXCEPT the 13.____

    A. cash flow statement
    B. federal income tax return

C. income statement
D. statement of financial position

14. _______ entries are used to zero out the balance in nominal accounts at the end of the period. 14.____

A. Reversing
B. Real
C. Closing
D. Adjusting

15. On October 1, Sterling Enterprises borrowed $100,000 from the bank. The loan is to be repaid in total in six months. The interest rate is 9%. On November 30, Sterling's total liability for this loan will be 15.____

A. $100,000
B. $101,500
C. $104,500
D. $109,000

16. Which of the following is shown on a bank statement? 16.____

I. Deposits in transit
II. Beginning and ending balances of the depositor's checking ac count
III. Petty cash amounts
IV. Outstanding checks

A. I and II
B. II only
C. I, II and IV
D. I, II, III and IV

17. Navanax had 25,000 shares of 8% preferred stock, $100 par, and 250,000 shares of $1 par common stock outstanding throughout the year. Net income for the year was $1,100,000, and Navanax declared and distributed a cash dividend of $2 per share on its common stock. Earnings per share equaled 17.____

A. $1.60
B. $2.10
C. $3.60
D. $4.40

18. A 120-day note, dated March 25, has a maturity date of July 18.____

A. 22
B. 23
C. 24
D. 25

19. Of the following steps in the accounting cycle, which is performed FIRST? 19.____

A. Adjusting accounts
B. Preparing an adjusted trial balance
C. Posting
D. Closing temporary accounts

Questions 20 and 21 refer to the following information: On March 1, Richie Corporation bought land by signing a note payable to the bank.

20. The March 1 journal entry would include a debit to the ______ account. 20.____

A. revenue
B. owners' equity
C. liability
D. asset

21. The March 1 journal entry would include a credit to the ______ account. 21.____

A. liability
B. asset
C. owners' equity
D. expense

22. A company's ______ activities are transactions with creditors to borrow money and/or repay the principal amounts of loans reported as cash flows. 22.____

A. leveraging
B. financing
C. investing
D. operating

23. Under the direct write-off method of accounting for uncollectible assets, 23.____

A. the matching principle is illustrated by the relationship between current period net sales and current period uncollectible accounts
B. when specific accounts receivable are determined to be worthless, the allowance for doubtful accounts is debited
C. accounts receivable are not recorded in the balance sheet at net realizable value, but in the balance of the accounts receivable ledger account
D. the uncollectible accounts expense is less than the expense would be under the income statement approach

24. The true interest rate of a note, computed only on the remaining balance of the unpaid debt for the specific time period, is known as the ______ interest rate. 24.____

A. adjusted
B. annual effective
C. net
D. annual compounded

25. An accountant is using the indirect method to calculate and report the net cash provided or used by operating activities. Under this method the accountant will have to adjust net income for 25.____

I. revenues and expenses that did not provide or use cash
II. changes in noncash current assets and current liabilities related to operating activities
III. changes in current liabilities related to operating activities
IV. gains and losses from investing and financing activities

A. I and II
B. I, II and III
C. II, III and IV
D. I, II, III and IV

# KEY (CORRECT ANSWERS)

1. A
2. D
3. C
4. C
5. B
6. B
7. A
8. D
9. C
10. A
11. B
12. A
13. B
14. C
15. B
16. B
17. C
18. B
19. A
20. D
21. A
22. C
23. C
24. B
25. D

# TEST 3

DIRECTIONS: Each question or incomplete statement is followed by several suggested answers or completions. Select the one that BEST answers the question or completes the statement. *PRINT THE LETTER OF THE CORRECT ANSWER IN THE SPACE AT THE RIGHT.*

1. An accountant is using the allowance method of recording bad debts. The journal entry to record the bad debts adjustment would 1.____

   A. debit the allowance for doubtful accounts
   B. credit the allowance for doubtful accounts
   C. debit accounts receivable
   D. credit accounts receivable

2. The primary consumers of financial accounting information are 2.____

   A. investors and creditors
   B. corporate boards of directors
   C. financial managers
   D. budget officers

3. The balance sheet of Fred's Fancies, a retailer, includes equipment, accounts receivable, cash, accounts payable, supplies, capital stock, notes payable, and notes receivable. This balance sheet contains ______ assets and ______ iabilities. 3.____

   A. 5; 2
   B. 5; 3
   C. 4; 4
   D. 6;1

4. The cost principle requires assets such as land, buildings, and equipment be recorded at 4.____

   A. appraisal value at the time of purchase
   B. appraisal value at the balance sheet date
   C. historical cost
   D. fair market value

5. Each of the following would affect the book side of a bank reconciliation, EXCEPT 5.____

   A. a bank debit memorandum
   B. bank service charges
   C. outstanding checks
   D. a check-printing fee from the bank

6. Ichthys Dive Shops borrowed $300,000 cash from the bank by signing a 5-year, 8% installment note. Given that the present value factor of an 8% annuity for 5 years is 3.9927 and each payment is $75,137, the present value of the note is 6.____

   A. $75,137
   B. $94,013
   C. $300,000
   D. $375,685

7. Before any year-end adjusting entries were made, the Tansu Mill's net income was $40,000. The following adjustments need to be made: 7.____

| | |
|---|---|
| Portion of insurance expiring | $300 |
| Interest accrued on company savings | $ 110 |
| Fees collected in advance now earned | $2,400 |

The income statement for the current year should show a net income of

A. $37,410
B. $38,010
C. $41,990
D. $42,210

8. If a substantial amount of a company's accounts payable are paid in cash, the company's current ratio would 8.____

A. increase
B. decrease
C. remain the same
D. change depending on the relationship between the payables and the current liabilities

9. Superscrubbers began providing janitorial services for a large corporation on January 15 for a monthly fee of $ 10,000. The first payment is to be received on February 15. The adjusting entry made by Superscrubbers on January 31 includes a 9.____

A. debit of $5000 to janitorial fees receivable
B. credit of $5000 to janitorial fees earned
C. credit of $10,000 to janitorial fees earned
D. debit of $5000 to unearned janitorial fees

10. Which of the following would NOT be closed during the closing process? 10.____

A. Advertising expense
B. Dividends
C. Interest revenue
D. Accumulated depreciation

11. The ______ principle requires that every business be accounted for separately and distinctly from its owner or owners. 11.____

A. realization
B. objectivity
C. business entity
D. compartmentalization

12. Funky Chic Decorating purchased a window treatment display for $25,000 and sold it several years later for $12,000. The original estimated residual value was $10,000, and the accumulated depreciation at the time of sale was $8000. The sale should be recorded as a 12.____

A. $3000 loss
B. $5000 loss

C. $2000 gain
D. $3000 gain

13. During a period of falling prices, the ______ method of inventory valuation will generally result in the highest amount of income taxes paid. 13.____

A. first in, first out (FIFO)
B. last in, first out (LIFO)
C. gross profit
D. weighted average

14. Which of the following statements about retained earnings is FALSE? 14.____

A. They are not subject to statutory restrictions.
B. They usually approximate a company's cumulative net income less dividends declared.
C. They may be subject to appropriations by corporate directors for the purpose of limiting dividends.
D. They may be subject to restrictions due to loan agreements.

15. On August 11 of the current year, Trachtenberg Corporation concluded that a customer's $8700 account receivable was uncollectible, and wrote the account off. Assuming the allowance method is used to account for bad debts, the write-off will 15.____

A. have no effect on either net income or total assets
B. decrease net income, but have no effect on total assets
C. have no effect on net income, but decrease total assets
D. decrease both net income and total assets

16. Chuzzlewit Enterprises sold equipment for $30,000. The cost was $70,000, and the equipment had accumulated depreciation of $50,000 at the time of the sale. In the investing section of the cash flow statement, the amount of ______ would be entered for this transaction. 16.____

A. $0 (no entry)
B. $10,000
C. $20,000
D. $30,000

Questions 17-19 refer to the following information: Multiplastics purchased a machine in January 1 that cost $300,000, has a residual value of $20,000, and a useful life of seven years.

17. The amount of depreciation expense for the second year, under the double-declining balance method, would be 17.____

A. $47,287
B. $53,576
C. $61,261
D. $85,800

18. The amount of depreciation expense for the third year, under the sum-of-the-years'-digits method, would be 18.____

A. $50,000
B. $53,576
C. $63,567
D. $70,000

19. The net book value of the machine at the end of the fourth year (after recording fourth-year depreciation), using the straight-line method, would be 19.____

A. $120,000
B. $140,000
C. $171,429
D. $188,888

20. The purpose of a classified balance sheet is to 20.____

A. organize assets and liabilities into important subgroups
B. show revenues, expenses, and net income
C. report operating, investing, and financing activities
D. measure a company's ability to pay its bills in a timely manner

21. What is the term for an expense resulting from a failure to take advantage of cash discounts on purchases? 21.____

A. Trade discounts
B. Shortfall
C. Sales discounts
D. Discounts lost

22. Accounts that appear on a postclosing trial balance are referred to as ______ accounts. 22.____

A. projected
B. real
C. prorata
D. nominal

23. Which of the following is an example of an operating activity? 23.____

A. Purchasing office equipment
B. Paying wages
C. Selling stock
D. Borrowing money from a bank

24. Landshark Corporation has operated with a gross profit rate of 30% for the last several years. On January 1 of the current year the company had an inventory with a cost of $50,000. Purchases of merchandise during January amounted to $60,000, and sales for the month were $90,000. Using the gross profit method, the estimated inventory on January 31 is 24.____

A. $27,000
B. $47,000
C. $59,000
D. $63,000

25. Earnings per share is an accounting item that is 25.____

A. optional for most companies
B. shown on the face of the income statement
C. computed for both preferred and common stock
D. expressed as "return on equity" in the ledger

---

# KEY (CORRECT ANSWERS)

| | | | |
|---|---|---|---|
| 1. | A | 11. | C |
| 2. | A | 12. | B |
| 3. | A | 13. | B |
| 4. | C | 14. | A |
| 5. | C | 15. | A |
| 6. | C | 16. | D |
| 7. | D | 17. | C |
| 8. | A | 18. | A |
| 9. | B | 19. | B |
| 10. | D | 20. | A |

| | |
|---|---|
| 21. | D |
| 22. | B |
| 23. | B |
| 24. | B |
| 25. | B |

---

# TEST 4

DIRECTIONS: Each question or incomplete statement is followed by several suggested answers or completions. Select the one that BEST answers the question or completes the statement. *PRINT THE LETTER OF THE CORRECT ANSWER IN THE SPACE AT THE RIGHT.*

1. After the Yan Company collects $ 10,000 of its notes receivable, total assets are 1.____

   A. increased by $10,000
   B. decreased by $10,000
   C. unchanged, but total liabilities are greater
   D. unchanged

2. Revenues, expenses, and owner's withdrawal accounts are examples of ______ accounts. 2.____

   A. real
   B. permanent
   C. temporary
   D. closing

3. At the end of the year, the owners' equity of Plebeian Enterprises is $240,000, and is equal to 75% of total liabilities. The amount of total assets is 3.____

   A. $80,000
   B. $320,000
   C. $420,000
   D. $560,000

4. The ______ ratio of a company shows the percent of total assets provided by creditors. 4.____

   A. total asset turnover
   B. acid
   C. return on total assets
   D. debt

5. Which of the following would be recorded as a current liability? 5.____

   A. Accrued wages payable
   B. Property taxes payable
   C. Vacation benefits
   D. Income taxes payable

Questions 6-9 refer to the following information:
Year-end inventory for the Standish Company, under the periodic inventory system, is $25,000. The inventory on the first day of the year was $20,000 and purchases made during the year cost $40,000. Purchase returns and allowances equaled $1500, transportation in cost $500, and net sales for the year totaled $75,000.

6. At year's end, the net cost of purchases for Standish was 6.____

   A. $38,500
   B. $39,000

C. $40,000
D. $40,500

7. At year's end, the cost of goods sold for Standish was 7.____

A. $31,500
B. $34,000
C. $44,000
D. $59,000

8. At year's end, the cost of goods available for sale for Standish was 8.____

A. $34,000
B. $44,000
C. $59,000
D. $64,000

9. At year's end, the gross margin on sales for Standish was 9.____

A. $41,000
B. $44,000
C. $59,000
D. $61,000

10. Which of the following is a common nonrecurring item on the income statement? 10.____

A. Discontinued operations
B. Operating income
C. Cumulative effect of a change in accounting estimate
D. Ordinary gains and losses

11. If a transaction causes an asset account to decrease, it may also result in an increase 11.____

A. in the combined total of liabilities and stockholders' equity
B. of an equal amount in another asset account
C. in a liability account
D. of an equal amount in a stockholders' equity account

12. Beverly Corp. had total operating expenses of $100,000 in the previous accounting period; depreciation of $2,000; and an increase in accrued liabilities of $5,000. The company's prepaid expenses at the beginning of the period were $18,000; at the ending, they were $12,000. 12.____

What was the cash paid by Beverly Corp. for operating expenses?

A. $87,000
B. $91,000
C. $99,000
D. $101,000

13. The ______ method of inventory valuation identifies the invoice cost of each item in ending inventory to determine the cost assigned to that inventory. 13.____

A. specific identification
B. first in, first out (FIFO)
C. last in, first out (LIFO)
D. weighted-average

14. In which of the following situations would revenue be recognized? 14.____

A. An order is received with cash payment, and the order will be filled next month.
B. An order has been shipped and will arrive at the customer's place of business after the end of the month. Shipping terms are FOB destination.
C. An order has been received, and the goods have been set aside for the customer to pick up at her convenience.
D. An order is received, and it will take about a week to manufacture enough goods to fill it.

15. A credit is used to record a(n) 15.____

A. increase in an asset
B. decrease in an expense
C. increase in a liability
D. increase in owners' equity

16. To balance the income statement columns of a worksheet, net income should be entered in the 16.____

A. adjustments debit column
B. balance sheet debit column
C. income statement debit column
D. income statement credit column

17. On May 1, Horticopia's accounts receivable totaled $6000. The allowance for doubtful accounts was $240. During the month of May, Horticopia made $20,000 in credit sales and collected $19,600 from its customers. On May 31, the not realizable value of accounts receivable is 17.____

A. $6000
B. $6160
C. $6400
D. $6640

18. Which of the following would affect the bank side of a bank reconciliation? 18.____

A. Interest earned on a checking account
B. Bank service charges
C. Bank credit memorandum
D. Deposits in transit

19. ______ preferred stock is a kind of stock on which the right to receive dividends is forfeited for any year in which dividends are not declared. 19.____

A. Convertible
B. Callable
C. Noncumulative
D. Cumulative

20. Which of the following are trade receivables? 20.____

A. Deposits with creditors
B. Cash advances to employees
C. Amounts owed by customers on account
D. Loans to affiliated companies

21. Which of the following is a term for the accounting procedure that estimates and reports bad debts expense from credit sales during the period of the sales, and also reports accounts receivable at the amount of cash proceeds that is expected from their collection? 21.____

A. Adjustment method for uncollectible debts
B. Aging of notes receivable
C. Direct write-off method of accounting for bad debts
D. Allowance method of accounting for bad debts

22. If Floracom accrues $200,000 for salaries payable at the end of the year, 22.____

A. assets and owners' equity will remain unchanged
B. assets decrease and liabilities increase by $200,000
C. liabilities decrease and owners' equity increases by $200,000
D. liabilities and expenses each increase $200,000

23. Each of the following is an operating activity, EXCEPT 23.____

A. the purchase of equipment for cash
B. the purchase of supplies for cash
C. interest paid on a note payable
D. cash sale

24. Compared to a perpetual inventory system, a periodic inventory system 24.____

A. provides more timely information
B. is based on estimates
C. requires updating inventory-related accounts only at the end of each period
D. allows a company to determine inventory and cost of goods sold at any time

25. On January 1, Uniqual Inc. purchased a machine for $60,000. The machine is estimated to have a useful life of 5 years and a salvage value of $10,000. Using the double-declining balance method of depreciation, what is the book value of the asset at the end of the year? 25.____

A. $21,600
B. $32,000
C. $38,400
D. $48,000

# KEY (CORRECT ANSWERS)

| | | | |
|---|---|---|---|
| 1. | D | 11. | B |
| 2. | C | 12. | A |
| 3. | D | 13. | A |
| 4. | D | 14. | C |
| 5. | A | 15. | B |
| 6. | B | 16. | C |
| 7. | B | 17. | B |
| 8. | C | 18. | D |
| 9. | A | 19. | C |
| 10. | A | 20. | C |

| | |
|---|---|
| 21. | D |
| 22. | D |
| 23. | A |
| 24. | C |
| 25. | A |

# READING COMPREHENSION
# UNDERSTANDING AND INTERPRETING WRITTEN MATERIAL

## EXAMINATION SECTION

## TEST 1

DIRECTIONS: Each question or incomplete statement is followed by several suggested answers or completions. Select the one that BEST answers the question or completes the statement. *PRINT THE LETTER OF THE CORRECT ANSWER IN THE SPACE AT THE RIGHT.*

Questions 1-4.

DIRECTIONS: Questions 1 through 4 are to be answered SOLELY on the basis of the following paragraph.

An annual leave allowance, which combines leaves previously given for vacation, personal business, family illness, and other reasons shall be granted members. Calculation of credits for such leave shall be on an annual basis beginning January 1st of each year. Annual leave credits shall be based on time served by members during preceding calendar year. However, when credits have been accrued and member retires during current year, additional annual leave credits shall, in this instance, be granted at accrual rate of three days for each completed month of service, excluding terminal leave. If accruals granted for completed months of service extend into following month, member shall be granted an additional three days accrual for completed month. This shall be the only condition where accruals in a current year are granted for vacation period in such year.

1. According to the above paragraph, if a fireman's wife were to become seriously ill so that he would take time off from work to be with her, such time off would be deducted from his _____ leave allowance. 1.____
   A. annual
   B. vacation
   C. personal business
   D. family illness

2. Terminal leave means leave taken 2.____
   A. at the end of the calendar year
   B. at the end of the vacation year
   C. immediately before retirement
   D. before actually earned, because of an emergency

3. A fireman appointed on July 1, 2017 will be able to take his first full or normal annual leave during the period 3.____
   A. July 1, 2017 to June 30, 2018
   B. Jan. 1, 2018 to Dec. 31, 2018
   C. July 1, 2018 to June 30, 2019
   D. Jan. 1, 2019 to Dec. 31, 2019

4. According to the above paragraph, a member who retires on July 15 of this year will be entitled to receive leave allowance based on this year of _____ days. 4.____
   A. 15
   B. 18
   C. 22
   D. 24

5. Fire alarm boxes are electromechanical devices for transmitting a coded signal. In each box, there is a trainwork of wheels. When the box is operated, a spring-activated code wheel begins to revolve. The code number of the box is etched on the circumference of the code wheel, and the latter is associated with the circuit in such a way that when it revolves it causes the circuit to open and close in a predetermined manner, thereby transmitting its particular signal to the central station. A fire alarm box is nothing more than a device for interrupting the flow of current in a circuit in such a way as to produce a coded signal that may be decoded by the dispatchers in the central office. 5.____
Based on the above, select the FALSE statement.
   A. Each standard fire alarm box has its own code wheel.
   B. The code wheel operates when the box is pulled.
   C. The code wheel is operated electrically.
   D. Only the break in the circuit by the notched wheel causes the alarm signal to be transmitted to the central office.

Questions 6-9.

DIRECTIONS: Questions 6 through 9 are to be answered SOLELY on the basis of the following paragraph.

Ventilation, as used in firefighting operations, means opening up a building or structure in which a fire is burning to release the accumulated heat, smoke, and gases. Lack of knowledge of the principles of ventilation on the part of firemen may result in unnecessary punishment due to ventilation being neglected or improperly handled. While ventilation itself extinguishes no fires, when used in an intelligent manner, it allows firemen to get at the fire more quickly, easily, and with less danger and hardship.

6. According to the above paragraph, the MOST important result of failure to apply the principles of ventilation at a fire may be 6.____
   A. loss of public confidence
   B. waste of water
   C. excessive use of equipment
   D. injury to firemen

7. It may be inferred from the above paragraph that the CHIEF advantage of ventilation is that it 7.____
   A. eliminates the need for gas masks
   B. reduces smoke damage
   C. permits firemen to work closer to the fire
   D. cools the fire

8. Knowledge of the principles of ventilation, as defined in the above paragraph, would be LEAST important in a fire in a 8.____
   A. tenement house
   B. grocery store
   C. ship's hold
   D. lumberyard

9. We may conclude from the above paragraph that for the well-trained and equipped fireman, ventilation is 9.____
   A. a simple matter
   B. rarely necessary
   C. relatively unimportant
   D. a basic tool

Questions 10-13.

DIRECTIONS: Questions 10 through 13 are to be answered SOLELY on the basis of the following passage.

Fire exit drills should be established and held periodically to effectively train personnel to leave their working area promptly upon proper signal and to evacuate the building, speedily but without confusion. All fire exit drills should be carefully planned and carried out in a serious manner under rigid discipline so as to provide positive protection in the event of a real emergency. As a general rule, the local fire department should be furnished advance information regarding the exact date and time the exit drill is scheduled. When it is impossible to hold regular drills, written instructions should be distributed to all employees.

Depending upon individual circumstances, fires in warehouses vary from those of fast development that are almost instantly beyond any possibility of employee control to others of relatively slow development where a small readily attackable flame may be present for periods of time up to 15 minutes or more during which simple attack with fire extinguishers or small building hoses may prevent the fire development. In any case, it is characteristic of many warehouse fires that at a certain point in development they flash up to the top of the stack, increase heat quickly, and spread rapidly. There is a degree of inherent danger in attacking warehouse type fires, and all employees should be thoroughly trained in the use of the types of extinguishers or small hoses in the buildings and well instructed in the necessity of always staying between the fire and a direct pass to an exit.

10. Employees should be instructed that, when fighting a fire, they MUST 10.____
    A. try to control the blaze
    B. extinguish any fire in 15 minutes
    C. remain between the fire and a direct passage to the exit
    D. keep the fire between themselves and the fire exit

11. Whenever conditions are such that regular fire drills cannot be held, then which one of the following actions should be taken? 11.____
    A. The local fire department should be notified.
    B. Rigid discipline should be maintained during work hours.
    C. Personnel should be instructed to leave their working area by whatever means are available.
    D. Employees should receive fire drill procedures in writing.

12. The above passage indicates that the purpose of fire exit drills is to train employees to 12.____
    A. control a fire before it becomes uncontrollable
    B. act as firefighters
    C. leave the working area promptly
    D. be serious

13. According to the above passage, fire exit drills will prove to be of UTMOST effectiveness if 13.____
    A. employee participation is made voluntary
    B. they take place periodically
    C. the fire department actively participates
    D. they are held without advance planning

Questions 14-16.

DIRECTIONS: Questions 14 through 16 are to be answered SOLELY on the basis of the following paragraph.

The heat output from unit heaters will depend on how fast and how completely dry hot steam fills the unit core. For complete and fast air removal and rapid drainage of condensate, use a trap actuated by water or vapor (inverted bucket trap) and not a trap operated by temperature only (thermostatic or bellows trap). A temperature-actuated trap will hold back the hot condensate until it cools to a point where the thermal element opens. When this happens, the condensate backs up in the heater and reduces the heat output. With a water-actuated trap, this will not happen as the water or condensate is discharged as fast as it is formed.

14. On the basis of the information given in the above paragraph, it can be concluded that the PROPER type of trap to use for a unit heater is a(n) _____ trap. 14.____
    A. thermostatic
    B bellows-type
    C. inverted bucket
    D. temperature

15. According to the above paragraph, the MAIN reason for using the type of trap specified for a unit heater is to 15.____
    A. bring the condensate up to steam temperature
    B. prevent reduction in the heat output of the unit heater
    C. permit cycling of the heater
    D. maintain constant temperature of condensate in the trap

16. As used in the above paragraph, the word *actuated* means MOST NEARLY 16.____
    A. clogged
    B. operated
    C. cleaned
    D. vented

Questions 17-25.

DIRECTIONS: Questions 17 through 25 are to be answered SOLELY on the basis of the following passage. Each question consists of a statement. You are to indicate whether the statement is TRUE (T) or FALSE (F).

<u>MOVING AN OFFICE</u>

An office with all its equipment is sometimes moved during working hours. This is a difficult task and must be done in an orderly manner to avoid confusion. The operation should be planned in such a way as not to interrupt the progress of work usually done in the office and to make possible the accurate placement of the furniture and records in the new location. If the office moves to a place inside the same building, the desks and files are moved with all their contents. If the movement is to another building, the contents of each desk and file are placed in boxes. Each box is marked with a letter showing the particular section in the new quarters to which it is to be moved. Also marked on each box is the number of the desk or file on which the box is to be placed. Each piece of equipment must have a numbered tag. The number of each piece of equipment is put in soft chalk on the floor in the new office to show the proper location, and several floor plans are made to show where each piece of equipment goes. When the moving is done, someone is stationed at each of the several exits of the old office to see that each box or piece of equipment has its destination clearly marked on it. At the new office, someone stands at each of the several entrances with a copy of the floor plan and directs the placing of the furniture and equipment according to the floor plan. No one should interfere at this point with the arrangements shown on the plan. Improvements in arrangement can be considered and made at a later date.

17. It is a hard job to move an office from one place to another during working hours. 17.____

18. Confusion cannot be avoided if an office is moved during working hours. 18.____

19. The work usually done in an office must be stopped for the day when the office is moved during working hours. 19.____

20. If an office is moved from one floor to another in the same building, the contents of a desk are taken out and put into boxes for moving. 20.____

21. If boxes are used to hold material from desks when moving an office, the box is numbered the same as the desk on which it is to be put. 21.____

22. Letters are marked in soft chalk on the floor at the new quarters to show where the desks should go when moved. 22.____

23. When the moving begins, a person is put at each exit of the old office to check that each box and piece of equipment has clearly marked on it where to go. 23.____

24. A person stationed at each entrance of the new quarters to direct the placing of the furniture and equipment has a copy of the floor plan of the new quarters. 24.____

25. If, while the furniture is being moved into the new office, a person helping at a doorway gets an idea of a better way to arrange the furniture, he should change the planned arrangement and make a record of the change. 25.____

# KEY (CORRECT ANSWERS)

| | | | |
|---|---|---|---|
| 1. | A | 11. | D |
| 2. | C | 12. | C |
| 3. | D | 13. | B |
| 4. | B | 14. | C |
| 5. | C | 15. | B |
| 6. | D | 16. | B |
| 7. | C | 17. | T |
| 8. | D | 18. | F |
| 9. | D | 19. | F |
| 10. | C | 20. | F |

| | |
|---|---|
| 21. | T |
| 22. | F |
| 23. | T |
| 24. | T |
| 25. | F |

# TEST 2

DIRECTIONS: Each question or incomplete statement is followed by several suggested answers or completions. Select the one that BEST answers the question or completes the statement. *PRINT THE LETTER OF THE CORRECT ANSWER IN THE SPACE AT THE RIGHT.*

Questions 1-4.

DIRECTIONS: Questions 1 through 4 are to be answered SOLELY on the basis of the following paragraph.

In all cases of homicide, members of the Police Department who investigate will make every effort to obtain statements from dying persons. Such statements are of the greatest importance to the District Attorney. In many cases, there may be a failure to solve the crime if they are not taken. The principal element to be considered in taking the declaration of a dying person is his mental attitude. In order to be admissible in evidence, the person must have no hope of recovery. The patient will be fully interrogated on that point before a statement is taken.

1. In cases of homicide, according to the above paragraph, members of the police force will 1.____
   A. try to change the mental attitude of the dying person
   B. attempt to obtain a statement from the dying person
   C. not give the information they obtain directly to the District Attorney
   D. be careful not to injure the dying person unnecessarily

2. The mental attitude of the person making the dying statement is of GREAT importance because it can determine, according to the above paragraph, whether the 2.____
   A. victim should be interrogated in the presence of witnesses
   B. victim will be willing to make a statement of any kind
   C. statement will tell the District Attorney who committed the crime
   D. the statement can be used as evidence

3. District Attorneys find that statements of a dying person are important, according to the above paragraph, because 3.____
   A. it may be that the victim will recover and then refuse to testify
   B. they are important elements in determining the mental attitude of the victim
   C. they present a point of view
   D. it may be impossible to punish the criminal without such a statement

4. A well-known gangster is found dying from a bullet wound. The patrolman first on the scene, in the presence of witnesses, tells the man that he is going to die and asks, *Who shot you?* The gangster says, *Jones shot me, but he hasn't killed me. I'll live to get him.* He then falls back dead. According to the above paragraph, this statement is 4.____
   A. *admissible* in evidence; the man was obviously speaking the truth
   B. *not admissible* in evidence; the man obviously did not believe that he was dying

C. *admissible* in evidence; there were witnesses to the statement
D. *not admissible* in evidence; the victim did not sign any statement and the evidence is merely hearsay

Questions 5-7.

DIRECTIONS: Questions 5 through 7 are to be answered SOLELY on the basis of the following paragraph.

The factors contributing to crime and delinquency are varied and complex. The home and its immediate environment have been found to be crucial in determining the behavior patterns of the individual, and criminality can frequently be traced to faulty family relationships and a bad neighborhood. But in the search for a clearer understanding of the underlying causes of delinquent and criminal behavior, the total environment must be taken into consideration.

5. According to the above paragraph, family relationships 5.____
   A. tend to become faulty in bad neighborhoods
   B. are important in determining the actions of honest people as well as criminals
   C. are the only important element in the understanding of causes of delinquency
   D. are determined by the total environment

6. According to the above paragraph, the causes of crime and delinquency are 6.____
   A. not simple
   B. not meaningless
   C. meaningless
   D. simple

7. According to the above paragraph, faulty family relationships FREQUENTLY are 7.____
   A. responsible for varied and complex results
   B. caused when one or both parents have a criminal behavior pattern
   C. independent of the total environment
   D. the cause of criminal acts

Questions 8-10.

DIRECTIONS: Questions 8 through 10 are to be answered SOLELY on the basis of the following paragraph.

A change in the specific problems which confront the police and in the methods for dealing with them has taken place in the last few decades. The automobile is a two-way symbol of this change in policing. It menaces every city with a complicated traffic problem and has speeded up the process of committing a crime and making a getaway, but at the same time has increased the effectiveness of police operations. However, the major concern of police departments continues to be the antisocial or criminal actions and behavior of human beings.

8. On the basis of the above paragraph, it can be stated that, for the most part, in the past few decades the specific problems of a police force 8.____
   A. have changed but the general problems have not
   B. as well as the general problems have changed
   C. have remained the same but the general problems have changed
   D. as well as the general problems have remained the same

9. According to the above paragraph, advances in science and industry have, in general, made the police 9.____
   A. operations less effective from the overall point of view
   B. operations more effective from the overall point of view
   C. abandon older methods of solving police problems
   D. concern themselves more with the antisocial acts of human beings

10. The automobile is a *two-way symbol*, according to the above paragraph, because its use 10.____
   A. has speeded up getting to and away from the scene of a crime
   B. both helps and hurts police operations
   C. introduces a new antisocial act—traffic violation—and does away with criminals like horse thieves
   D. both increases and decreases speed by introducing traffic problems

Questions 11-14.

DIRECTIONS: Questions 11 through 14 are to be answered SOLELY on the basis of the following passage on INSTRUCTIONS TO COIN AND TOKEN CASHIERS.

<u>INSTRUCTIONS TO COIN AND TOKEN CASHIERS</u>

Cashiers should reset the machine registers to an even starting number before commencing the day's work. Money bags received directly from collecting agents shall be counted and receipted for on the collecting agent's form. Each cashier shall be responsible for all coin or token bags accepted by him. He must examine all bags to be used for bank deposits for cuts and holes before placing them in use. Care must be exercised so that bags are not cut in opening them. Each bag must be opened separately and verified before another bag is opened. The machine register must be cleared before starting the count of another bag. The amount shown on the machine register must be compared with the amount on the bag tag. The empty bag must be kept on the table for re-examination should there be a difference between the amount on the bag tag and the amount on the machine register.

11. A cashier should BEGIN his day's assignment by 11.____
   A. counting and accepting all money bags
   B. resetting the counting machine register
   C. examining all bags for cuts and holes
   D. verifying the contents of all money bags

12. In verifying the amount of money in the bags received from the collecting agent, it is BEST to 12.____
    A. check the amount in one bag at a time
    B. base the total on the amount on the collecting agent's form
    C. repeat the total shown on the bag tag
    D. refer to the bank deposit receipt

13. A cashier is instructed to keep each empty coin bag on his table while verifying its contents CHIEFLY because, as long as the bag is on the table 13.____
    A. it cannot be misplaced
    B. the supervisor can see how quickly the cashier works
    C. cuts and holes are easily noticed
    D. a recheck is possible in case the machine count disagrees with the bag tag total

14. The INSTRUCTIONS indicate that it is NOT proper procedure for a cashier to 14.____
    A. assume that coin bags are free of cuts and holes
    B. compare the machine register total with the total shown on the bag tag
    C. sign a form when he receives coin bags
    D. reset the machine register before starting the day's counting

Questions 15-17.

DIRECTIONS: Questions 15 through 17 are to be answered SOLELY on the basis of the following passage.

The mass media are an integral part of the daily life of virtually every American. Among these media the youngest, television, is the most pervasive. Ninety-five percent of American homes have at least one T.V. set, and on the average that set is in use for about 40 hours each week. The central place of television in American life makes this medium the focal point of a growing national concern over the effects of media portrayals of violence on the values, attitudes, and behavior of an ever-increasing audience.

In our concern about violence and its causes, it is easy to make television a scapegoat. But we emphasize the fact that there is no simple answer to the problem of violence—no single explanation of its causes, and no single prescription for its control. It should be remembered that America also experienced high levels of crime and violence in periods before the advent of television.

The problem of balance, taste and artistic merit in entertaining programs on television are complex. We cannot <u>countenance</u> government censorship of television. Nor would we seek to impose arbitrary limitations on programming which might jeopardize television's ability to deal in dramatic presentations with controversial social issues. Nonetheless, we are deeply troubled by television's constant portrayal of violence, not in any genuine attempt to focus artistic expression on the human condition, but rather in pandering to a public preoccupation with violence that television itself has helped to generate,

15. According to the above passage, television uses violence MAINLY 15.____
    A. to highlight the reality of everyday existence
    B. to satisfy the audience's hunger for destructive action

C. to shape the values and attitudes of the public
D. when it films documentaries concerning human conflict

16. Which one of the following statements is BEST supported by the above passage? 16.____
A. Early American history reveals a crime pattern which is not related to television.
B. Programs should give presentations of social issues and never portray violent acts.
C. Television has proven that entertainment programs can easily make the balance between taste and artistic merit a simple matter.
D. Values and behavior should be regulated by governmental censorship.

17. Of the following, which word has the same meaning as *countenance*, as used in the above passage? 17.____
A. Approve B. Exhibit C. Oppose D. Reject

Questions 18-21.

DIRECTIONS: Questions 18 through 21 are to be answered SOLELY on the basis of the following passage.

Maintenance of leased or licensed areas on public parks or land has always been a problem. A good rule to follow in the administration and maintenance of such areas is to limit the responsibility of any lessee or licensee to the maintenance of the structures and grounds essential to the efficient operation of the concession, not including areas for the general use of the public, such as picnic areas, public comfort stations, etc.; except where such facilities are leased to another public agency or where special conditions make such inclusion practicable, and where a good standard of maintenance can be assured and enforced. If local conditions and requirements are such that public use areas are included, adequate safeguards to the public should be written into contracts and enforced in their administration, to insure that maintenance by the concessionaire shall be equal to the maintenance standards for other park property.

18. According to the above passage, when an area on a public park is leased to a concessionaire, it is usually BEST to 18.____
A. confine the responsibility of the concessionaire to operation of the facilities and leave the maintenance function to the park agency
B. exclude areas of general public use from the maintenance obligation of the concessionaire
C. make the concessionaire responsible for maintenance of the entire area including areas of general public use
D. provide additional comfort station facilities for the area

19. According to the above passage, a valid reason for giving a concessionaire responsibility for maintenance of a picnic area within his leased area is that 19.____
A. local conditions and requirements make it practicable
B. more than half of the picnic area falls within his leased area
C. the concessionaire has leased picnic facilities to another public agency
D. the picnic area falls entirely within his leased area

20. According to the above passage, a precaution that should be taken when a concessionaire is made responsible for maintenance of an area of general public use in a park is  20.____
   A. making sure that another public agency has not previously been made responsible for this area
   B. providing the concessionaire with up-to-date equipment, if practicable
   C. requiring that the concessionaire take out adequate insurance for the protection of the public
   D. writing safeguards to the public into the contract

# KEY (CORRECT ANSWERS)

| | | | |
|---|---|---|---|
| 1. | B | 11. | B |
| 2. | D | 12. | A |
| 3. | D | 13. | D |
| 4. | B | 14. | A |
| 5. | B | 15. | B |
| 6. | A | 16. | A |
| 7. | D | 17. | A |
| 8. | A | 18. | B |
| 9. | B | 19. | A |
| 10. | B | 20. | D |

# TEST 3

DIRECTIONS: Each question or incomplete statement is followed by several suggested answers or completions. Select the one that BEST answers the question or completes the statement. *PRINT THE LETTER OF THE CORRECT ANSWER IN THE SPACE AT THE RIGHT.*

Questions 1-5.

DIRECTIONS: Questions 1 through 5 are to be answered SOLELY on the basis of the following paragraph.

Physical inspections are an important tool for the examiner because he will have to decide the case in many instances on the basis of the inspection report. Most proceedings in a rent office are commenced by the filing of a written application or complaint by an interested party; that is, either the landlord or the tenant. Such an application or complaint must be filed in duplicate in order that the opposing party may be served with a copy of the application or complaint and thus be given an opportunity to answer and oppose it. Sometimes, a further opportunity is given the applicant to file a written rebuttal or reply to his adversary's answer. Often an examiner can make a determination or decision based on the written application, the answer, and the reply to the answer; and, of course, it would speed up operations if it were always possible to make decisions based on written documents only. Unfortunately, decisions can't always be made that way. There are numerous occasions where disputed issues of fact remain which cannot be resolved on the basis of the written statements of the parties. Typical examples are the following: The tenant claims that the refrigerator or stove or bathroom fixture is not functioning properly and the landlord denies this It is obvious that in such cases an inspection of the accommodations is almost the only means of resolving such disputed issues,

1. According to the above paragraph, 1.____
   A. physical inspections are made in all cases
   B. physical inspections are seldom made
   C. It is sometimes possible to determine the facts in a case without a physical inspection
   D. physical inspections are made when it is necessary to verify the examiner's determination

2. According to the above paragraph, in MOST cases, proceedings are started by a(n) 2.____
   A. inspector discovering a violation
   B. oral complaint by a tenant or landlord
   C. request from another agency, such as the Building Department
   D. written complaint by a tenant or landlord

3. According to the above paragraph, when a tenant files an application with the rent office, the landlord is 3.____
   A. not told about the proceeding until after the examiner makes his determination
   B. given the duplicate copy of the application

C. notified by means of an inspector visiting the premises
D. not told about the proceeding until after the inspector has visited the premises

4. As used in the above paragraph, the word *disputed* means MOST NEARLY 4.____
A. unsettled B. contested C. definite D. difficult

5. As used in the above paragraph, the word *resolved* means MOST NEARLY 5.____
A. settled B. fixed C. helped D. amended

Questions 6-10.

DIRECTIONS: Questions 6 through 10 are to be answered SOLELY on the basis of the following paragraph.

The examiner should order or request an inspection of the housing accommodations. His request for a physical inspection should be in writing, identify the accommodations and the landlord and the tenant, and specify <u>precisely</u> just what the inspector is to look for and report on. Unless this request is specific and lists <u>in detail</u> every item which the examiner wishes to be reported, the examiner will find that the inspection has not served its purpose and that even with the inspector's report, he is still in no position to decide the case due to loose ends which have not been completely tied up. The items that the examiner is interested in should be separately numbered on the inspection request and the same number referred to in the inspector's report. You can see what it would mean if an inspector came back with a report that did not cover everything. It may mean a tremendous waste of time and often require a re-inspection.

6. According to the above paragraph, the inspector makes an inspection on the order of 6.____
A. the landlord B. the tenant
C. the examiner D. both the landlord and the tenant

7. According to the above paragraph, the reason for numbering each item that an inspector reports on is so that 7.____
A. the report is neat
B. the report can be easily read and referred to
C. none of the examiner's requests for information is missed
D. the report will be specific

8. The one of the following items that is NOT necessarily included in the request for inspection is 8.____
A. location of dwelling B. name of landlord
C. item to be checked D. type of building

9. As used in the above paragraph, the word *precisely* means MOST NEARLY 9.____
A. exactly B. generally C. usually D. strongly

10. As used in the above paragraph, the words *in detail* mean MOST NEARLY 10.____
A. clearly B. item by item C. substantially D. completely

Questions 11-13.

DIRECTIONS: Questions 11 through 13 are to be answered SOLELY on the basis of the following passage.

The agreement under which a tenant rents property from a landlord is known as a lease. Generally speaking, leases are classified as either short-term or long-term in duration. They are further subdivided according to the method used to determine the amount of periodic rent payments. Of the following types of lease in use, the more commonly used ones are the following:

1. The straight or fixed lease is one in which rent may be paid in equal amounts throughout the duration of the lease. These are usually restricted to short-term leasing, or somewhat longer-term if clauses in the lease provide for periodic escalation of payments as the economy shifts.
2. Percentage leasing, used for short-term commercial leasing, provides the landlord with a stipulated percentage of a tenant's gross sales from goods and services sold on the premises, in addition to a fixed amount of rent.
3. The net lease, generally long-term (ten years or more), requires the tenant to pay all operating costs, including real estate taxes and insurance. In a net-net lease, the tenant further agrees to meet mortgage interest and principal payments.
4. An escalated lease, which is a long-term lease, requires rent to be of a stipulated base amount which periodically is subject to escalation in accordance with cost-of-living index scales, or in direct proportion to taxes, insurance, and operating costs.

11. Based on the information given in the passage, which type of lease is MOST likely to be advantageous to a landlord if there is a high rate of inflation? 11.____
______ lease.
A. Fixed B. Percentage C. Net D. Escalated

12. On the basis of thee above passage, which types of lease would generally be MOST suitable for a well-established textile company which requires permanent facilities for its large operations? 12.____
_____ lease and _____ lease.
A. Percentage; escalated
B. Escalated; net
C. Straight; net
D. Straight; percentage

13. According to the above passage, the ONLY type of lease which assures the same amount of rent throughout a specified interval is the _____ lease. 13.____
A. straight B. percentage C. net-net D. escalated

Questions 14-15.

DIRECTIONS: Questions 14 and 15 are to be answered SOLELY on the basis of the following passage.

If you like people, if you seek contact with them rather than hide yourself in a corner, if you study your fellow men sympathetically, if you try consistently to contribute something to their success and happiness, if you are reasonably generous with your thought and your time, if you have a partial reserve with everyone but a seeming reserve with no one, you will get along with your superiors, your subordinates, and the human race.

By the scores of thousands, precepts and platitudes have been written for the guidance of personal conduct. The odd part of it is that, despite all of this labor, most of the frictions in modern society arise from the individual's feeling of inferiority, his false pride, his vanity, his unwillingness to yield space to any other man and his consequent urge to throw his own weight around. Goethe said that the quality which best enables a man to renew his own life, in his relation to others, is his capability of renouncing particular things at the right moment in order warmly to embrace something new in the next.

14. On the basis of the above passage, it may be INFERRED that 14.____
    A. a person should be unwilling to renounce privileges
    B. a person should realize that loss of a desirable job assignment may come at an opportune moment
    C. it is advisable for a person to maintain a considerable amount of reserve in his relationship with unfamiliar people
    D. people should be ready to contribute generously to a worthy charity

15. Of the following, the MOST valid implication made by the above passage is that 15.____
    A. a wealthy person who spends a considerable amount of money entertaining his friends is not really getting along with them
    B. if a person studies his fellow men carefully and impartially, he will tend to have good relationships with them
    C. individuals who maintain seemingly little reserve in their relationships with people have in some measure overcome their own feelings of inferiority
    D. most precepts that have been written for the guidance of personal conduct in relationships with other people are invalid

Questions 16-17.

DIRECTIONS: Questions 16 and 17 are to be answered SOLELY on the basis of the following passage.

When a design for a new bank note of the Federal Government has been prepared by the Bureau of Engraving and Printing and has been approved by the Secretary of the Treasury, the engravers begin the work of cutting the design in steel. No one engraver does all the work. Each man is a specialist. One works only on portraits, another on lettering, another on scroll work, and so on. Each engraver, with a steel tool known as a graver, and aided by a powerful magnifying glass, carefully carves his portion of the design into the steel. He knows that one false cut or a slip of his tool, or one miscalculation of width or depth of line, may destroy the merit of his work. A single mistake means that months or weeks of labor will have been in vain. The bureau is proud of the fact that no counterfeiter ever has duplicated the excellent work of its expert engravers.

16. According to the above passage, each engraver in the Bureau of Engraving and Printing 16.____
    A. must be approved by the Secretary of the Treasury before he can begin work on the design for a new bank note
    B. is responsible for engraving a complete design of a new bank note by himself
    C. designs new bank notes and submits them for approval to the Secretary of the Treasury
    D. performs sonly a specific part of the work of engraving a design for a new bank note

17. According to the above passage, 17.____
    A. an engraver's tools are not available to a counterfeiter
    B. mistakes made in engraving a design can be corrected immediately with little delay in the work of the Bureau
    C. the skilled work of the engravers has not been successfully reproduced by counterfeiter
    D. careful carving and cutting by the engraver is essential to prevent damage to equipment

Questions 18-21.

DIRECTIONS: Questions 18 through 21 are to be answered SOLELY on the basis of the following passage.

In the late fifties, the average American housewife spent $4.50 per day for a family of four on food and 5.15 hours in food preparation, if all of her food was *home prepared*; she spent $5.80 per day and 3.245 hours if all of her food was purchased *partially prepared*; and $6.70 per day and 1.64 hours if all of her food was purchased *ready-to-serve.*

Americans spent about 20 billion dollars for food products in 1941. They spent nearly 70 billion dollars in 1958. They spent 25 percent of their cash income on food in 1958. For the same kinds and quantities of food that consumers bought in 1941, they would have spent only 16% of their cash income in 1958. It is obvious that our food does cost more. Many factors contribute to this increase besides the additional cost that might be attributed to processing. Consumption of more expensive food items, higher marketing margins, and more food eaten in restaurants are other factors.

The Census of Manufacturers gives some indication of the total bill for processing. The value added by manufacturing of food and kindred products amounted to 3.5 billion of the 20 billion dollars spent for food in 1941. In the year 1958, the comparable figure had climbed to 14 billion dollars.

18. According to the above passage, the cash income of Americans in 1958 was MOST NEARLY _____ billion dollars. 18.____
    A. 11.2 B. 17.5 C. 70 D. 280

19. According to the above passage, if Americans bought the same kinds and quantities of food in 1958 as they did in 1941, they would have spent MOST NEARLY _____ billion dollars. 19.____
    A. 20 B. 45 C. 74 D. 84

20. According to the above passage, the percent increase in money spent for food in 1958 over 1941, as compared with the percentage increase in money spent for food processing in the same years, 20.____
    A. was greater
    B. was less
    C. was the same
    D. cannot be determined from the passage

21. In 1958, an American housewife who bought all of her food ready-to-serve saved time, as compared with the housewife who prepared all of her food at home 21.____
    A. 1.6 hours daily
    B. 1.9 hours daily
    C. 3.5 hours daily
    D. an amount of time which cannot be determined from the above passage

Questions 22-25.

DIRECTIONS: Questions 22 through 25 are to be answered SOLELY on the basis of the following passage.

Any member of the retirement system who is in city service, who files a proper application for service credit and agrees to deductions from his compensation at triple his normal rate of contribution, shall be credited with a period of city service previous to the beginning of his present membership in the retirement system. The period of service credited shall be equal to the period throughout which such triple deductions are made, but may not exceed the total of the city service the number rendered between his first day of eligibility for membership in the retirement system and the day he last became a member. After triple contributions for all of the first three years of service credit claimed, the remaining service credit may be purchased by a single payment of the sum of the remaining payments. If the total time purchasable exceeds ten years, triple contributions may be made for one-half of such time, and the remaining time purchased by a single payment of the sum of the remaining payments. Credit for service acquired in the above manner may be used only in determining the amount of any retirement benefit. Eligibility for such benefit will, in all cases, be based upon service rendered after the employee's membership last began, and will be exclusive of service credit purchased as described above.

22. According to the above passage, in order to obtain credit for city service previous to the beginning of an employee's present membership in the retirement system, the employee must 22.____
    A. apply for the service credit and consent to additional contributions to the retirement system
    B. apply for the service credit before he renews his membership in the retirement system
    C. have previous city service which does not exceed ten years
    D. make contributions to the retirement system for three years

23. According to the information in the above passage, credit for city service previous to the beginning of an employee's present membership in the retirement system is 23.____
    A. credited up to a maximum of ten years
    B. credited to any member of the retirement system
    C. used in determining the amount of the employee's benefits
    D. used in establishing the employee's eligibility to receive benefits

24. According to the information in the above passage, a member of the retirement system may purchase service credit for 24.____
    A. the period of time between his first day of eligibility for membership in the retirement system and the date he applies for the service credit
    B. one-half of the total of his previous city service if the total time exceeds ten years
    C. the period of time throughout which triple deductions are made
    D. the period of city service between his first day of eligibility for membership in the retirement system and the day he last became a member

25. Suppose that a member of the retirement system has filed an application for service credit for five years of previous city service. 25.____
    Based on the information in the above passage, the employee may purchase credit for this previous city service by making
    A. triple contributions for three years
    B. triple contributions for one-half of the time and a single payment of the sum of the remaining payments
    C. triple contributions for three years and a single payment of the sum of the remaining payments
    D. a single payment of the sum of the payments

# KEY (CORRECT ANSWERS)

1. C
2. D
3. B
4. B
5. A

6. C
7. C
8. D
9. A
10. B

11. D
12. B
13. A
14. B
15. C

16. D
17. C
18. D
19. B
20. B

21. C
22. A
23. C
24. D
25. C

# EXAMINATION SECTION

## TEST 1

DIRECTIONS: Each question or incomplete statement is followed by several suggested answers or completions. Select the one that BEST answers the question or completes the statement. *PRINT THE LETTER OF THE CORRECT ANSWER IN THE SPACE AT THE RIGHT.*

1. When a supervisor in a large office introduces a change in the regular office procedure, it is USUAL to expect 1.____
   A. immediate acceptance by office staff, unless the change is unnecessary
   B. an immediate production increase, since new procedures are more stimulating than old ones
   C. a temporary production loss, even if the change is really an overall improvement
   D. resistance to the change only if it has been put into writing

2. A supervisor evaluates the performance of subordinates and then applies measures, where needed, which result in bringing performance up to desired standards. 2.____
   Which of the following functions of management might he BEST be described as performing?
   A. Organizing B. Controlling C. Directing D. Planning

3. Assume that, as a supervisor, you have been assigned responsibility for a new and complex project which entails collection and analysis of data. You have prepared general written instructions which explain the project and procedures to be followed by several statisticians. 3.____
   Which of the following procedures would be MOST advisable for you, as the supervisor, to follow?
   A. Distribute the instructions to your subordinates to come to you with any important questions
   B. Distribute the instructions and advise subordinates to come to you with any important questions
   C. Meet with subordinates as a group and explain the project using the written instructions as a handout
   D. Delegate responsibility for further explanation of the project to an immediate qualified subordinate to free you for concentration on research design

4. Supervisors have an obligation to make careful and thorough appraisals and reports of probationary employees. 4.____
   Of the following, the MOST important justification for this statement is that the probationary period
   A. should be used for positive development of the employee's understanding of the organization
   B. is the most effective period for changing a new employee's knowledges, skills, and attitudes

C. insures that the employee will meet work standard requirements on future assignments
D. should be considered as the final step in the selection process

5. Many studies of management indicate that a principal reason for failure of supervisors lies in their ability to delegate duties effectively. Which one of the following practices by a supervisor would NOT be a block to successful delegation? 5.____
A. Instructing the delegate to follow a set procedure in carrying out the assignment
B. Maintaining point-by-point control over the process delegated
C. Transferring ultimate responsibility for the duties assigned to the delegate
D. Requiring the delegate to keep the delegator informed of his progress

6. Crosswise communication occurs between personnel at lower or middle levels of different organizational units. It often speeds information and improves understanding, but has certain dangers. Of the following proposed policies, which would NOT be important as a safeguard in crosswise communication? 6.____
A. Supervisors should agree as to how crosswise communication should occur.
B. Crosswise relationships must exist only between employees of equal status.
C. Subordinates must keep their superiors informed about their interdepartmental communications.
D. Subordinates must refrain from making commitments beyond their authority.

7. Systems theory has given us certain principles which are as applicable to organizational and social activities as they are to those of science. With regard to the training of employees in an organization, which of the following is likely to be MOST consistent with the modern systems approach? Training can be effective ONLY when it is 7.____
A. related to the individual abilities of the employees
B. done on all levels of the organizational hierarchy
C. evaluated on the basis of experimental and control groups
D. provided on the job by the immediate supervisor

8. The management of a large agency, before making a decision as to whether or not to computerize its operations, should have a feasibility study made. Of the following, the one which is LEAST important to include in such a study is 8.____
A. the current abilities of management and staff to use a computer
B. projected workloads and changes in objectives of functional units in the agency
C. the contributions expected of each organizational unit towards achievement of agency objectives
D. the decision-making activity and informational needs of each management function

9. Managing information covers the creation, collection, processing, storage, and transmission of information that appears in a variety of forms. A supervisor responsible for a statistical unit can be considered, in many respects, an information manager. 9.____
Of the following, which would be considered the LEAST important aspect of the information manager's job?
   A. Establishing better information standards and forms
   B. Reducing the amount of unnecessary paperwork performed
   C. Producing progressively greater numbers of informational reports
   D. Developing a greater appreciation for information among management members

10. Because of the need for improvement in information systems throughout industry and government, various techniques for improving these systems have been developed. 10.____
Of these, *systems simulation* is a technique for improving systems which
   A. creates new ideas and concepts through the use of a computer
   B. deals with time controlling of interrelated systems which make up an overall project
   C. permits experimentation with various ideas to see what results might be obtained
   D. does not rely on assumptions which condition the value of the results

11. The one of the following which it is NOT advisable for a supervisor to do when dealing with individual employees is to 11.____
   A. recognize a person's outstanding service as well as his mistakes
   B. help an employee satisfy his need to excel
   C. encourage an efficient employee to seek better opportunities even if this action may cause the supervisor to lose a good worker
   D. take public notice of an employee's mistakes so that fewer errors will be made in the future

12. Suppose that you are in a department where you are given the responsibility for teaching seven new assistants a number of routine procedures that all assistants should know. 12.____
Of the following, the BEST method for you to follow in teaching these procedures is to
   A. separate the slower learners from the faster learners and adapt your presentation to their level of ability
   B. instruct all the new employees in a group without attempting to assess differences in learning rates
   C. restrict your approach to giving them detailed written instructions in order to save time
   D. avoid giving the employees written instructions in order to force them to memorize job procedures quickly

13. Suppose that you are a supervisor to whom several assistants must hand in work for review. You notice that one of the assistants gets very upset whenever you discover an error in his work, although all the assistants make mistakes from time to time. 13.____
Of the following, it would be BEST for you to
   A. arrange discreetly for the employee's work to be reviewed by another supervisor
   B. ignore his reaction since giving attention to such behavior increases its intensity
   C. suggest that the employee seek medical help since he has such great difficulty in accepting normal criticism
   D. try to build the employee's self-confidence by emphasizing those parts of his work that are done well

14. Suppose you are a supervisor responsible for supervising a number of assistants in an agency where each assistant receives a manual of policies and procedures when he first reports for work. You have been asked to teach your subordinates a new procedure which requires knowledge of several items of policy and procedure found in the manual. 14.____
The one of the following techniques which it would be BEST for you to employ is to
   A. give verbal instructions which include a review of the appropriate standard procedures as well as an explanation of new tasks
   B. give individual instruction restricted to the new procedure to each assistant as the need arises
   C. provide written instructions for new procedural elements and refer employees to their manuals for explanation of standard procedures
   D. ask employees to review appropriate sections of their manual and then explain those aspects of the new procedure which the manual did not cover

15. Supposes that you are a supervisor in charge of a unit in which changes in work procedures are about to be instituted. 15.____
The one of the following which you, as the supervisor, should anticipate as being MOST likely to occur during the changeover is
   A. a temporary rise in production because of interest in the new procedures
   B. uniform acceptance of these procedures on the part of your staff
   C. varying interpretations of the new procedures by your staff
   D. general agreement among staff members that the new procedures are advantageous

16. Suppose that a supervisor and one of the assistants under his supervision are known to be friends who play golf together on weekends. 16.____
The maintenance of such a friendship on the part of the supervisor is GENERALLY
   A. *acceptable* as long as this assistant continues to perform his duties satisfactorily
   B. *unacceptable* since the supervisor will find it difficult to treat the assistant as a subordinate

C. *acceptable* if the supervisor does not favor this assistant above other employees
D. *unacceptable* because the other assistants will resent the friendship regardless of the supervisor's behavior on the job

17. Suppose that you are a supervisor assigned to review the financial records of an agency which has recently undergone a major reorganization. 17.____
Which of the following would it be BEST for you to do FIRST?
A. Interview the individual in charge of agency financial operations to determine whether the organizational changes affect the system of financial review
B. Discuss the nature of the reorganization with your own supervisor to anticipate and plan a new financial review procedure
C. Carry out the financial review as usual, and adjust your methods to any problems arising from the reorganization
D. Request a written report from the agency head explaining the nature of the reorganization and recommending changes in the system of financial review

18. Suppose that a newly assigned supervisor finds that he must delegate some of his duties to subordinates in order to get the work done. 18.____
Which one of the following would NOT be a block to his delegating these duties effectively?
A. Inability to give proper directions as to what he wants done
B. Reluctance to take calculated risks
C. Lack of trust in his subordinates
D. Retaining ultimate responsibility for the delegated work

19. A supervisor sometimes performs the staff function of preparing and circulating reports among bureau chiefs. 19.____
Which of the following is LEAST important as an objective in designing and writing such reports?
A. Providing relevant information on past, present, and future actions
B. Modifying his language in order to insure goodwill among the bureau chiefs
C. Helping the readers of the report to make appropriate decisions
D. Summarizing important information to help readers see trends or outstanding points

20. Suppose you are a supervisor assigned to prepare a report to be read by all bureau chiefs in your agency. 20.____
The MOST important reason for avoiding highly technical accounting terminology in writing this report is to
A. ensure the accuracy and relevancy of the text
B. insure winning the readers' cooperation
C. make the report more interesting to the readers
D. make it easier for the readers to understand

21. Which of the following conditions is MOST likely to cause low morale in an office? 21.____
   A. Different standards of performance for individuals in the same title
   B. A requirement that employees perform at full capacity
   C. Standards of performance that vary with titles of employees
   D. Careful attention to the image of the division or department

22. A wise supervisor or representative of management realizes that, in the relationship between supervisor and subordinates, all power is not on the side of management, and that subordinates do sometimes react to restrictive authority in such a manner as to seriously retard management's objectives. A wise supervisor does not stimulate such reactions. 22.____
In the subordinate's attempt to retaliate against an unusually authoritative management style, which of the following actions would generally be LEAST successful for the subordinate? He
   A. joins with other employees in organizations to deal with management
   B. obviously delays in carrying out instructions which are given in an arrogant or incisive manner
   C. performs assignments exactly as instructed even when he recognizes errors in instructions
   D. holds back the flow of feedback information to superiors

23. Which of the following is the MOST likely and costly effect of vague and indefinite instructions given to subordinates by a supervisor? 23.____
   A. Misunderstanding and ineffective work on the part of the subordinates
   B. A necessity for the supervisor to report identical instructions with each assignment
   C. A failure of the supervisor to adequately keep the attention of subordinates
   D. Inability of subordinates to assist each other in the absence of the supervisor

24. At the professional level, there is a kind of informal authority which exercises itself even though no delegation of authority has taken place from higher management. It occurs within the context of knowledge required and professional competence in a special area. 24.____
An example of the kind of authority described in this statement is MOST clearly exemplified in the situation where a senior supervisor influences associates and subordinates by virtue of the
   A. salary level fixed for his particular set of duties
   B. amount of college training he possesses
   C. technical position he has gained and holds on the work team
   D. initiative and judgment he has demonstrated to his supervisor

25. An assistant under your supervision attempts to conceal the fact that he has made an error. 25.____
Under this circumstance, it would be BEST for you, as the supervisor, to proceed on the assumption that

A. this evasion indicates something wrong in the fundamental relationship between you and the assistant
B. this evasion is not deliberate, if the error is subsequently corrected by the assistant
C. this evasion should be overlooked if the error is not significant
D. detection and correction of errors will come about as an automatic consequence of internal control procedures

---

## KEY (CORRECT ANSWERS)

| | | | |
|---|---|---|---|
| 1. | C | 11. | D |
| 2. | B | 12. | B |
| 3. | C | 13. | D |
| 4. | D | 14. | A |
| 5. | D | 15. | C |
| 6. | B | 16. | C |
| 7. | B | 17. | A |
| 8. | A | 18. | D |
| 9. | C | 19. | B |
| 10. | C | 20. | D |

| | |
|---|---|
| 21. | A |
| 22. | B |
| 23. | A |
| 24. | C |
| 25. | A |

---

# TEST 2

DIRECTIONS: Each question or incomplete statement is followed by several suggested answers or completions. Select the one that BEST answers the question or completes the statement. *PRINT THE LETTER OF THE CORRECT ANSWER IN THE SPACE AT THE RIGHT.*

1. The unit which you supervise has a number of attorneys, accountants, examiners, statisticians, and clerks who prepare some of the routine papers required to be filed. In order to be certain that nothing goes out of your office that is improper, you have instituted a system that requires that you review and initial all moving papers, memoranda of law and briefs that are prepared. As a result, you put in a great deal of overtime and even must take work home with you frequently. A situation such as this is 1.____
   A. inevitable if you are to keep proper controls over the quality of the office work product
   B. indicative of the fact that the agency must provide an additional position within your office for an assistant supervisor who would do all the reviewing, leaving you free for other pressing administrative work and to handle the most difficult work in your unit
   C. the logical result of an ever-increasing caseload
   D. symptomatic of poor supervision and management

2. Your unit has been assigned a new employee who has never worked for the city. To orient him to his job in your unit, of the following, the BEST procedure is first to 2.____
   A. assign him to another employee to whatever work that employee gives him so that he can become familiar with your work and at the same time be productive
   B. give him copies of the charter and code provisions affecting your operations plus any in-office memoranda or instructions that are available and have him read them
   C. assign him to work on a relatively simple problem and then, after he has finished it, tell him politely what he did wrong
   D. explain to him the duties of his position and the functions of the office

3. A bureau chief who supervises other supervisors makes it a practice to assign them more cases than they can possibly handle. This approach is 3.____
   A. *right*, because it results in getting more work done than would otherwise be the case
   B. *right*, because it relieves the bureau chief making the assignments of the responsibility of getting the work done
   C. *wrong*, because it builds resistance on the part of those called upon to handle the caseload
   D. *wrong*, because superiors lose track of cases

4. Assume you are a supervisor and are expected to exercise *authority* over subordinates. 4.____
Which of the following BEST defines *authority*? The
   A. ability to control the nature of the contribution a subordinate is desirous of making
   B. innate inability to get others to do for you what you want to get done irrespective of their own wishes
   C. legal right conferred by the agency to control the actions of others
   D. power to determine a subordinate's attitude toward his agency and his superiors

5. Paternalistic leadership stresses a paternal or fatherly influence in the relationships between the leader and the group and is manifest in a watchful care for the comfort and welfare of the followers. 5.____
Which one of the following statements regarding paternalistic leadership is MOST accurate?
   A. Employees who work well under paternalistic leadership come to expect such leadership even when the paternal leader has left the organization.
   B. Most disputes arising out of supervisor-subordinate relationships develop because group leaders do not understand the principles of paternalistic leadership.
   C. Paternalistic leadership frequently destroys office relationships because most employees are turned into non-thinking dependent robots.
   D. Paternalistic leadership is rarely, if ever, successful because employees resent paternalistic leadership which they equate with weakness.

6. Employees who have extensive dealings with members of the public should have, as much as possible, *real acceptance* of all people and a willingness to serve everyone impartially and objectively. 6.____
Assuming that this statement is correct, the one of the following which would be the BEST demonstration of *real acceptance* is
   A. condoning antisocial behavior
   B. giving the appearance of agreeing with everyone encountered
   C. refusing to give opinions on anyone's behavior
   D. understanding the feelings expressed through a person's behavior

7. Assume that the agency chief has requested you to help plan a public relations program because of recent complaints from citizens about the unbecoming conduct and language of various groups of city employees who have dealings with the public. 7.____
In carrying out this assignment, the one of the following steps which should be undertaken FIRST is to
   A. study the characteristics of the public clientele dealt with by employees in your agency
   B. arrange to have employees attend several seminars on human relations
   C. develop several procedures for dealing with the public and allow the staff to choose the one which is best
   D. find out whether the employees in your agency may oppose any plan proposed by you

8. The one of the following statements which BEST expresses the relationship between the morale of government employees and the public relations aspects of their work is: 8.____
   A. There is little relationship between employee morale and public relations, chiefly because public opinion is shaped primarily by response to departmental policy formulation.
   B. Employee morale is closely related to public relations, chiefly because the employee's morale will largely determine the manner in which he deals with the public.
   C. There is little relationship between employee morale and public relations, chiefly because public relations is primarily a function of the agency's public relations department.
   D. Employee morale is closely related to public relations, chiefly because employee morale indicates the attitude of the agency's top officials toward the public.

9. As a supervisor, you are required to deal extensively with the public. The agency chief has indicated that he is considering holding a special in-service training course for employees in communications skills 9.____
   Holding this training course would be
   A. *advisable*, chiefly because government employees should receive formal training in public relations skills
   B. *inadvisable*, chiefly because the public regards such training as a *waste of the taxpayers money*
   C. *advisable*, chiefly because such training will enable the employee to aid in drafting departmental press releases
   D. *inadvisable*, chiefly because of the great difficulty involved in developing skills through formal instruction

10. Assume that you have extensive contact with the public. In dealing with the public, sensitivity to an individual's attitudes is important because these attitudes can be used to predict behavior. 10.____
    However, the MAIN reason that attitudes CANNOT successfully predict all behavior is that
    A. attitudes are highly resistant to change
    B. an individual acquires attitudes as a function of growing up in a particular cultural environment
    C. attitudes are only one of many factors which determine a person's behavior
    D. an individual's behavior is not always observable

11. Rotation of employees from assignment to assignment is sometimes advocated by management experts. 11.____
    Of the following, the MOST probable advantage to the organization of this practice is that it leads to
    A. higher specialization of duties so that excessive identification with the overall organization is reduced
    B. increased loyalty of employees to their immediate supervisors

C. greater training and development of employees
D. intensified desire of employees to obtain additional, outside formal education

12. Usually, a supervisor should attempt to standardize the work for which he is responsible. 12.____
The one of the following which is a BASIC reason for doing this is to
A. eliminate the need to establish priorities
B. permit the granting of exceptions to rules and special circumstances
C. facilitate the taking of action based on applicable standards
D. learn the identity of outstanding employees

13. The differences between line and staff authority are often quite ambiguous. 13.____
Of the following, the ESSENTIAL difference is that
A. *line authority* is exercised by first-level supervisors; *staff authority* is exercised by higher-level supervisors and managerial staff
B. *staff authority* is the right to issue directives; *line authority* is entirely consultative
C. *line authority* is the power to make decisions regarding intra-agency matters; *staff authority* involves decisions regarding inter-agency matters
D. *staff authority* is largely advisory; *line authority* is the right to command

14. Modern management theory stresses work-centered motivation as one way of increasing the productivity of employees. 14.____
The one of the following which is PARTICULARLY characteristic of such motivation is that it
A. emphasizes the crucial role of routinization of procedures
B. stresses the satisfaction to be found in performing work
C. features the value of wages and fringe benefits
D. uses a firm but fair method of discipline

15. The agency's informal communications network is called the *grapevine.* 15.____
If employees are learning about important organizational developments primarily through the grapevine, this is MOST likely an indication that
A. official channels of communication are not functioning so efficiently as they should
B. supervisory personnel are making effective use of the grapevine to communicate with subordinates
C. employees already have a clear understanding of the agency's policies and procedures
D. upward formal channels of communication within the agency are informing management of employee grievances

16. Of the following, a flow chart is BEST described as a chart which shows 16.____
A. the places through which work moves in the course of the job process
B. which employees perform specific functions leading to the completion of a job

C. the schedules for production and how they eliminate waiting time between jobs
D. how work units are affected by the actions of related work units

17. Evaluation of the results of training is necessary in order to assess its value. Of the following, the BEST technique for the supervisor to use in determining whether the training under consideration actually resulted in the desired modification of the behavior of the employee concerned is through 17.____
A. inference B. job analysis C. observation D. simulation

18. The usual distinction between line and staff authority is that staff authority is mainly advisory, whereas line authority is the right to command. However, a third category has been suggested-prescriptive-to distinguish those personnel whose functions may be formally defined as staff but in practice exercise considerable authority regarding decisions relating to their specialties. 18.____
The one of the following which indicates the MAJOR purpose of creating this third category is to
A. develop the ability of each employee to perform a greater number of tasks
B. reduce line-staff conflict
C. prevent over-specialization of functions
D. encourage decision-making by line personnel

19. It is sometimes considered desirable to train employees to a standard of proficiency higher than that deemed necessary for actual job performance. 19.____
The MOST likely reason for such overtraining would be to
A. eliminate the need for standards
B. increase the value of refresher training
C. compensate for previous lack of training
D. reduce forgetting or loss of skill

20. Assume that you have been directed to immediately institute various new procedures in the handling of records. 20.____
Of the following, the BEST method for you to use to insure that your subordinates know exactly what to do is to
A. circulate a memorandum explaining the new procedure have your subordinates initial it
B. explain the new procedures to one or two subordinates and ask them to tell the others
C. have a meeting with your subordinates to give them copies of the procedures and discuss it with them
D. post the new procedures where they can be referred to by all those concerned

21. A supervisor decided to hold a problem-solving conference with his entire staff and distributed an announcement and agenda one week before the meeting. 21.____
Of the following, the BEST reason for providing each participant with an agenda is that
   A. participants will feel that something will be accomplished
   B. participants may prepare for the conference
   C. controversy will be reduced
   D. the top man should state the expected conclusions

22. In attempting to motivate employees, rewards are considered preferable to punishment PRIMARILY because 22.____
   A. punishment seldom has any effect on human behavior
   B. punishment usually results in decreased production
   C. supervisors find it difficult to punish
   D. rewards are more likely to result in willing cooperation

23. In an attempt to combat the low morale in his organization, a high-level supervisor publicized an *open-door* policy to allow employees who wished to do so to come to him with their complaints. 23.____
Which of the following is LEAST likely to account for the fact that no employee came in with a complaint?
   A. Employees are generally reluctant to go over the heads of their immediate supervisors.
   B. The employees did not feel that management would help them.
   C. The low morale was not due to complaints association with the job
   D. The employees felt that they had more to lose than to gain.

24. It is MOST desirable to use written instructions rather than oral instructions for a particular job when 24.____
   A. a mistake on the job will not be serious
   B. the job can be completed in a short time
   C. there is no need to explain the job minutely
   D. the job involves many details

25. You have been asked to prepare for public distribution a statement dealing with a controversial matter. 25.____
Of the following approaches, the one which would usually be MOST effective is to present your department's point of view
   A. as tersely as possible with no reference to any other matters
   B. developed from ideas and facts well known to most readers
   C. and show all the statistical data and techniques which were used in arriving at it
   D. in such a way that the controversial parts are omitted

# KEY (CORRECT ANSWERS)

1. D
2. D
3. C
4. C
5. A

6. D
7. A
8. B
9. A
10. C

11. C
12. C
13. D
14. B
15. A

16. A
17. C
18. B
19. D
20. C

21. B
22. D
23. C
24. D
25. B

# TEST 3

DIRECTIONS: Each question or incomplete statement is followed by several suggested answers or completions. Select the one that BEST answers the question or completes the statement. *PRINT THE LETTER OF THE CORRECT ANSWER IN THE SPACE AT THE RIGHT.*

1. An administrator who supervises other supervisors makes it a practice to set deadline dates for completion of assignments. 1.____
A NATURAL consequence of setting deadline dates is that
   A. supervisors will usually wait until the deadline date before they give projects their wholehearted attention
   B. projects are completed sooner than if no deadline dates are set
   C. such dates are ignored even though they are conspicuously posted
   D. the frequency of errors sharply increases resulting in an inability to meet deadlines

2. Assume that you are chairing a meeting of the members of your staff. You throw out a question to the group. No one answers your question immediately, so that you find yourself faced with silence. 2.____
In the circumstances, it would probably be BEST for you to
   A. ask the member of the group who appears to be least attentive to repeat the question
   B. change the topic quickly
   C. repeat the question carefully, pronouncing each word, and if there is still no response, repeat the question an additional time
   D. wait for an answer since someone will usually say something to break the tension

3. Assume that you are holding a meeting with the members of your staff. John, a member of the unit, keeps sidetracking the subject of the discussion by bringing up extraneous matters. You deal with the situation by saying to him after he has raised an immaterial point, *"That's an interesting point John, but can you show me how it ties in with what we're talking about?"* 3.____
Your approach in this situation would GENERALLY be considered
   A. *bad*; you have prevented the group from discussing not only extraneous matters but pertinent material as well
   B. *bad*; you have seriously humiliated John in front of the entire group
   C. *good*; you have pointed out how the discussion is straying from the main topic
   D. *good*; you have prevented John from presenting extraneous matters at future meetings

4. Assume that a senior supervisor is asked to supervise a group of staff personnel. The work of one of these staff men meets minimum standards of acceptability. However, this staff man constantly looks for something at which to take offense. In any conversation with either a fellow staff man or with a superior, he views the slightest criticism as a grave insult. 4.____

In this case, the senior supervisor should

A. advise the staff man that the next time he refuses to accept criticism, he will be severely reprimanded
B. ask member of the group for advice on how to deal with this staff man
C. make it a practice to speak calmly, slowly, and deliberately to this staff man and question him frequently to make sure that there is no breakdown in communications
D. recognize that professional help may be required and that this problem may not be conducive to a solution by a supervisor

5. Assume that you discover that one of the staff in preparing certain papers has made a serious mistake which has become obvious. 5.____
In dealing with this situation, it would be BEST for you to begin by
A. asking the employee how the mistake happened
B. asking the employee to read through the papers to see whether he can correct the mistake
C. pointing out to the employee that, while an occasional error is permissible, frequent errors can prove a source of embarrassment to all concerned
D. pointing to the mistake and asking the employee whether he realizes the consequences of the mistake

6. You desire to develop teamwork among the members of your staff. You are assigned a case which will require that two of the staff work together if the papers are to be prepared in time. You decided to assign two employees, whom you know to be close friends, to work on these papers. 6.____
Your action in this regard would GENERALLY be considered
A. *bad*; friends working together tend to do as little as they can get away with
B. *bad*; people who are friends socially often find that the bonds of friendship disintegrate in work situations
C. *good*; friends who are permitted to work together show their appreciation by utilizing every opportunity to reinforce the group leader's position of authority
D. *good*; the evidence suggests that more work can be done in this way

7. You notice that all of the employees, without exception, take lunch hours which in your view are excessively long. You call each of them to your desk and point out that unless this practice is brought to a stop, appropriate action will be taken. 7.____
The way in which you handled this problem would GENERALLY be considered
A. *proper*, primarily because a civil servant, no matter what his professional status, owes the public a full day's work for a full day's pay
B. *proper*, primarily because employees need to have a clear picture of the rewards and penalties that go with public employment
C. *improper*, primarily because group problems require group discussion which need not be formal in character
D. *improper*, primarily because professional personnel resent having such matters as lunch hours brought to their attention

8. In communicating with superiors or subordinates, it is well to bear in mind a phenomenon known as the *halo effect*. An example of this *halo effect* occurs when we 8.____
   A. employ informal language in a formal setting as a means of attracting attention
   B. ignore the advice of someone we distrust without evaluating the advice
   C. ask people to speak up who have a tendency to speak softly or occasionally indistinctly
   D. react to a piece of good work by inquiring into the motivations of those who did the work

9. Which of the following dangers is MOST likely to arise when a work group becomes too tightly knit? The 9.____
   A. group may appoint an informal leader who gradually sets policies and standards for the group to the detriment of the agency
   B. group may be reluctant to accept new employees as members
   C. quantity and quality of work produced may tend to diminish sharply despite the group's best efforts
   D. group may focus too strongly on employee benefits at inappropriate times

10. The overall managerial problem has become more complex because each group of management specialists will tend to view the interests of the enterprise in terms which are compatible with the survival or the increase of its special function. That is, each group will have a trained capacity for its own function and a *trained incapacity* to see its relation to the whole. 10.____
    The *trained incapacity* to which the foregoing passage refers PROBABLY results from
    A. an imbalance in the number of specialists as compared with the number of generalists
    B. development by each specialized group of a certain dominant value or goal that shapes its entire way of doing things
    C. low morale accompanied by lackadaisical behavior by large segments of the managerial staff
    D. supervisory failure to inculcate pride in workmanship

11. Of the following, the MOST important responsibility of a supervisor in charge of a section is to 11.____
    A establish close personal relationships with each of his subordinates in the section
    B. insure that each subordinate in the section knows the full range of his duties and responsibilities
    C. maintain friendly relations with his immediate supervisor
    D. protect his subordinates from criticism from any source

12. The BEST way to get a good work output from employees is to 12.____
    A. hold over them the threat of disciplinary action or removal
    B. maintain a steady, unrelenting pressure on them
    C. show them that you can do anything they can do faster and better
    D win their respect and liking so they want to work for you

13. Supervisors should GENERALLY 13.____
    A. lean more toward management than toward their subordinates
    B. lean neither toward subordinates nor management
    C. lean more toward their subordinates than toward their management
    D. maintain a proper balance between management and subordinates

14. For a supervisor in charge of a section to ask occasionally the opinion of a subordinate concerning a problem is 14.____
    A. *desirable*; but it would be even better if the subordinate were consulted routinely on every problem
    B. *desirable*; subordinates may make good suggestions and will be pleased by being consulted
    C. *undesirable*; subordinates may be resentful if their advice is not followed
    D. *undesirable*; the supervisor should not attempt to shift his responsibilities to subordinates

15. The PRIMARY responsibility of a supervisor is to 15.____
    A. gain the confidence and make friends of all his subordinates
    B. get the work done properly
    C. satisfy his superior and gain his respect
    D. train the men in new methods for doing the work

16. In starting a work simplification study, the one of the following steps that should be taken FIRST is to 16.____
    A. break the work down into its elements
    B. draw up a chart of operations
    C. enlist the interest and cooperation of the personnel
    D. suggest alternative procedures

17. Of the following, the MOST important value of a manual of procedures is that it usually 17.____
    A. eliminates the need for on-the-job training
    B. decreases the span of control which can be exercised by individual supervisory personnel
    C. outlines methods of operation for ready reference
    D. provides concrete examples of work previously performed by employees

18. Reprimanding a subordinate when he has done something wrong should be done PRIMARILY in order to 18.____
    A. deter others from similar acts
    B. improve the subordinate in future performance
    C. maintain discipline
    D. uphold departmental rules

19. Most of the training of new employees in a public agency is USUALLY accomplished by 19.____
    A. formal classes
    B. general orientation
    C. internship
    D. on-the-job activities

20. You find that delivery of a certain item cannot possibly be made to a using agency by the date the using agency requested. 20.____
Of the following, the MOST advisable course of action for you to take FIRST is to
   A. cancel the order and inform the using agency
   B. discuss the problem with the using agency
   C. notify the using agency to obtain the item through direct purchase
   D. schedule the delivery for the earliest possible date

21. Assume that one of your subordinates has gotten into the habit of regularly and routinely referring every small problem which arises in his work to you. 21.____
In order to help him overcome this habit, it is generally MOST advisable for you to
   A. advise him that you do not have time to discuss each problem with him and that he should do whatever he wants
   B. ask your subordinate for his solution and approve any satisfactory approach that he suggests
   C. refuse to discuss such routine problems with him
   D. tell him that he should consider looking for another position if he does not feel competent to solve such routine problems

22. The BEST of the following reasons for developing understudies to supervisory staff is that this practice 22.____
   A. assures that capable staff will not leave their jobs since they are certain to be promoted
   B. helps to assure continued efficiency when persons in important positions leave their jobs
   C. improves morale by demonstrating to employees the opportunities for advancement
   D. provides an opportunity for giving on-the-job training

23. When a supervisor delegates some of his work to a subordinate, the 23.____
   A. supervisor retains final responsibility for the work
   B. supervisor should not check on the work until it has been completed
   C. subordinate assumes full responsibility for the successful completion of the work
   D. subordinate is likely to lose interest and get less satisfaction from the work

24. Sometimes it is necessary to give out written orders or to post written or typed information on a bulletin board rather than to merely give spoken orders. The supervisor must decide how he will do it. 24.____
In which of the following situations would it be BETTER for him to give written rather than spoken orders?
   A. He is going to reassign a man from one unit to another under his supervision.
   B. His staff must be informed of a permanent change in a complicated operating procedure.

C. A man must be transferred from a clerical unit to an operating unit.
D. He must order a group of staff men to do a difficult and tedious inventory job to which most of them are likely to object.

25. Of the following symbolic patterns, which one is NOT representative of a normal direction in which formal organizational communications flow? 25.____

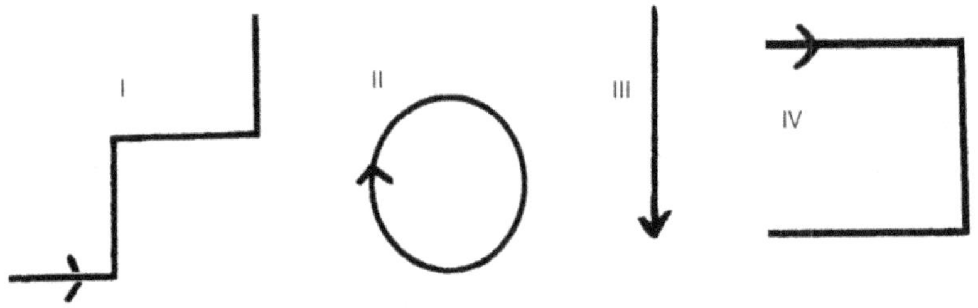


A. I B. II C. III D. IV

---

## KEY (CORRECT ANSWERS)

| | | | |
|---|---|---|---|
| 1. | B | 11. | B |
| 2. | D | 12. | D |
| 3. | C | 13. | D |
| 4. | D | 14. | B |
| 5. | A | 15. | B |
| 6. | D | 16. | C |
| 7. | C | 17. | C |
| 8. | B | 18. | B |
| 9. | B | 19. | D |
| 10. | B | 20. | B |

21. B
22. B
23. A
24. B
25. B

# EXAMINATION SECTION

## TEST 1

DIRECTIONS: Each question or incomplete statement is followed by several suggested answers or completions. Select the one that BEST answers the question or completes the statement. *PRINT THE LETTER OF THE CORRECT ANSWER IN THE SPACE AT THE RIGHT.*

1. Which one of the following generalizations is MOST likely to be INACCURATE and lead to judgmental errors in communication? 1.____
   A. A supervisor must be able to read with understanding.
   B. Misunderstanding may lead to dislike.
   C. Anyone can listen to another person and understand what he means.
   D. It is usually desirable to let a speaker talk until he is finished.

2. Assume that, as a supervisor, you have been directed to inform your subordinates about the implementation of a new procedure which will affect their work. 2.____
   While communicating this information, you should do all of the following EXCEPT
   A. obtain the approval of your subordinates regarding the new procedure
   B. explain the reason for implementing the new procedure
   C. hold a staff meeting at a time convenient to most of your subordinates
   D. encourage a productive discussion of the new procedure

3. Assume that you are in charge of a section that handles requests for information on matters received from the public. One day, you observe that a clerk under your supervision is using a method to log-in requests for information that is different from the one specified by you in the past. Upon questioning the clerk, you discover that instructions changing the old procedure were delivered orally by your supervisor on a day on which you were absent from the office. 3.____
   Of the following, the MOST appropriate action for you to take is to
   A. tell the clerk to revert to the old procedure at once
   B. ask your supervisor for information about the change
   C. call your staff together and tell them that no existing procedure is to be changed unless you direct that it be done
   D. write a memo to your supervisor suggesting that all future changes in procedure are to be in writing and that they be directed to you

4. At the first meeting with your staff after appointment as a supervisor, you find considerable indifference and some hostility among the participants. 4.____
   Of the following, the MOST appropriate way to handle this situation is to
   A. disregard the attitudes displayed and continue to make your presentation until you have completed it
   B. discontinue your presentation but continue the meeting and attempt to find out the reasons for their attitudes

C. warm up your audience with some good-natured statements and anecdotes and then proceed with your presentation
D. discontinue the meeting and set up personal interviews with the staff members to try to find out the reason for their attitude

5. In order to start the training of a new employee, it has been a standard practice to have him read a manual of instructions or procedures. 5.____
This method is currently being replaced by the _____ method.
A. audio-visual
B. conference
C. lecture
D. programmed instruction

6. Of the following subjects, the one that can usually be successfully taught by a first-line supervisor who is training his subordinates is: 6.____
A. theory and philosophy of management
B. human relations
C. responsibilities of a supervisor
D. job skills

7. Assume that as supervisor you are training a clerk who is experiencing difficulty learning a new task. 7.____
Which of the following would be the LEAST effective approach to take when trying to solve this problem? To
A. ask questions which will reveal the clerk's understanding of the task
B. take a different approach in explaining the task
C. give the clerk an opportunity to ask questions about the task
D. make sure the clerk knows you are watching his work closely

8. One school of management and supervision involves participation by employees in the setting of group goals and in the sharing of responsibility for the operation of the unit. 8.____
If this philosophy were applied to a unit consisting of professional and clerical personnel, one should expect
A. the professional and clerical personnel to participate with equal effectiveness in operating areas and policy areas
B. the professional personnel to participate with greater effectiveness than the clerical personnel in policy areas
C. the clerical personnel to participate with greater effectiveness than the professional personnel in operating areas
D. greater participation by clerical personnel but with less responsibility for their actions

9. With regard to productivity, high morale among employees generally indicates a 9.____
A. history of high productivity
B. nearly absolute positive correlation with high productivity
C. predisposition to be productive under facilitating leadership and circumstances
D. complacency which has little effect on productivity

10. Assume that you are going to organize the professionals and clerks under your supervision into work groups or team of two or three employees. 10.____
Of the following, the step which is LEAST likely to foster the successful development of each group is to
   A. allow friends to work together in the group
   B. provide special help and attention to employees with no friends in their group
   C. frequently switch employees from group to group
   D. rotate jobs within the group in order to strengthen group identification

11. Following are four statements which might be made by an employee to his supervisor during a performance evaluation interview. 11.____
Which of the statements BEST provides a basis for developing a plan to improve the employee's performance?
   A. *I understand that you are dissatisfied with my work and I will try harder in the future.*
   B. *I feel that I've been making too many careless clerical errors recently.*
   C. *I am aware that I will be subject to disciplinary action if my work does not improve within one month.*
   D. *I understand that this interview is simply a requirement of your job and not a personal attack on me.*

12. Three months ago, Mr. Smith and his supervisor, Mrs. Jones, developed a plan which was intended to correct Mr. Smith's inadequate job performance. Now, during a follow-up interview, Mr. Smith, who thought his performance had satisfactorily improved, has been informed that Mrs. Jones is still dissatisfied with his work. 12.____
Of the following, it is MOST likely that the disagreement occurred because, when formulating the plan, they did NOT
   A. set realistic goals for Mr. Smith's performance
   B. set a reasonable time limit for Mr. Smith to effect his improvement in performance
   C. provide for adequate training to improve Mr. Smith's skills
   D. establish performance standards for measuring Mr. Smith's progress

13. When a supervisor delegates authority to subordinates, there are usually many problems to overcome, such as inadequately trained subordinates and poor planning. 13.____
All of the following are means of increasing the effectiveness of delegation EXCEPT:
   A. Defining assignments in the light of results expected
   B. Maintaining open lines of communication
   C. Establishing tight controls so that subordinates will stay within the bounds of the area of delegation
   D. Providing rewards for successful assumption of authority by a subordinate

14. Assume that one of your subordinates has arrived late for work several times during the current month. The last time he was late you had warned him that another unexcused lateness would result informal disciplinary action. If the employee arrives late for work again during this month, the FIRST action you should take is to 14.____
   A. give the employee a chance to explain this lateness
   B. give the employee a written copy of your warning
   C. tell the employee that you are recommending formal disciplinary action
   D. tell the employee that you will give him only one more chance before recommending formal disciplinary action

15. In trying to decide how many subordinates a manager can control directly, one of the determinants is how much the manager can reduce the frequency and time consumed in contacts with his subordinates. Of the following, the factor which LEAST influences the number and direction of these contacts is: 15.____
   A. How well the manager delegates authority
   B. The rate at which the organization is changing
   C. The control techniques used by the manager
   D. Whether the activity is line or staff

16. Systematic rotation of employees through lateral transfer within a government organization to provide for managerial development is 16.____
   A. *good*, because systematic rotation develops specialists who learn to do many jobs well
   B. *bad*, because the outsider upsets the status quo of the existing organization
   C. *good*, because rotation provides challenge and organizational flexibility
   D. *bad*, because it is upsetting to employees to be transferred within a service

17. Assume that you are required to provide an evaluation of the performance of your subordinates. Of the following factors, it is MOST important that the performance evaluation include a rating of each employee's 17.____
   A. initiative B. productivity C. intelligence D. personality

18. When preparing performance evaluations of your subordinates, one way to help assure that you are rating each employee fairly is to 18.____
   A. prepare a list of all employees and all the rating factors and rate all employees on one rating factor before going on to the next factor
   B. prepare a list of all your employees and all the rating factors and rate each employee on all factors before going on to the next employee
   C. discuss all the ratings you anticipate giving with another supervisor in order to obtain an unbiased opinion
   D. discuss each employee with his co-workers in order to obtain peer judgment of worth before doing any rating

19. A managerial plan which would include the GREATEST control is a plan which is 19.____
    A. spontaneous and geared to each new job that is received
    B. detailed and covering an extended time period
    C. long-range and generalized, allowing for various interpretations
    D. specific and prepared daily

20. Assume that you are preparing a report which includes statistical data covering increases in budget allocations of four agencies for the past ten years. 20.____
For you to represent the statistical data pictorially or graphically within the report is a
    A. *poor* idea, because you should be able to make statistical data understandable through the use of words
    B. *good* idea, because it is easier for the reader to understand pictorial representation rather than quantities of words conveying statistical data
    C. *poor* idea, because using pictorial representation in a report may make the report too expensive to print
    D. *good* idea, because a pictorial representation makes the report appear more attractive than the use of many words to convey the statistical data

# KEY (CORRECT ANSWERS)

| | | | |
|---|---|---|---|
| 1. | C | 11. | A |
| 2. | A | 12. | B |
| 3. | B | 13. | C |
| 4. | D | 14. | A |
| 5. | D | 15. | D |
| 6. | D | 16. | C |
| 7. | D | 17. | B |
| 8. | B | 18. | A |
| 9. | C | 19. | B |
| 10. | C | 20. | B |

# TEST 2

DIRECTIONS: Each question or incomplete statement is followed by several suggested answers or completions. Select the one that BEST answers the question or completes the statement. *PRINT THE LETTER OF THE CORRECT ANSWER IN THE SPACE AT THE RIGHT.*

1. Research studies have shown that supervisors of groups with high production records USUALLY 1.____
   A. give detailed instructions, constantly check on progress, and insist on approval of all decisions before implementation
   B. do considerable paperwork and other work similar to that performed by subordinates
   C. think of themselves as team members on the same level as others in the work group
   D. perform tasks traditionally associated with managerial functions

2. Mr. Smith, a bureau chief, is summoned by his agency's head in a conference to discuss Mr. Jones, an accountant who works in one of the divisions of his bureau. Mr. Jones has committed an error of such magnitude as to arouse the agency head's concern. 2.____
   After agreeing with the other conferees that a severe reprimand would be the appropriate punishment, Mr. Smith SHOULD
   A. arrange for Mr. Jones to explain the reasons for his error to the agency head
   B. send a memorandum to Mr. Jones, being careful that the language emphasizes the nature of the error rather than Mr. Jones' personal faults
   C. inform Mr. Jones' immediate supervisor of the conclusion reached at the conference, and let the supervisor take the necessary action
   D. suggest to the agency head that no additional action be taken against Mr. Jones because no further damage will be caused by the error

3. Assume that Ms. Thomson, a unit chief, has determined that the findings of an internal audit have been seriously distorted as a result of careless errors. The audit had been performed by a group of auditors in her unit and the errors were overlooked by the associate accountant in charge of the audit. Ms. Thomson has decided to delay discussing the matter with the associate accountant and the staff who performed the audit until she verifies certain details, which may require prolonged investigation. 3.____
   Mrs. Thomson's method of handling this situation is
   A. *appropriate*; employees should not be accused of wrongdoing until all the facts have been determined
   B. *inappropriate*; the employees involved may assume that the errors were considered unimportant
   C. *appropriate*; employees are more likely to change their behavior as a result of disciplinary action taken after a *cooling off* period
   D. *inappropriate*; the employees involved may have forgotten the details and become emotionally upset when confronted with the facts

4. After studying the financial situation in his agency, an administrative accountant decides to recommend centralization of certain accounting functions which are being performed in three different bureaus of the organization 4.____
The one of the following which is MOST likely to be a DISADVANTAE if this recommendation is implemented is that
   A. there may be less coordination of the accounting procedure because central direction is not so close to the day-to-day problems as the personnel handling them in each specialized accounting unit
   B. the higher management levels would not be able to make emergency decisions in as timely a manner as the more involved, lower-level administrators who are closer to the problem
   C. it is more difficult to focus the attention of the top management in order to resolve accounting problems because of the many other activities top management is involved in at the same time
   D. the accuracy of upward and inter-unit communication may be reduced because centralization may require insertion of more levels of administration in the chain of command

5. Of the following assumptions about the role of conflict in an organization, the one which is the MOST accurate statement of the approach of modern management theorists is that conflict 5.____
   A. can usually be avoided or controlled
   B. serves as a vital element in organizational change
   C. works against attainment of organizational goals
   D. provides a constructive outlet for problem employees

6. Which of the following is generally regarded as the BEST approach for a supervisor to follow in handling grievances brought by subordinates? 6.____
   A. Avoid becoming involved personally
   B. Involve the union representative in the first stage of discussion
   C. Settle the grievance as soon as possible
   D. Arrange for arbitration by a third party

7. Assume that supervisors of similar-sized accounting units in city, state, and federal offices were interviewed and observed at their work. It was found that the ways they acted in and viewed their roles tended to be very similar, regardless of who employed them. 7.____
Which of the following is the BEST explanation of this similarity
   A. A supervisor will ordinarily behave in conformance to his own self-image.
   B. Each role in an organization, including the supervisory role, calls for a distinct type of personality.
   C. The supervisor role reflects an exceptionally complex pattern of human response.
   D. The general nature of the duties and responsibilities of the supervisory position determines the role.

8. Which of the following is NOT consistent with the findings of recent research about the characteristics of successful top managers? 8.____
   A. They are *inner-directed* and not overly concerned with pleasing others.
   B. They are challenged by situations filled with high risk and ambiguity.
   C. They tend to stay on the same job for long periods of time.
   D. They consider it more important to handle critical assignments successfully than to do routine work well.

9. As a supervisor, you have to give subordinates operational guidelines. 9.____
   Of the following, the BEST reason for providing them with information about the overall objectives within which their operations fit is that the subordinates will
   A. be more likely to carry out the operation according to your expectations
   B. know that there is a legitimate reason for carrying out the operation in the way you have prescribed
   C. be more likely to handle unanticipated problems that may arise without having to take up your time
   D. more likely to transmit the operating instructions correctly to their subordinates

10. A supervisor holds frequent meetings with his staff. 10.____
    Of the following, the BEST approach he can take in order to elicit productive discussions at these meetings is for him to
    A. ask questions of those who attend
    B. include several levels of supervisors at the meetings
    C. hold the meetings at a specified time each week
    D. begin each meeting with a statement that discussion is welcomed

11. Of the following, the MOST important action that a supervisor can take to increase the productivity of a subordinate is to 11.____
    A. increase his uninterrupted work time
    B. increase the number of reproducing machines available in the office
    C. provide clerical assistance whenever he requests it
    D. reduce the number of his assigned tasks

12. Assume that, as a supervisor, you find out that you often must countermand or modify your original staff memos. 12.____
    If this practice continues, which one of the following situations is MOST likely to occur? The
    A. staff will not bother to read your memos
    B. office files will become cluttered
    C. staff will delay acting on your memos
    D. memos will be treated routinely

13. In making management decisions, the committee approach is often used by managers. 13.____
    Of the following, the BEST reason for using this approach is to
    A. prevent any one individual from assuming too much authority
    B. allow the manager to bring a wider range of experience and judgment to bear on the problem

C. allow the participation of all staff members, which will make them feel more committed to the decisions reached
D. permit the rapid transmission of information about decisions reached to the staff members concerned

14. In establishing standards for the measurement of the performance of a management project team, it is MOST important for the project manager to 14.____
A. identify and define the objectives of the project
B. determine the number of people who will be assigned to the project team
C. evaluate the skills of the staff who will be assigned to the project team
D. estimate fairly accurately the length of time required to complete each phase of the project

15. It is virtually impossible to tell an employee either that he is not good as another employee or that he does not measure up to a desirable level of performance, without having him feel threatened, rejected, and discouraged. 15.____
In accordance with the foregoing observation, a supervisor who is concerned about the performance of the less efficient members of his staff should realize that
A. he might obtain better results by not discussing the quality and quantity of their work with them, but by relying instead on the written evaluation of their performance to motivate their improvement
B. since he is required to discuss their performance with them, he should do so in words of encouragement and in so friendly a manner as to not destroy their morale
C. he might discuss their work in a general way, without mentioning any of the specifics about the quality of their performance, with the expectation that they would understand the full implications of his talk
D. he should make it a point, while telling them of their poor performance, to mention that their work is as good as that of some of the other employees in the unit

16. Some advocates of management-by-objectives procedures in public agencies have been urging that this method of operations be expanded to encompass all agencies of the government, for one or more of the following reasons, not all of which may be correct: 16.____
I. The MBO method is likely to succeed because it embraces the practice of setting near-term goals for the subordinate manager, reviewing accomplishments at an appropriate time, and repeating this process indefinitely
II. Provision for authority to perform the tasks assigned as goals in the MBO method is normally not needed because targets are set in quantitative or qualitative terms and specific times for accomplishment are arranged in short-term, repetitive intervals
III. Many other appraisal-of-performance programs failed because both supervisors and subordinates resisted them, while the MBO approach is not instituted until there is an organizational commitment to it
IV. Personal accountability is clearly established through the MBO approach because verifiable results are set up in the process of formulating the targets

Which of the choices below includes ALL of the foregoing statements that are CORRECT?

A. I, III B. II, IV C. I, II, III, IV D. I, III, IV

17. In preparing an organizational structure, the PRINCIPAL guideline for locating staff units is to place them 17.____
    A. all under a common supervisor
    B. as close as possible to the activities they serve
    C. as close to the chief executive as possible without over-extending his span of control
    D. at the lowest operational level

18. The relative importance of any unit in a department can be LEAST reliably judged by the 18.____
    A. amount of office space allocated to the unit
    B. number of employees in the unit
    C. rank of the individual who heads the unit
    D. rank of the individual to whom the unit head reports directly

19. Those who favor Planning-Programming-Budgeting Systems (PPBS) as a new method of governmental financial administration emphasize that PPBS 19.____
    A. applies statistical measurements which correlate highly with criteria
    B. makes possible economic systems analysis, including an explicit examination of alternatives
    C. makes available scarce government resources which can be coordinated on a government-wide basis and shared between local units of government
    D. shifts the emphasis in budgeting methods to an automated system of data processing

20. The term applied to computer processing which processes data concurrently with a given activity and provides results soon enough to influence the selection of a course of action is _____ processing. 20.____
    A. realtime
    B. batch
    C. random access
    D. integrated data

---

# KEY (CORRECT ANSWERS)

| | | | |
|---|---|---|---|
| 1. | D | 11. | A |
| 2. | C | 12. | C |
| 3. | B | 13. | B |
| 4. | D | 14. | A |
| 5. | B | 15. | B |
| 6. | C | 16. | D |
| 7. | D | 17. | B |
| 8. | C | 18. | B |
| 9. | C | 19. | B |
| 10. | A | 20. | A |

# INTERPRETING STATISTICAL DATA
# GRAPHS, CHARTS AND TABLES
# EXAMINATION SECTION
# TEST 1

DIRECTIONS: Each questioner incomplete statement is followed by several suggested answers or completions. Select the one that BEST answers the question or completes the statement. *PRINT THE LETTER OF THE CORRECT ANSWER IN THE SPACE AT THE RIGHT.*

Questions 1-3.

DIRECTIONS: Questions 1 through 3 are to be answered SOLELY on the basis of the following table.

QUARTERLY SALES REPORTED BY MAJOR INDUSTRY GROUPS

DECEMBER 2021 – FEBRUARY 2023

Reported Sales, Taxable & Non-Taxable (in Millions)

| Industry Groups | 12/21-2/22 | 3/22-5/22 | 6/22-8/22 | 9/22-11/22 | 12/22-2/23 |
|---|---|---|---|---|---|
| Retailers | 2,802 | 2,711 | 2,475 | 2,793 | 2,974 |
| Wholesalers | 2,404 | 2,237 | 2,269 | 2,485 | 2,974 |
| Manufacturers | 3,016 | 2,888 | 3,001 | 3,518 | 3,293 |
| Services | 1,034 | 1,065 | 984 | 1,132 | 1,092 |

1. The trend in total reported sales may be described as

   A. downward
   B. downward and upward
   C. horizontal
   D. upward

2. The two industry groups that reveal a similar seasonal pattern for the period December 2021 through November 2022 are

   A. retailers and manufacturers
   B. retailers and wholesalers
   C. wholesalers and manufacturers
   D. wholesalers and service

3. Reported sales were at a MINIMUM between

   A. December 2021 and February 2022
   B. March 2022 and May 2022
   C. June 2022 and August 2022
   D. September 2022 and November 2022

# TEST 2

DIRECTIONS: Each question or incomplete statement is followed by several suggested answers or completions. Select the one that BEST answers the question or completes the statement. *PRINT THE LETTER OF THE CORRECT ANSWER IN THE SPACE AT THE RIGHT*

Questions 1-4.

DIRECTIONS: Questions 1 through 4 are to be answered SOLELY on the basis of the following information.

The income elasticity of demand for selected items of consumer demand in the United States are:

| Item | Elasticity |
|---|---|
| Airline Travel | 5.66 |
| Alcohol | .62 |
| Dentist Fees | 1.00 |
| Electric Utilities | 3.00 |
| Gasoline | 1.29 |
| Intercity Bus | 1.89 |
| Local Bus | 1.41 |
| Restaurant Meals | .75 |

1. The demand for the item listed below that would be MOST adversely affected by a decrease in income is

   A. alcohol
   B. electric utilities
   C. gasoline
   D. restaurant meals

2. The item whose relative change in demand would be the same as the relative change in income would be

   A. dentist fees
   B. gasoline
   C. restaurant meals
   D. none of the above

3. If income increases by 12 percent, the demand for restaurant meals may be expected to increase by

   A. 9 percent
   B. 12 percent
   C. 16 percent
   D. none of the above

4. On the basis of the above information, the item whose demand would be MOST adversely affected by an increase in the sales tax from 7 percent to 8 percent to be passed on to the consumer in the form of higher prices

   A. would be airline travel
   B. would be alcohol
   C. would be gasoline
   D. cannot be determined

# TEST 3

DIRECTIONS: Each question or incomplete statement is followed by several suggested answers or completions. Select the one that BEST answers the question or completes the statement. *PRINT THE LETTER OF THE CORRECT ANSWER IN THE SPACE AT THE RIGHT.*

Questions 1-3.

DIRECTIONS: Questions 1 through 3 are to be answered SOLELY on the basis of the following graphs depicting various relationships in a single retail store.

GRAPH 1
RELATIONSHIP BETWEEN NUMBER OF CUSTOMERS
STORE AND TIME OF DAY

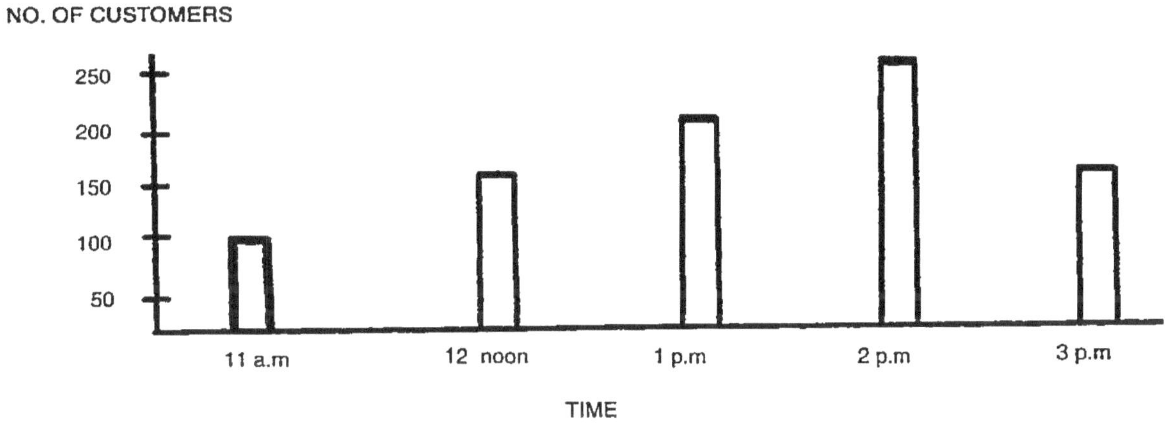


GRAPH II
RELATIONSHIP BETWEEN NUMBER OF CHECK-OUT LANES AVAILABLE IN STORE AND
WAIT TIME FOR CHECK-OUT

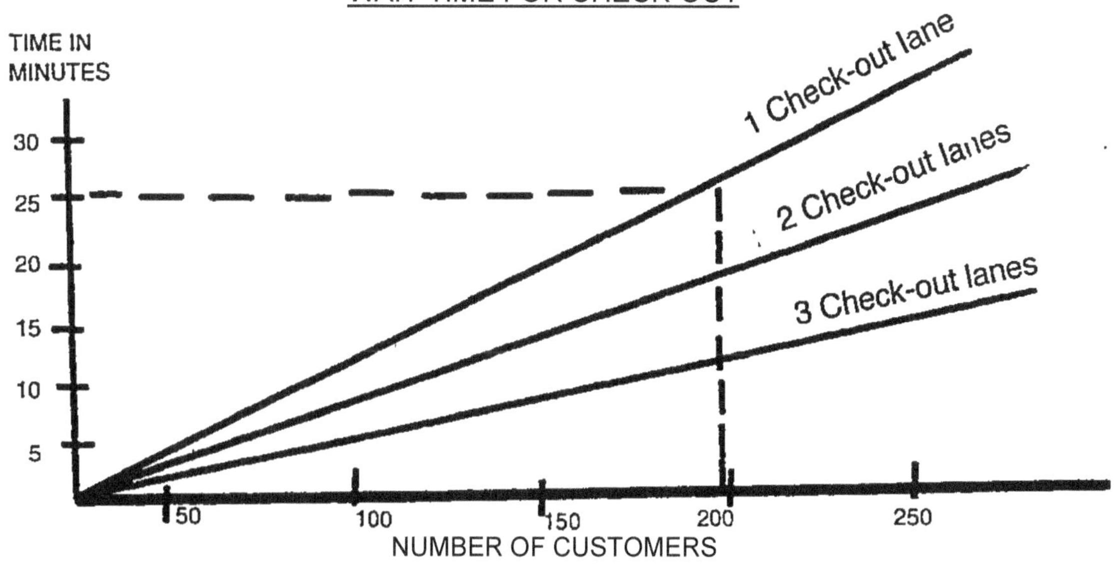


Note the dotted lines in Graph II. They demonstrate that, if there are 200 people in the store and only one check-out lane is open, the wait time will be 25 minutes.

1. At what time would a person be most likely NOT to have to wait more than 15 minutes if only one check-out lane is open?

   A. 11 A.M. B. 12 Noon C. 1 P.M. D. 3 P.M.

2. At what time of day would a person have to wait the LONGEST to check out if three check-out lanes are available?

   A. 11 A.M. B. 12 Noon C. 1 P.M. D. 2 P.M

3. The difference in wait times between 1 and 3 check-out lanes at 3 P.M. is MOST NEARLY

   A. 5 B. 10 C. 15 D. 20

# TEST 4

DIRECTIONS: Each question or incomplete statement is followed by several suggested answers or completions. Select the one that BEST answers the question or completes the statement. *PRINT THE LETTER OF THE CORRECT ANSWER IN THE SPACE AT THE RIGHT.*

Questions 1-4.

DIRECTIONS: Questions 1 through 4 are to be answered SOLELY on the basis of the graph below.

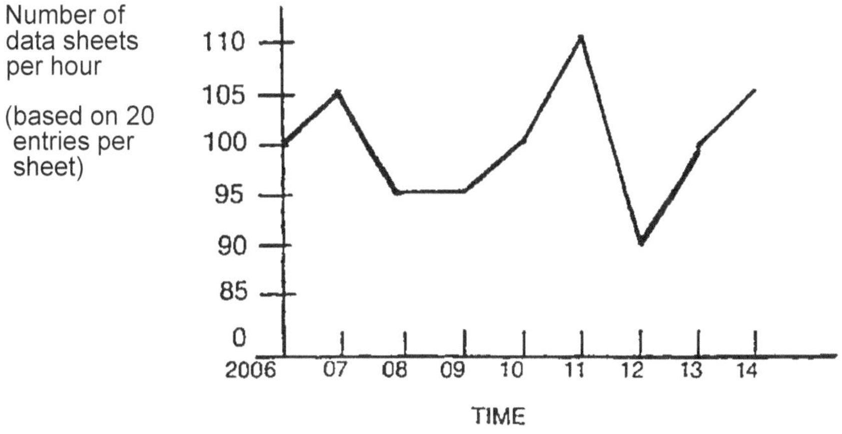


1. Of the following, during what four-year period did the average output of computer operators fall BELOW 100 sheets per hour?

   A. 2007-10 B. 2008-11 C. 2010-13 D. 2011-14

2. The average percentage change in output over the previous year's output for the years 2009 to 2012 is MOST NEARLY

   A. 2 B. 0 C. -5 D. -7

3. The difference between the actual output for 2012 and the projected figure based upon the average increase from 2006-2011 is MOST NEARLY

   A. 18 B. 20 C. 22 D. 24

4. Assume that after constructing the above graph you, an analyst, discovered that the average number of entries per sheet in 2012 was 25 (instead of 20) because of the complex nature of the work performed during that period.
   The average output in sheets per hour for the period 2010-13, expressed in terms of 20 items per sheet, would then be MOST NEARLY

   A. 95 B. 100 C. 105 D. 110

# TEST 6

DIRECTIONS: Each question or incomplete statement is followed by several suggested answers or completions. Select the one that BEST answers the question or completes the statement. *PRINT THE LETTER OF THE CORRECT ANSWER IN THE SPACE AT THE RIGHT.*

Questions 1-3.

DIRECTIONS: Questions 1 through 3 are to be answered on the basis of the following data assembled for a cost-benefit analysis.

| | Cost | Benefit |
|---|---|---|
| No program | 0 | 0 |
| Alternative W | $ 3,000 | $ 6,000 |
| Alternative X | $10,000 | $17,000 |
| Alternative Y | $17,000 | $25,000 |
| Alternative Z | $30,000 | $32,000 |

1. From the point of view of selecting the alternative with the best cost benefit ratio, the BEST alternative is Alternative

   A. W  B. X  C. Y  D. Z

2. From the point of view of selecting the alternative with the best measure of net benefit, the BEST alternative is Alternative

   A. W  B. X  C. Y  D. Z

3. From the point of view of pushing public expenditure to the point where marginal benefit equals or exceeds marginal cost, the BEST alternative is Alternative

   A. W  B. X  C. Y  D. Z

# TEST 6

DIRECTIONS: Each question or incomplete statement is followed by several suggested answers or completions. Select the one that BEST answers the question or completes the statement. *PRINT THE LETTER OF THE CORRECT ANSWER IN THE SPACE AT THE RIGHT.*

Questions 1-3.

DIRECTIONS: Questions 1 through 3 are to be answered SOLELY on the basis of the following data.

A series of cost-benefit studies of various alternative health programs yields the following results:

| Program | Benefit | Cost |
|---|---|---|
| K | 30 | 15 |
| L | 60 | 60 |
| M | 300 | 150 |
| N | 600 | 500 |

In answering Questions 1 and 2, assume that all programs can be increased or decreased in scale without affecting their individual benefit-to-cost ratios.

1. The benefit-to-cost ratio of Program M is

   A. 10:1  B. 5:1  C. 2:1  D. 1:2

2. The budget ceiling for one or more of the programs included in the study is set at 75 units. It may MOST logically be concluded that

   A. Programs K and L should be chosen to fit within the budget ceiling
   B. Program K would be the most desirable one that could be afforded
   C. Program M should be chosen rather than Program K
   D. the choice should be between Programs M and K

3. If no assumptions can be made regarding the effects of change of scale, the MOST logical conclusion, on the basis of the data available, is that

   A. more data are needed for a budget choice of program
   B. Program K is the most preferable because of its low cost and good benefit-to-cost ratio
   C. Program M is the most preferable because of its high benefits and good benefit-to-cost ratio
   D. there is no difference between Programs K and M, and either can be chosen for any purpose

# TEST 7

DIRECTIONS: Each question or incomplete statement is followed by several suggested answers or completions. Select the one that BEST answers the question or completes the statement. *PRINT THE LETTER OF THE CORRECT ANSWER IN THE SPACE AT THE RIGHT.*

Questions 1-6.

DIRECTIONS: Questions 1 through 6 are to be answered SOLELY on the basis of the information contained in the charts below which relate to the budget allocations of City X, a small suburban community. The charts depict the annual budget allocations by Department and by expenditures over a five-year period.

CITY X BUDGET IN MILLIONS OF DOLLARS
TABLE I. Budget Allocations by Department

| Department | 2017 | 2018 | 2019 | 2020 | 2021 |
|---|---|---|---|---|---|
| Public Safety | 30 | 45 | 50 | 40 | 50 |
| Health and Welfare | 50 | 75 | 90 | 60 | 70 |
| Engineering | 5 | 8 | 10 | 5 | 8 |
| Human Resources | 10 | 12 | 20 | 10 | 22 |
| Conservation & Environment | 10 | 15 | 20 | 20 | 15 |
| Education & Development | 15 | 25 | 35 | 15 | 15 |
| TOTAL BUDGET | 120 | 180 | 225 | 150 | 180 |

TABLE II. Budget Allocations by Expenditures

| Category | 2017 | 2018 | 2019 | 2020 | 2021 |
|---|---|---|---|---|---|
| Raw Materials & Machinery | 36 | 63 | 68 | 30 | 98 |
| Capital Outlay | 12 | 27 | 56 | 15 | 18 |
| Personal Services | 72 | 90 | 101 | 105 | 64 |
| TOTAL BUDGET | 120 | 180 | 225 | 150 | 180 |

1. The year in which the SMALLEST percentage of the total annual budget was allocated to the Department of Education and Development is

   A. 2017   B. 2018   C. 2020   D. 2021

2. Assume that in 2020 the Department of Conservation and Environment divided its annual budget into the three categories of expenditures and in exactly the same proportion as the budget shown in Table II for the year 2020. The amount allocated for capital outlay in the Department of Conservation and Environment's 2020 budget was MOST NEARLY ______ million.

   A. $2   B. $4   C. $6   D. $10

3. From the year 2018 to the year 2020, the sum of the annual budgets for the Departments of Public Safety and Engineering showed an overall ______ million.

   A. decline; SB  B. increase; $7
   C. decline; S15  D. increase; S22

4. The LARGEST dollar increase in departmental budget allocations from one year to the next was in ______ from ______.

   A. Public Safety; 2017 to 2018
   B. Health and Welfare; 2017 to 2018
   C. Education and Development; 2019 to 2020
   D. Human Resources; 2019 to 2020

5. During the five-year period, the annual budget of the Department of Human Resources was GREATER than the annual budget for the Department of Conservation and Environment in ______ of the years.

   A. none  B. one  C. two  D. three

6. If the total City X budget increases at the same rate from 2021 to 2022 as it did from 2020 to 2021, the total City X budget for 2022 will be MOST NEARLY ______ million.

   A. $180  B. $200  C. $210  D. $215

# TEST 8

DIRECTIONS: Each question or incomplete statement is followed by several suggested answers or completions. Select the one that BEST answers the question or completes the statement. *PRINT THE LETTER OF THE CORRECT ANSWER IN THE SPACE AT THE RIGHT.*

Questions 1-3.

DIRECTIONS: Questions 1 through 3 are to be answered SOLELY on the basis of the following information.

Assume that in order to encourage Program A, the State and Federal governments have agreed to make the following reimbursements for money spent on Program A, provided the unreimbursed balance is paid from City funds.

During Fiscal Year 2021-2022 - For the first $2 million expended, 50% Federal reimbursement and 30% State reimbursement; for the next $3 million, 40% Federal reimbursement and 20% State reimbursement; for the next $5 million, 20% Federal reimbursement and 10% State reimbursement. Above $10 million expended, no Federal or State reimbursement.

During Fiscal Year 2022-2023 - For the first $1 million expended, 30% Federal reimbursement and 20% State reimbursement; for the next $4 million, 15% Federal reimbursement and 10% State reimbursement. Above $5 million expended, no Federal or State reimbursement.

1. Assume that the Program A expenditures are such that the State reimbursement for Fiscal Year 2021-2022 will be $1 million.
   Then, the Federal reimbursement for Fiscal Year 2021-2022 will be

   A. $1,600,000 B. $1,800,000
   C. $2,000,000 D. $2,600,000

2. Assume that $8 million were to be spent on Program A in Fiscal Year 2022-2023.
   The TOTAL amount of unreimbursed City funds required would be

   A. $3,500,000 B. $4,500,000
   C. $5,500,000 D. $6,500,000

3. Assume that the City desires to have a combined total of $6 million spent in Program A during both the Fiscal Year 2021-2022 and the Fiscal Year 2022-2023.
   Of the following expenditure combinations, the one which results in the GREATEST reimbursement of City funds is ______ in Fiscal Year 2021-2022 and ______ in Fiscal Year 2022-2023.

   A. $5 million; $1 million B. $4 million; $2 million
   C. $3 million; $3 million D. $2 million; $4 million

# KEY (CORRECT ANSWERS)

### TEST 1

1. D
2. C
3. C

### TEST 2

1. B
2. A
3. A
4. D

### TEST 3

1. A
2. D
3. B

### TEST 4

1. A
2. B
3. C
4. C

### TEST 5

1. A
2. C
3. C

### TEST 6

1. C
2. D
3. A

### TEST 7

1. D
2. A
3. A
4. B
5. B
6. D

### TEST 8

1. B
2. D
3. A

# PREPARING WRITTEN MATERIAL

# EXAMINATION SECTION

## TEST 1

DIRECTIONS: Each of the sentences in this test may be classified under one of the following four categories:

A. *Incorrect* because of faulty grammar or sentence structure
B. *Incorrect* because of faulty punctuation
C. *Incorrect* because of faulty capitalization
D. *Correct*

Examine each sentence carefully to determine under which of the above four options it is best classified. Then, in the space at the right, print the capital letter preceding the option which is the BEST of the four suggested above.

(Each incorrect sentence contains but one type of error. Consider a sentence to be correct if it contains none of the types of errors mentioned, even though there may be other correct ways of expressing the same thought.)

1. This fact, together with those brought out at the previous meeting, prove that the schedule is satisfactory to the employees. 1.____

2. Like many employees in scientific fields, the work of bookkeepers and accountants requires accuracy and neatness. 2.____

3. "What can I do for you," the secretary asked as she motioned to the visitor to take a seat. 3.____

4. Our representative, Mr. Charles will call on you next week to determine whether or not your claim has merit. 4.____

5. We expect you to return in the spring; please do not disappoint us. 5.____

6. Any supervisor, who disregards the just complaints of his subordinates, is remiss in the performance of his duty. 6.____

7. Because she took less than an hour for lunch is no reason for permitting her to leave before five o'clock. 7.____

8. "Miss Smith," said the supervisor, "Please arrange a meeting of the staff for two o'clock on Monday." 8.____

9. A private company's vacation and sick leave allowance usually differs considerably from a public agency. 9.____

10. Therefore, in order to increase the efficiency of operations in the department, a report on the recommended changes in procedures was presented to the departmental committee in charge of the program. 10.____

11. We told him to assign the work to whoever was available. 11.____

12. Since John was the most efficient of any other employee in the bureau, he received the highest service rating. 12.____

13. Only those members of the national organization who resided in the middle West attended the conference in Chicago. 13.____

14. The question of whether the office manager has as yet attained, or indeed can ever hope to secure professional status is one which has been discussed for years. 14.____

15. No one knew who to blame for the error which, we later discovered, resulted in a considerable loss of time. 15.____

## KEY (CORRECT ANSWERS)

| | | | | | |
|---|---|---|---|---|---|
| 1. | A | 6. | B | 11. | D |
| 2. | A | 7. | A | 12. | A |
| 3. | B | 8. | C | 13. | C |
| 4. | B | 9. | A | 14. | B |
| 5. | D | 10. | D | 15. | A |

# TEST 2

DIRECTIONS: Each of the sentences in this test may be classified under one of the following four categories:

A. *Incorrect* because of faulty grammar or sentence structure
B. *Incorrect* because of faulty punctuation
C. *Incorrect* because of faulty capitalization
D. *Correct*

1. The National alliance of Businessmen is trying to persuade private businesses to hire youth in the summertime. 1.____

2. The supervisor who is on vacation, is in charge of processing vouchers. 2.____

3. The activity of the committee at its conferences is always stimulating. 3.____

4. After checking the addresses again, the letters went to the mailroom. 4.____

5. The director, as well as the employees, are interested in sharing the dividends. 5.____

# KEY (CORRECT ANSWERS)

1. C
2. B
3. D
4. A
5. A

# TEST 3

DIRECTIONS: In each of the following groups of sentences, one of the four sentences is faulty in grammar, punctuation, or capitalization. Select the INCORRECT sentence in each case.

1. A. Sailing down the bay was a thrilling experience for me. 1.____
   B. He was not consulted about your joining the club.
   C. This story is different than the one I told you yesterday.
   D. There is no doubt about his being the best player.

2. A. He maintains there is but one road to world peace. 2.____
   B. It is common knowledge that a child sees much he is not supposed to see.
   C. Much of the bitterness might have been avoided if arbitration had been resorted to earlier in the meeting.
   D. The man decided it would be advisable to marry a girl somewhat younger than him.

3. A. In this book, the incident I liked least is where the hero tries to put out the forest fire. 3.____
   B. Learning a foreign language will undoubtedly give a person a better understanding of his mother tongue.
   C. His actions made us wonder what he planned to do next.
   D. Because of the war, we were unable to travel during the summer vacation.

4. A. The class had no sooner become interested in the lesson than the dismissal bell rang. 4.____
   B. There is little agreement about the kind of world to be planned at the peace conference.
   C. "Today," said the teacher, "we shall read 'The Wind in the Willows,' I am sure you'll like it.
   D. The terms of the legal settlement of the family quarrel handicapped both sides for many years.

5. A. I was so surprised that I was not able to say a word. 5.____
   B. She is taller than any other member of the class.
   C. It would be much more preferable if you were never seen in his company.
   D. We had no choice but to excuse her for being late.

# KEY (CORRECT ANSWERS)

1. C
2. D
3. A
4. C
5. C

# TEST 4

DIRECTIONS: In each of the following groups of sentences, one of the four sentences is faulty in grammar, punctuation, or capitalization. Select the INCORRECT sentence in each case.

1. A. Please send me these data at the earliest opportunity. 1.____
   B. The loss of their material proved to be a severe handicap.
   C. My principal objection to this plan is that it is impracticable.
   D. The doll had laid in the rain for an hour and was ruined.

2. A. The garden scissors, left out all night in the rain, were in a badly rusted condition. 2.____
   B. The girls felt bad about the misunderstanding which had arisen
   C. Sitting near the campfire, the old man told John and I about many exciting adventures he had had.
   D. Neither of us is in a position to undertake a task of that magnitude.

3. A. The general concluded that one of the three roads would lead to the besieged city. 3.____
   B. The children didn't, as a rule, do hardly anything beyond what they were told to do.
   C. The reason the girl gave for her negligence was that she had acted on the spur of the moment.
   D. The daffodils and tulips look beautiful in that blue vase.

4. A. If I was ten years older, I should be interested in this work. 4.____
   B. Give the prize to whoever has drawn the best picture.
   C. When you have finished reading the book, take it back to the library.
   D. My drawing is as good as or better than yours.

5. A. He asked me whether the substance was animal or vegetable. 5.____
   B. An apple which is unripe should not be eaten by a child.
   C. That was an insult to me who am your friend.
   D. Some spy must of reported the matter to the enemy.

6. A. Limited time makes quoting the entire message impossible. 6.____
   B. Who did she say was going?
   C. The girls in your class have dressed more dolls this year than we.
   D. There was such a large amount of books on the floor that I couldn't find a place for my rocking chair.

7. A. What with his sleeplessness and his ill health, he was unable to assume any responsibility for the success of the meeting. 7.____
   B. If I had been born in February, I should be celebrating my birthday soon.
   C. In order to prevent breakage, she placed a sheet of paper between each of the plates when she packed them.
   D. After the spring shower, the violets smelled very sweet.

8. A. He had laid the book down very reluctantly before the end of the lesson. 8.____
   B. The dog, I am sorry to say, had lain on the bed all night.
   C. The cloth was first lain on a flat surface; then it was pressed with a hot iron.
   D. While we were in Florida, we lay in the sun until we were noticeably tanned.

9. A. If John was in New York during the recent holiday season, I have no doubt he spent most of the time with his parents. 9.____
   B. How could he enjoy the television program; the dog was barking and the baby was crying.
   C. When the problem was explained to the class, he must have been asleep.
   D. She wished that her new dress were finished so that she could go to the party.

10. A. The engine not only furnishes power but light and heat as well. 10.____
    B. You're aware that we've forgotten whose guilt was established, aren't you?
    C. Everybody knows that the woman made many sacrifices for her children.
    D. A man with his dog and gun is a familiar sight in this neighborhood.

# KEY (CORRECT ANSWERS)

| | | | |
|---|---|---|---|
| 1. | D | 6. | D |
| 2. | C | 7. | B |
| 3. | B | 8. | C |
| 4. | A | 9. | B |
| 5. | D | 10. | A |

# TEST 5

DIRECTIONS: Each of Questions 1 through 5 consists of a sentence which may be classified appropriately under one of the following four categories:

A. *Incorrect* because of faulty grammar
B. *Incorrect* because of faulty punctuation
C. *Incorrect* because of faulty spelling
D. *Correct*

Examine each sentence carefully. Then, print in the space at the right the letter preceding the category which is the BEST of the four suggested above

(Note: Each incorrect sentence contains only one type of error. Consider a sentence correct if it contains no errors, although there may be other correct ways of writing the sentence.)

1. Of the two employees, the one in our office is the most efficient. 1.____

2. No one can apply or even understand, the new rules and regulations. 2.____

3. A large amount of supplies were stored in the empty office. 3.____

4. If an employee is occassionally asked to work overtime, he should do so willingly. 4.____

5. It is true that the new procedures are difficult to use but, we are certain that you will learn them quickly. 5.____

6. The office manager said that he did not know who would be given a large allotment under the new plan. 6.____

7. It was at the supervisor's request that the clerk agreed to postpone his vacation. 7.____

8. We do not believe that it is necessary for both he and the clerk to attend the conference. 8.____

9. All employees, who display perseverance, will be given adequate recognition. 9.____

10. He regrets that some of us employees are dissatisfied with our new assignments. 10.____

11. "Do you think that the raise was merited," asked the supervisor? 11.____

12. The new manual of procedure is a valuable supplament to our rules and regulations. 12.____

13. The typist admitted that she had attempted to pursuade the other employees to assist her in her work. 13.____

14. The supervisor asked that all amendments to the regulations be handled by you and I. 14.____

15. The custodian seen the boy who broke the window. 15.____

---

# KEY (CORRECT ANSWERS)

| | | | | | |
|---|---|---|---|---|---|
| 1. | A | 6. | D | 11. | B |
| 2. | B | 7. | D | 12. | C |
| 3. | A | 8. | A | 13. | C |
| 4. | C | 9. | B | 14. | A |
| 5. | B | 10. | D | 15. | A |

---

# BASIC FUNDAMENTALS OF A FINANCIAL STATEMENT

## TABLE OF CONTENTS

# BASIC FUNDAMENTALS OF A FINANCIAL STATEMENT

## COMMENTARY

The ability to read and understand a financial statement is a basic requirement for the accountant, auditor, account clerk, bookkeeper, bank examiner, budget examiner, and, of course, for the executive who must manage and administer departmental affairs.

## FINANCIAL REPORTS

Are financial reports really as difficult as all that? Well, if you know they are not so difficult because you have worked with them before, this section will be of auxiliary help for you. However, if you find financial statements a bit murky, but realize their great importance to you, we ought to get along fine together. For "mathematics," all we'll use is fourth-grade arithmetic.

Accountants, like all other professionals, have developed a specialized vocabulary. Sometimes this is helpful and sometimes plain confusing (like their practice of calling the income account, "Statement of Profit and Loss," when it is bound to be one or the other). But there are really only a score or so technical terms that you will have to get straight in mind. After that is done, the whole foggy business will begin to clear and in no time at all you'll be able to talk as wisely as the next fellow.

## BALANCE SHEET

Look at the sample balance sheet printed on Page 2, and we'll have an insight into how it is put together. This particular report is neither the simplest that could be issued, nor the most complicated. It is a good average sample of the kind of report issues by an up-to-date manufacturing company.

Note particularly that the balance sheet represents the situation as it stood on one particular day, December 31, not the record of a year's operation. This balance sheet is broken into two parts on the left are shown *ASSETS* and on the right *LIABILITIES*. Under the asset column, you will find listed the value of things the company owns or are owed to the company. Under liabilities are listed the things the company owes to others, plus reserves, surplus, and the stated value of the stockholders' interest in the company.

One frequently hears the comment, "Well, I don't see what a good balance sheet is anyway, because the assets and liabilities are always the same whether the company is successful or not."

It is true that they always balance and, by itself, a balance sheet doesn't tell much until it is analyzed. Fortunately, we can make a balance sheet tell its story without too much effort–often an extremely revealing story, particularly, if we compare the records of several years.

## *ASSETS*

The first notation on the asset side of the balance sheet is *CURRENT ASSETS* (Item 1). In general, current assets include cash and things that can be turned into cash in a hurry, or that, in the normal course of business, will be turned into cash in the reasonably near future, usually within a year.

Item 2 on our sample sheet is *CASH*. Cash is just what you would expect–bills and silver in the till and money on deposit in the bank.

*UNITED STATES GOVERNMENT SECURITIES* is Item 3. The general practice is to show securities listed as current assets at cost or market value, whichever is lower. The figure, for all reasonable purposes, represents the amount by which total cash could be easily increased if the company wanted to sell these securities.

The next entry is *ACCOUNTS RECEIVABLE* (Item 4). Here we find the total amount of money owed to the company by its regular business creditors and collectable within the next year. Most of the money is owed to the company by its customers for goods that the company delivered on credit. If this were a department store instead of a manufacturer, what you owed the store on our charge account would be included here. Because some people fail to pay their bills, the company sets up a reserve for doubtful accounts, which it subtracts from all the money owed.

THE ABC MANUFACTURING COMPANY, INC.
CONSOLIDATED BALANCE SHEET – DECEMBER 31

| Item | | | Item | | |
|---|---|---|---|---|---|
| 1. CURRENT ASSETS | | | 16. CURRENT LIABILITIES | | |
| 2. Cash | | | 17. Accts. Payable | | $300,000 |
| 3. U.S. Government Securities | | | 18. Accrued Taxes | | 800,000 |
| 4. Accounts Receivable | | 2,000,000 | 19. Accrued Wages, interest | | |
| (less reserves) | | | and Other Expenses | | 370,000 |
| 5. Inventories (at lower of cost or | | | 20. Total Current Liabilities | | $1,470,000 |
| market) | | 2,000,000 | 21. FIRST MORTGAGE SINK- | | |
| 6. Total Current Assets | | $7,000,000 | ING FUND BONDS, 3½ % | | |
| 7. INVESTMENT IN AFFILIATED | | | DUE 2020 | | $2,000,000 |
| COMPANY | | | 22. RESERVE FOR | | |
| Not consolidated (at cost, not in | | | CONTINGENCIES | | 200,000 |
| excess of net assets) | | 200,000 | 23. CAPITAL STOCK: | | |
| 8. OTHER INVESTMENTS | | | 24. 5% Preferred Stock | | |
| At cost, less than market | | 100,000 | (authorized and issued | | |
| 9. PLANT IMPROVEMENT FUND | | 550,000 | 10,000 shares of $100 par | | |
| 10. PROPERTY, PLANT AND | | | shares of $100 | | |
| EQUIPMENT: | | | (par value) | $1,000,000 | |
| Cost | $8,000,000 | | 25. Common stock | | |
| 11. Less Reserve | | | (authorized and issued | | |
| for Depreciation | 5,000,000 | | 400,000 shares of no | | |
| 12. NET PROPERTY | | 3,000,000 | par value) | 1,000,000 | |
| 13. PREPAYMENTS | | 50,000 | 26. SURPLUS: | | 2,000,000 |
| 14. DEFERRED CHARGES | | 100,000 | 27. Earned | 3,530,000 | |
| 15. PATENTS AND GOODWILL | | 100,000 | 28. Capital (arising from sale | | |
| | | | of common capital stock | | |
| | | | at price in excess of | | |
| | | | stated value) | 1,900,000 | |
| | | | | | 5,430,000 |
| TOTAL | | $11,000,000 | TOTAL | | $11,100,000 |

Item 5, *INVENTORIES*, is the value the company places on the supplies it owns. The inventory of a manufacturer may contain raw materials that it uses in making the things it sells, partially finished goods in process of manufacture, and, finally, completed merchandise that it is ready to sell. Several methods are used to arrive at the value placed on these various items. The most common is to value them at their cost or present market value, whichever is lower.

You can be reasonably confident, however, that the figure given is an honest and significant one for the particular industry if the report is certified by a reputable firm of public accountants.

Next on the asset side is *TOTAL CURRENT ASSETS* (Item 6). This is an extremely important figure when used in connection with other items in the report, which we will come to presently. Then we will discover how to make total current assets tell their story.

*INVESTMENT IN AFFILIATED COMPANY* Item 7) represents the cost to our parent company of the capital stock of its subsidiary or affiliated company. A subsidiary is simply one company that is controlled by another. Most corporations that own other companies outright lump the figures in a CONSOLIDATED BALANCE SHEET. This means that, under cash, for example, one would find a total figure that represented all of the cash of the parent company and of its wholly owned subsidiary. This is a perfectly reasonable procedure because, in the last analysis, all of the money is controlled by the same persons.

Our typical company shows that it has *OTHER INVESTMENTS* (Item 8), in addition to its affiliated company. Sometimes good marketable securities other than Government bonds are carried as current assets, but the more conservative practice is to list these other security holdings separately. If they have been bought as a permanent investment, they would always be shown by themselves. "At cost, less than market" means that our company paid $100,000 for these other investments, but they are now worth more.

Among our assets is a *PLANT IMPROVEMENT FUND* (Item 9). Of course, this item does not appear in all company balance sheets, but is typical of special funds that companies set up for one purpose or another. For example, money set aside to pay off part of the bonded debt of a company might be segregated into a special fund. The money our directors have put aside to improve the plant would often be invested in Government bonds,

**FIXED ASSETS**

The next item (10) is *PROPERTY, PLANT, AND EQUIPMENT*, but it might just as well be labeled Fixed Assets as these items are used more or less interchangeably, Under Item 10, the report gives the value of land, buildings, and machinery and such movable things as trucks, furniture, and hand tools. Historically, probably more sins were committed against this balance sheet item than any other.

In olden days, cattlemen used to drive their stock to market in the city. It was a common trick to stop outside of town, spread out some salt for the cattle to make them thirsty and then let them drink all the water they could hold. When they were weighed for sale, the cattlemen would collect cash for the water the stock had drunk. Business buccaneers, taking the cue from their farmer friends, would often "write up" the value of their fixed assets. In other words, they would increase the value shown on the balance sheet, making the capital stock appear to be worth a lot more than it was. *Watered stock* proved a bad investment for most stockholders. The practice has, fortunately, been stopped, though it took major financial reorganizations to squeeze the water out of some securities.

The most common practice today is to list fixed assets at cost. Often, there is no ready market for most of the things that fall under this heading, so it is not possible to give market value. A good report will tell what is included under fixed assets and how it has been valued. If the value has been increased by *write-up* or decreased by *write-down*, a footnote explanation is usually given. A *write-up* might occur, for instance, if the value of real estate increased substantially. A *write-down* might follow the invention of a new machine that put an important part of the company's equipment out of date.

**DEPRECIATION**

Naturally, all of the fixed property of a company will wear out in time (except, of course, non-agricultural land). In recognition of this fact, companies set up a *RESERVE FOR APPRECIATION* (Item 11). If a truck costs $4,000 and is expected to last four years, it will be depreciated at the rate of $1,000 a year.

Two other items also frequently occur in connection with depreciation—*depletion* and *obsolescence*. Companies may lump depreciation, depletion, and obsolescence under a single title, or list them separately.

*Depletion* is a term used primarily by mining and oil companies (or any of the so-called extractive industries). Depletion means exhaust or use up. As the oil or other natural resource is used up, a reserve is set up, to compensate for the natural wealth the company no longer owns. This reserve is set up in recognition of the fact that, as the company sells its natural product, it must get back not only the cost of extracting but also the original cost of the natural resource.

*Obsolescence* represents the loss in value because a piece of property has gone out of date before it wore out. Airplanes are modern examples of assets that tend to get behind the times long before the parts wear out. (Women and husbands will be familiar with the speed at which ladies' hats "obsolesce.")

In our sample balance sheet we have placed the reserve for depreciation under fixed assets and then subtracted, giving us *NET PROPERTY* (Item 12), which we add into the asset column. Sometimes, companies put the reserve for depreciation in the liability column. As you can see, the effect is just the same whether it is *subtracted* from assets or *added* to liabilities.

The manufacturer, whose balance sheet we use, rents a New York showroom and pays his rent yearly, in advance. Consequently, he has listed under assets *PREPAYMENTS* (Item 13). This is listed as an asset because he has paid for the use of the showroom, but has not yet received the benefit from its use. The use is something coming to the firm in the following year and, hence, is an asset. The dollar value of this asset will decrease by one-twelfth each month during the coming year.

DEFERRED CHARGES (Item 14) represents a type of expenditure similar to prepayment. For example, our manufacturer brought out a new product last year, spending $100,000 introducing it to the market. As the benefit from this expenditure will be returned over months or even years to come, the manufacturer did not think it reasonable to charge the full expenditure against costs during the year. He has *deferred* the charges and will write them off gradually.

**INTANGIBLES**

The last entry in our asset column is *PATENTS AND GOODWILL* (Item 15). If our company were a young one, set up to manufacturer some new patented product, it would probably carry its patents at a substantial figure. In fact, *intangibles* of both old and new companies are often of great but generally unmeasurable worth.

Company practice varies considerably in assigning value to intangibles. Proctor & Gamble, despite the tremendous goodwill that has been built up for *Ivory Soap*, has reduced all of its intangibles to the nominal $1. Some of the big cigarette companies, on the contrary, place a high dollar value on the goodwill their brand names enjoy. Companies that spend a good deal for research and the development of new products are more inclined than others to reflect this fact in the value assigned to patents, license agreements, etc.

**LIABILITIES**

The liability side of the balance sheet appears a little deceptive at first glance. Several of the entries simply don't sound like liabilities by any ordinary definition of the term.

The first term on the liability side of any balance sheet is usually *CURRENT LIABILITIES* (Item 16). This is a companion to the Current Assets item across the page and includes all debts that fall due within the next year. The relation between current assets and current liabilities is one of the most revealing things to be gotten from the balance sheet, but we will go into that quite thoroughly later on.

*ACCOUNTS PAYABLE* (Item 17) represents the money that the company owes to its ordinary business creditors–unpaid bills for materials, supplies, insurance, and the like. Many companies itemize the money they owe in a much more detailed fashion than we have done, but, as you will see, the totals are the most interesting thing to us.

Item 18, *ACCRUED TAXES*, is the tax bill that the company estimates it still owes for the past year. We have lumped all taxes in our balance sheet, as many companies do. However, sometimes you will find each type of tax given separately. If the detailed procedure is followed, the description of the tax is usually quite sufficient to identify the separate items.

Accounts Payable was defined as the money the company owed to its regular business creditors. The company also owes, on any given day, wages to its own employees; interest to its bondholders and to banks from which it may have borrowed money; fees to its attorneys; pensions, etc. These are all totaled under *ACCRUED WAGES, INTEREST AND OTHER EXPENSES* (Item 19).

*TOTAL CURRENT LIABILITIES* (Item 20) is just the sum of everything that the company owed on December 31 and which must be paid sometime in the next twelve months.

It is quite clear that all of the things discussed above are liabilities. The rest of the entries on the liability side of the balance sheet, however, do not seem at first glance to be liabilities.

Our balance sheet shows that the company, on December 31, had $2,000,000 of 3½ percent First Mortgage BONDS outstanding (Item 21). Legally, the money received by a company when it sells bonds is considered a loan to the company. Therefore, it is obvious that the company owes to the bondholders an amount equal to the face value or the *call price* of the bonds it has outstanding. The call price is a figure usually larger than the face value of the bonds at which price the company can *call* the bonds in from the bondholders and pay them off before they ordinarily fall due. The date that often occurs as part of the name of a bond is the date at which the company has promised to pay off the loan from the bondholders.

**RESERVES**

The next heading, *RESERVE FOR CONTINGENCIES* (Item 22) sounds more like an asset than a liability. "My reserves," you might say, "are dollars in the bank, and dollars in the bank are assets.

No one would deny that you have something there. In fact, the corporation treasurer also has his reserve for contingencies balanced by either cash or some kind of unspecified investment on the asset side of the ledger. His reason for setting up a reserve on the liability side of the balance sheet is a precaution against making his financial position seem better than it is. He decided that the company might have to pay out this money during the coming year if certain things happened. If he did not set up the "reserve," his surplus would appear larger by an amount equal to his reserve.

A very large reserve for contingencies or a sharp increase in this figure from the previous year should be examined closely by the investor. Often, in the past, companies tried to hide their true earnings by transferring funds into a contingency reserve. As a reserve looks somewhat like a true liability, stockholders were confused about the real value of their securities. When a reserve is not set up for protection against some very probable loss or expenditure, it should be considered by the investor as part of surplus.

## CAPITAL STOCK

Below reserves there is a major heading, *CAPITAL STOCK* (Item 23). Companies may have one type of security outstanding, or they may have a dozen. All of the issues that represent shares of ownership are capital, regardless of what they are called on the balance sheet—preferred stock, preference stock, common stock, founders' shares, capital stock, or something else.

Our typical company has one issue of 5 percent *PREFERRED STOCK* (Item 24). It is called *preferred* because those who own it have a right to dividends and assets before the *common* stockholders—that is, the holders are in a preferred position as owners. Usually, preferred stockholders do not have a voice in company affairs unless the company fails to pay them dividends at the promised rate. Their rights to dividends are almost always *cumulative*. This simply means that all past dividends must be paid before the other stockholders can receive anything. Preferred stockholders are not creditors of the company so it cannot properly be said that the company *owes* them the value of their holdings. However, in case the company decided to go out of business, preferred stockholders would have a prior claim on anything that was left in the company treasury after all of the creditors, including the bondholders, were paid off. In practice, this right does not always mean much, but it does explain why the book value of their holdings is carried as a liability.

*COMMON STOCK* (Item 25) is simple enough as far as definition is concerned. It represents the rights of the ordinary owner of the company. Each company has as many owners as it has stockholders. The proportion of the company that each stockholder owns is determined by the number of shares he has. However, neither the book value of a no-par common stock, nor the par value of an issue that has a given par, can be considered as representing either the original sale price, the market value, or what would be left for the stockholders if the company were liquidated.

A profitable company will seldom be dissolved. Once things have taken such a turn that dissolution appears desirable, the stated value of the stock is generally nothing but a fiction. Even if the company is profitable as a going institution, once it ceases to function even its tangible assets drop in value because there is not usually a ready market for its inventory of raw materials and semi-finished goods, or its plant and machinery.

## SURPLUS

The last major heading on the liability side of the balance sheet is *SURPLUS* (Item 26). The surplus, of course, is not a liability in the popular sense at all. It represents, on our balance sheet, the difference between the stated value of our common stock and the net assets behind the stock.

Two different kinds of surplus frequently appear on company balance sheets, and our company has both kinds. The first type listed is *EARNED* surplus (Item 27). Earned surplus is roughly similar to your own savings. To the corporation, earned surplus is that part of net income which has not been paid to stockholders as dividends. It still belongs to you, but the directors have decided that it is best for the company and the stockholders to keep it in the business. The surplus may be invested in the plant just as you might invest part of your savings in your home. It may also be in cash or securities.

In addition to the earned surplus, our company also has a *CAPITAL* surplus (Item 28) of $1,900.00, which the balance sheet explains arose from selling the stock at a higher cost per share than is given as its stated value. A little arithmetic shows that the stock is carried on the books at $2.50 a share while the capital surplus amounts to $4.75 a share. From this we know that the company actually received an average of $7.25 net a share for the stock when it was sold.

**WHAT DOES THE BALANCE SHEET SHOW?**

Before we undertake to analyze the balance sheet figures, a word on just what an investor can expect to learn is in order. A generation or more ago, before present accounting standards had gained wide acceptance, considerable imagination went into the preparation of balance sheets. This, naturally, made the public skeptical of financial reports. Today, there is no substantial ground for skepticism. The certified public accountant, the listing requirements of the national stock exchanges, and the regulations of the Securities and Exchange Commission have, for all practical purposes, removed the grounds for doubting the good faith of financial reports.

The investor, however, is still faced with the task of determining the significance of the figures. As we have already seen, a number of items are based, to a large degree, upon estimates, while others are, of necessity, somewhat arbitrary.

**NET WORKING CAPITAL**

There is one very important thing that we can find from the balance sheet and accept with the full confidence that we know what we are dealing with. That is net working capital, sometimes simply called working capital.

On the asset side of our balance sheet, we have added up all of the current assets and show the total as Item 6. On the liability side, Item 20 gives the total of current liabilities. *Net working capital* or *net current assets* is the difference left after subtracting current liabilities from current assets. If you consider yourself an investor rather than a speculator, you should always insist that any company in which you invest have a comfortable amount of working capital. The ability of a company to meet its obligations with ease, expand its volume as business expands and take advantage of opportunities as they present themselves, is, to an important degree, determined by its working capital.

Probably the question in your mind is: "*Just what does 'comfortable amount*' of working capital mean?" Well, there are several methods used by analysts to judge whether a particular company has a sound working capital position. The first rough test for an industrial company is to compare the working capital figure with the current liability total. Most analysts say that minimum safety requires that net working capital at least equal current liabilities. Or, put another way, current assets should be at least twice as large as current liabilities.

There are so many different kinds of companies, however, that this test requires a great deal of modification if it is to be really helpful in analyzing companies in different industries. To help you interpret the current position of a company in which you are considering investing, the *current ratio* is more helpful than the dollar total of working capital. The current ratio is current assets divided by current liabilities.

In addition to working capital and current ratio, there are two other ways of testing the adequacy of the current position. *Net quick assets* provide a rigorous and important test of a company's ability to meet its current obligations. Net quick assets are found by taking total current assets (Item 6) and subtracting the value of inventories (Item 5). A well-fixed industrial company should show a reasonable excess of quick assets over current liabilities.

Finally, many analysts say that a good industrial company should have at least as much working capital (current assets less current liabilities) as the total book value of its bonds and preferred stock. In other words, current liabilities, bonded debt, and preferred stock *altogether* should not exceed the current assets.

**INVENTORY AND INVENTORY TURNOVER**

In the recent past, there has been much talk of inventories. Many commentators have said that these carry a serious danger to company earnings if management allows them to increase too much. Of course, this has always been true, but present high prices have made everyone more inventory-conscious than usual.

There are several dangers in a large inventory position. In the first place, sharp drop in price may cause serious losses; also, a large inventory may indicate that the company has accumulated a big supply of unsalable merchandise. The question still remains, however: "What do we mean by large inventory?"

As you certainly realize, an inventory is large or small only in terms of the yearly turnover and the type of business. We can discover the annual turnover of our sample company by dividing inventories (Item 5) into total annual sales (item "a" on the income account).

It is also interesting to compare the value of the inventory of a company being studied with total current assets. Again, however, there is considerable variation between different types of companies, so that the relationship becomes significant only when compared with similar companies.

**NET BOOK VALUE OF SECURITIES**

There is one other very important thing that can be gotten from the balance sheet, and that is the net book or equity value of the company's securities. We can calculate the net book value of each of the three types of securities our company has outstanding by a little very simple arithmetic. *Book value* means *the value at which something is carried on the books of the company.*

The full rights of the bondholders come before any of the rights of the stockholders, so, to find the net book value or net tangible assets backing up the bonds we add together the balance sheet value of the bonds, preferred stock, common stock, reserve, and surplus. This gives us a total of $9,630,000, (We would not include contingency reserve if we were reasonably sure the contingency was going to arise, but, as general reserves are often equivalent to surplus, it is, usually, best to treat the reserve just as though it were surplus.) However, part of this value represents the goodwill and patents carried at $100,000, which is not a tangible item, so, to be conservative, we subtract this amount, leaving $9,530,000 as the total net book value of the bonds. This is equivalent to $4,765 for each $1,000 bond, a generous figure. To calculate the net book value of the preferred stock, we must eliminate the face value of the bonds, and then, following the same procedure, add the value of the preferred stock, common stock, reserve, and surplus, and subtract goodwill. This gives us a total net book value for the preferred stock of $7,530 or $753 for each share of $100 par value preferred. This is also very good coverage for the preferred stock, but we must examine current earnings before becoming too enthusiastic about the value of any security.

The net book value of the common stock, while an interesting figure, is not so important as the coverage on the senior securities. In case of liquidation, there is seldom much left for the common stockholders because of the normal loss in value of company assets when they are put up for sale, as mentioned before. The book value figure, however, does give us a basis for comparison with other companies. Comparisons of net book value over a period of years also show us if the company is a soundly growing one or, on the other hand, is losing ground. Earnings, however, are our important measure of common stock values, as we will see shortly.

The net book value of the common stock is found by adding the stated value of the common stock, reserves, and surplus and then subtracting patents and goodwill. This gives us a total net book value of $6,530,000. As there are 400,000 shares of common outstanding, each share has a net book value of $16.32. You must be careful not to be misled by book value figures, particularly of common stock. Profitable companies (Coca-Cola, for example) often show a very low net book value and very substantial earnings. Railroads, on the other hand, may show a high book value for their common stock but have such low or irregular earnings that the market price of the stock is much less than its apparent book value. Banks, insurance companies, and investment trusts are exceptions to what we have said about common stock net book value. As their assets are largely liquid (i.e., cash, accounts receivable, and marketable securities), the book value of their common stock sometimes indicates its value very accurately.

**PROPORTION OF BONDS, PREFERRED AND COMMON STOCK**

Before investing, you will want to know the proportion of each kind of security issued by the company you are considering. A high proportion of bonds reduces the attractiveness of both the preferred and common stock, while too large an amount of preferred detracts from the value of the common.

The *bond ratio* is found by dividing the face value of the bonds (Item 21), or $2,000,000, by the total value of the bonds, preferred stock, common stock, reserve, and surplus, or $9,630,000. This shows that bonds amount to about 20 percent of the total of bonds, capital, and surplus.

The *preferred stock ratio* is found in the same way, only we divide the stated value of the preferred stock by the total of the other five items. Since we have half as much preferred stock as we have bonds, the preferred ratio is roughly 10.

Naturally, the *common stock ratio* will be the difference between 100 percent and the totals of the bonds and preferred, or 70 percent in our sample company. You will want to remember that the most valuable method of determining the common stock ratio is in combination with reserve and surplus. The surplus, as we have noted, is additional backing for the common stock and usually represents either original funds paid in to the company in excess of the stated value of the common stock (capital surplus), or undistributed earnings (earned surplus).

Most investment analysts carefully examine industrial companies that have more than about a quarter of their capitalization represented by bonds, while common stock should total at least as much as all senior securities (bonds and preferred issues). When this is not the case, companies often find it difficult to raise new capital. Banks don't like to lend them money because of the already large debt, and it is sometimes difficult to sell common stock because of all the bond interest or preferred dividends that must be paid before anything is available for the common stockholder.

Railroads and public utility companies are exceptions to most of the rules of thumb that we use in discussing The ABC Manufacturing Company, Inc. Their situation is different because of the tremendous amounts of money they have invested in their fixed assets, their small inventories and he ease with which they can collect their receivables. Senior securities of railroads and utility companies frequently amount to more than half of their capitalization, Speculators often interest themselves in companies that have a high proportion of debt or preferred stock because of the *leverage factor.* A simple illustration will show why. Let us take, for example, a company with $10,000,000 of 4 percent bonds outstanding. If the company is earning $440,000 before bond interest, there will be only $40,000 left for the common stock ($10,000,000 at 4% equals $400,000). However, an increase of only 10 percent in earnings (to $484,000) will leave $84,000 for common stock dividends, or an increase of more than 100 percent. If there is only a small common issue, the increase in earnings per share would appear very impressive.

You have probably already noticed that a decline of 10 percent in earnings would not only wipe out everything available for the common stock, but result in the company being unable to cover its full interest on its bonds without dipping into surplus. This is the great danger of so-called high leverage stocks and also illustrates the fundamental weakness of companies that have a disproportionate amount of debt or preferred stock. Investors would do well to steer clear of them. Speculators, however, will continue to be fascinated by the market opportunities they offer.

**THE INCOME ACCOUNT**

The fundamental soundness of a company, as shown by its balance sheet, is important to investors, but of even greater interest is the record of its operation. Its financial structure shows much of its ability to weather storms and pick up speed when times are good. It is the income record, however, that shows us how a company is actually doing and gives us our best guide to the future.

The *Consolidated Income and Earned Surplus* account of our company is stated on the next page. Follow the items given there and we will find out just how our company earned its money, what it did with its earnings, and what it all means in terms of our three classes of securities. We have used a combined income and surplus account because it is the form most frequently followed by industrial companies. However, sometimes the two statements are given separately. Also, a variety of names are used to describe this same part of the financial report. Sometimes it is called profit and loss account, sometimes *record of earnings*, and, often, simply *income account.* They are all the same thing.

The details that you will find on different income statements also vary a great deal. Some companies show only eight or ten separate items, while others will give a page or more of closely spaced entries that break down each individual type of revenue or cost. We have tried to strike a balance between extremes; give the major items that are in most income statements, omitting details that are only interesting to the expert analyst.

The most important source of revenue always makes up the first item on the income statement. In our company, it is *Net Sales* (Item "a"). If it were a railroad or a utility instead of a manufacturer, this item would be called *gross revenues.* In any case, it represents the money paid into the company by its customers. Net sales are given to show that the figure represents the amount of money actually received after allowing for discounts and returned goods.

Net sales or gross revenues, you will note, is given before any kind of miscellaneous revenue that might have been received from investments, the sale of company property, tax refunds, or the like. A well-prepared income statement is always set up this way so that the stockholder can estimate the success of the company in fulfilling its major job of selling goods or service. If this were not so, you could not tell whether the company was really losing or making money on its operations, particularly over the last few years when tax rebates and other unusual things have often had great influence on final net income figures.

The ABC Manufacturing Company, Inc.
CONSOLIDATED INCOME AND EARNED SURPLUS
For the Year Ended December 31

| Item | | |
|---|---|---|
| a. Sales | | $10,000,000 |
| b. COST OF SALES, EXPENSES AND OTHER OPERATING CHARGES: | | |
| c. Cost of Goods Sold | $7,000,000 | |
| d. Selling, Administrative & Gen. Expenses | 500,000 | |
| e. Depreciation | 200,000 | |
| f. Maintenance and Repairs | 400,000 | |
| g. Taxes (Other than Federal Inc. Taxes) | 300,000 | |
| h. NET PROFIT FROM OPERATIONS | | 8,400,000 |
| i. OTHER INCOME: | | $1,600,000 |
| j. Royalties and Dividends | $250,000 | |
| k. Interest | 25,000 | |
| l. TOTAL | | $1,875,000 |
| m. INTEREST CHARGES: | | |
| n. Interest on Funded Debt | $70,000 | |
| o. Other Interest | 20,000 | 90,000 |
| p. NET INCOME BEFORE PROVISION FOR FED. INCOME TAXES | | $1,785,000 |
| q. PROVISION FOR FEDERAL INCOME TAXES | | 678,300 |
| r. NET INCOME | | $1,106,700 |
| s. DIVIDENDS | | |
| t. Preferred Stock - $5.00 Per Share | $50,000 | |
| u. Common Stock - $1.00 Per Share | 400,000 | |
| v. PROVISION FOR CONTINGENCIES | 200,000 | 650,000 |
| w. BALANCE CARRIED TO EARNED SURPLUS | | 456,700 |
| x, EARNED SURPLUS – JANUARY 1 | | 3,073,000 |
| y. EARNED SURPLUS – DECEMBER 31 | | $3,530,000 |

**COST OF SALES**

A general heading, *Cost of Sales, Expenses, and Other Operating Charges* (Item "b") is characteristic of a manufacturing company, but a utility company or railroad would call all of these things *operating expenses*.

The most important subdivision is *Cost of Goods Sold* (Item "c"). Included under cost of goods sold are all of the expenses that go directly into the manufacture of the products the company sells–raw materials, wages, freight, power, and rent. We have lumped these expenses together, as many companies do. Sometimes, however, you will find each item listed separately. Analyzing a detailed income account is a pretty technical operation and had best be left to the expert.

We have shown separately, opposite "d," the *Selling, Administrative and General Expenses* of the past year. Unfortunately, there is little uniformity among companies in their treatment of these important non-manufacturing costs. Our figure includes the expenses of management; that is, executive salaries and clerical costs; commissions and salaries paid to salesmen; advertising expenses, and the like.

*Depreciation* ("e") shows us the amount that the company transferred from income during the year to the depreciation reserve that we ran across before as Item "11" on the balance sheet (Page 2). Depreciation must be charged against income unless the company is going to live on its own fat, something that no company can do for long and stay out of bankruptcy.

**MAINTENANCE**

*Maintenance and Repairs* (Item "f") represents the money spent to keep the plant in good operating order. For example, the truck that we mentioned under depreciation must be kept running day by day. The cost of new tires, recharging the battery, painting and mechanical repairs are all maintenance costs. Despite this day-to-day work on the truck, the company must still provide for the time when it wears out–hence, the reserve for depreciation.

You can readily understand from your own experience the close connection between maintenance and depreciation. If you do not take good care of your own car, you will have to buy a new one sooner than you would had you maintained it well. Corporations face the same problem with all of their equipment. If they do not do a good job of maintenance, much more will have to be set aside for depreciation to replace the abused tools and property.

Taxes are always with us. A profitable company always pays at least two types of taxes. One group of taxes are paid without regard to profits, and include real estate taxes, excise taxes, social security, and the like (Item "g"). As these payments are a direct part of the cost of doing business, they must be included before we can determine the *Net Profit From Operations* (Item "h").

*Net Profit From Operations* (sometimes called *gross profit*) tells us what the company made from manufacturing and selling its products. It is an interesting figure to investors because it indicates how efficiently and successfully the company operates in its primary purpose as a creator of wealth. As a glance at the income account will tell you, there are still several other items to be deducted before the stockholder can hope to get anything. You can also easily imagine that for many companies these other items may spell the difference between profit and loss. For these reasons, we use net profit from operations as an indicator of progress in manufacturing and merchandising efficiency, not as a judge of the investment quality of securities.

*Miscellaneous Income* not connected with the major purpose of the company is generally listed after net profit from operations. There are quite a number of ways that corporations increase their income, including interest and dividends on securities they own, fees for special services performed, royalties on patents they allow others to use, and tax refunds. Our income statement shows *Other Income* as Item "i," under which is shown income from *Royalties* and *Dividends* (Item "j"), and as a separate entry, *Interest* (Item "k") which the company received from its bond investments. The *Total* of other income (Item "l") shows us how much The ABC Manufacturing Company received from so-called *outside activities*. Corporations with diversified interests often receive tremendous amounts of other income.

**INTEREST CHARGES**

There is one other class of expenses that must be deducted from our income before we can determine the base on which taxes are paid, and that is *Interest Charges* (Item "m"). As our company has $2,000,000 worth of 3 ½ percent bonds outstanding, it will pay *Interest* on Funded Debt of $70,000 (Item "n"). During the year, the company also borrowed money from the bank, on which it, of course, paid interest, shown as *Other Interest* (Item "o").

*Net Income Before Provision for Federal Income Taxes* ("Item "p") is an interesting figure for historical comparison. It shows us how profitable the company was in all of its various operations. A comparison of this entry over a period of years will enable you to see how well the company had been doing as a business institution before the government stepped in for its share of net earnings. Federal taxes have varied so much in recent years that earnings before taxes are often a real help in judging business progress.

A few paragraphs back we mentioned that a profitable corporation pays two general types of taxes. We have already discussed those that are paid without reference to profits. *Provision for Federal Income Taxes* (Item "q") is ordinarily figured on the total income of the company after normal business expenses, and so appears on our income account below these charges. Bond interest, for example, as it is payment on a loan, is deducted beforehand. Preferred and common stock dividends, which are profits that go to owners of the company, come after all charges and taxes.

**NET INCOME**

After we have deducted all of our expenses and income taxes from total income, we get *Net Income* (Item "r"). Net income is the most interesting figure of all to the investor. Net income is the amount available to pay dividends on the preferred and common stock. From the balance sheet, we have learned a good deal about the company's stability and soundness of structure; from net profit from operations, we judge whether the company is improving in industrial efficiency. Net income tells us whether the securities of the company are likely to be a profitable investment.

The figure given for a single year is not nearly all of the store, however. As we have noted before, the historical record is usually more important than the figure for any given year. This is just as true of net income as any other item. So many things change from year to year that care must be taken not to draw hasty conclusions. During the war, Excess Profits Taxes had a tremendous effect on the earnings of many companies. In the next few years, carryback tax credits allowed some companies to show a net profit despite the fact that they had operated at a loss. Even net income can be a misleading figure unless one examines it carefully. A rough and easy way of judging how sound a figure it is would be to compare it with previous years.

The investor in stocks has a vital interest in *Dividends* (Item "s"). The first dividend that our company must pay is that on its *Preferred Stock* (Item "t"). Some companies will even pay preferred dividends out of earned surplus accumulated in the past if the net income is not large enough, but such a company is skating on thin ice unless the situation is most unusual.

The directors of our company decided to pay dividends totaling ($400,000 on the *Common Stock*, or $1 a share (Item "u"). As we have noted before, the amount of dividends paid is not determined by net income, but by a decision of the stockholders' representatives–the company's directors. Common dividends, just like preferred dividends, can be paid out of surplus if there is little or no net income. Sometimes companies do this if they have a long history of regular payments and don't want to spoil the record because of some special temporary situation that caused them to lose money. This occurs even less frequently and is more dangerous than paying preferred dividends out of surplus.

It is much more common, on the contrary, to plough earnings back into the business–a phrase you frequently see on the financial pages and in company reports. The directors of our typical company have decided to pay only $1 on the common stock, though net income would have permitted them to pay much more. They decided that the company should save the difference.

The next entry on our income account, *Provision for Contingencies* (Item "v") shows us where our reserve for contingencies arose. The treasurer of our typical company has put the provision for contingencies after dividends. However, you will discover, if you look at very many financial reports, that it is sometimes placed above net income.

All of the net income that was not paid out as dividends, or set aside for contingencies, is shown as *Balance Carried to Earned Surplus* (Item "w"). In other words, it is kept in the business. In previous years, the company had also earned more than it paid out so it had already accumulated by the beginning of the year an earned surplus of $3,073,000 (Item "x"). When we total the earned surplus accumulated during the year to that which the company had at the first of the year, we get the total earned surplus at the end of the year (Item "y"). You will notice that the total here is the same as that which we ran across on the balance sheet as Item 27.

Not all companies combine their income and surplus account. When they do not, you will find that *balance carried to surplus* will be the last item on the income account. The statement of consolidated surplus would appear as a third section of the corporation's financial report. A separate surplus account might be used if the company shifted funds for reserves to surplus during the year or made any other major changes in its method of treating the surplus account.

## ANALYZING THE INCOME ACCOUNT

The income account, like the balance sheet, will tell us a lot more if we make a few detailed comparisons. The size of the totals on an income account doesn't mean much by itself. A company can have hundreds of millions of dollars in net sales and be a very bad investment. On the other hand, even a very modest profit in round figure may make a security attractive if there are only a small number of shares outstanding.

Before you select a company for investment, you will want to know something of its *margin of profit*, and how this figure has changed over the years. Finding the margin of profit is very simple. We just divide the net profit from operations (Item "h") by net sales (Item "a"). The figure we get (0.16) shows us that the company made a profit of 16 percent from operations. By itself, though, this is not very helpful. We can make it significant in two ways.

In the first place, we can compare it with the margin of profit in previous years, and, from this comparison, learn if the company excels other companies that do a similar type of business. If the margin of profit of our company is very low in comparison with other companies in the same field, it is an unhealthy sign. Naturally, if it is high, we have grounds to be optimistic.

Analysts also frequently use *operating ratio* for the same purpose. The operating ratio is the complement of the margin of profit. The margin of profit of our typical company is 16. The operating ratio is 84. You can find the operating ratio either by subtracting the margin of profit from 100 or dividing the total of operating costs ($8,400,000) by net sales ($10,000,000).

The margin of profit figure and the operating ratio, like all of those ratios we examined in connection with the balance sheet, give us general information about the company, help us judge its prospects for the future. All of these comparisons have significance for the long term as they tell us about the fundamental economic condition of the company. But you still have the right to ask: "Are the securities good investments for me now?"

Investors, as opposed to speculators, are primarily interested in two things. The first is safety for their capital and the second, regularity of income. They are also interested in the rate of return on their investment but, as you will see, the rate of return will be affected by the importance placed on safety and regularity. High income implies risk. Safety must be bought by accepting a lower return.

The safety of any security is determined primarily by the earnings of the company that are available to pay interest or dividends on the particular issues. Again, though, round dollar figures aren't of much help to us. What we want to know is the relationship between the total money available and the requirements for each of the securities issued by the company.

**INTEREST COVERAGE**

As the bonds of our company represent part of its debt, the first thing we want to know is how easily the company can pay the interest. From the income account we see that the company had total income of $1,875,000 (Item "1"). The interest charge on our bonds each year is $70,000 (3½ percent of $2,000,000–Item 21 on the balance sheet). Dividing total income by bond interest charges ($1,875,000 by $70,000) shows us that the company earned its bond interest 26 times over. Even after income taxes, bond interest was earned 17 times, a method of testing employed by conservative analysts. Before an industrial bond should be considered a safe investment, so our company has a wide margin of safety.

To calculate the *preferred dividend coverage* (i.e., the number of times preferred dividends were earned), we must use net income as our base, as Federal Income Taxes and all interest charges must be paid before anything is available for stockholders. As we have 10,000 shares of $100 par value of preferred stock which pays a dividend of 5 percent, the total dividend requirement for the preferred stock is $50,000 (Items 24 on the balance sheet and "t" on the income account).

**EARNINGS PER COMMON SHARE**

The buyer of common stocks is often more concerned with the earnings per share of his stock than he is with the dividend. It is usually earnings per share or, rather, prospective earnings per share, that influence stock market prices. Our income account does not show the earnings available for the common stock, so we must calculate it ourselves. It is net income less preferred dividends (Items "r"- "t"), or $1,056,700. From the balance sheet, we know that there are 400,000 shares outstanding, so the company earned about $2.64 per share.

All of these ratios have been calculated for a single year. It cannot be emphasized too strongly, however, that the record is more important to the investor than the report of any single year. By all the tests we have employed, both the bonds and the preferred stock of our typical company appear to be very good investments, if their market prices were not too high. The investor would want to look back, however, to determine whether the operations were reasonably typical of the company.

Bonds and preferred stocks that are very safe usually sell at pretty high prices, so the yield to the investor is small. For example, if our company has been showing about the same coverage on its preferred dividends for many years and there is good reason to believe that the future will be equally kind, the company would probably replace the old 5 percent preferred with a new issue paying a lower rate, perhaps 4 percent.

**STOCK PRICES**

As the common stock does not receive a guaranteed dividend, its market value is determined by a great variety of influences in addition to the present yield of the stock measured by its dividends. The stock market, by bringing together buyers and sellers from all over the world, reflects their composite judgment of the present and future value of the stock. We cannot attempt here to write a treatise on the stock market. There is one important ratio, however, that every common stock buyer considers. That is the ratio of earnings to market price.

The so-called *price-earnings ratio* is simply the earnings per share on the common stock divided into the market price. Our typical company earned $2.64 a common share in the year. If the stock were selling at $30 a share, its price-earnings ratio would be about 11.4. This is the basis figure that you would want to use in comparing the common stock of this particular company with other similar stocks.

IMPORTANT TERMS AND CONCEPTS

LIABILITIES

WHAT THE COMPANY OWES—+ RESERVES + SURPLUS + STOCKHOLDERS INTEREST IN THE COMPANY

ASSETS

WHAT THE COMPANY OWNS— + WHAT IS OWED TO THE COMPANY

FIXED ASSETS

MACHINERY, EQUIPMENT, BUILDINGS, ETC.

EXAMPLES OF FIXED ASSETS

DESKS, TABLES, FILING CABINETS, BUILDINGS, LAND, TIMBERLAND, CARS AND TRUCKS, LOCOMOTIVES AND FREIGHT CARS, SHIPYARDS, OIL LANDS, ORE DEPOSITS, FOUNDRIES

EXAMPLES OF:

PREPAID EXPENSES

PREPAID INSURANCE, PREPAID RENT, PREPAIDD ROYALTIES AND PREPAID INTEREST

DEFERRED CHARGES

AMORTIZATION OF BOND DISCOUNT, ORGANIZATION EXPENSE, MOVING EXPENSES, DEVELOPMENT EXPENSES

ACCOUNTS PAYABLE

BILLS THE COMPANY OWES TO OTHERS

BONDHOLDERS ARE CREDITORS

BOND CERTIFICATES ARE IOU'S ISSUED BY A COMPANY BACKED BY A PLEDGE

BONDHOLDERS ARE OWNERS

A STOCK CERTIFICATE IS EVIDENCE OF THE SHAREHOLDER'S OWNERSHIP

EARNED SURPLUS

INCOME PLOWED BACK INTO THE BUSINESS

NET SALES

GROSS SALES MINUS DISCOUNTS AND RETURNED GOODS

NET INCOME

= TOTAL INCOME MINUS ALL EXPENSES AND INCOME TAXES

## PHILOSOPHY, PRINCIPLES, PRACTICES, AND TECHNICS OF SUPERVISION, ADMINISTRATION, MANAGEMENT, AND ORGANIZATION

## TABLE OF CONTENTS

# PHILOSOPHY, PRINCIPLES, PRACTICES, AND TECHNICS
# OF
# SUPERVISION, ADMINISTRATION, MANAGEMENT, AND ORGANIZATION

## MEANING OF SUPERVISION

The extension of the democratic philosophy has been accompanied by an extension in the scope of supervision. Modern leaders and supervisors no longer think of supervision in the narrow sense of being confined chiefly to visiting employees, supplying materials, or rating the staff. They regard supervision as being intimately related to all the concerned agencies of society, they speak of the supervisor's function in terms of "growth," rather than the "improvement" of employees.

This modern concept of supervision may be defined as follows: Supervision is leadership and the development of leadership within groups which are cooperatively engaged in inspection, research, training, guidance, and evaluation.

## THE OLD AND THE NEW SUPERVISION

TRADITIONAL

1. Inspection
2. Focused on the employee
3. Visitation
4. Random and haphazard
5. Imposed and authoritarian
6. One person usually

MODERN

1. Study and analysis
2. Focused on aims, materials, methods, supervisors, employees, environment
3. Demonstrations, intervisitation, workshops, directed reading, bulletins, etc.
4. Definitely organized and planned (scientific)
5. Cooperative and democratic
6. Many persons involved (creative)

## THE EIGHT (8) BASIC PRINCIPLES OF THE NEW SUPERVISION

I. Principle of Responsibility
   Authority to act and responsibility for acting must be joined.
   A. If you give responsibility, give authority.
   B. Define employee duties clearly.
   C. Protect employees from criticism by others.
   D. Recognize the rights as well as obligations of employees.
   E. Achieve the aims of a democratic society insofar as it is possible within the area of your work.
   F. Establish a situation favorable to training and learning.
   G. Accept ultimate responsibility for everything done in your section, unit, office, division, department.
   H. Good administration and good supervision are inseparable.

II. Principle of Authority

The success of the supervisor is measured by the extent to which the power of authority is not used.

A. Exercise simplicity and informality in supervision
B. Use the simplest machinery of supervision
C. If it is good for the organization as a whole, it is probably justified.
D. Seldom be arbitrary or authoritative.
E. Do not base your work on the power of position or of personality.
F. Permit and encourage the free expression of opinions.

III. Principle of Self-Growth

The success of the supervisor is measured by the extent to which, and the speed with which, he is no longer needed.

A. Base criticism on principles, not on specifics.
B. Point out higher activities to employees.
C. Train for self-thinking by employees to meet new situations.
D. Stimulate initiative, self-reliance, and individual responsibility
E. Concentrate on stimulating the growth of employees rather than on removing defects.

IV. Principle of Individual Worth

Respect for the individual is a paramount consideration in supervision.

A. Be human and sympathetic in dealing with employees.
B. Don't nag about things to be done.
C. Recognize the individual differences among employees and seek opportunities to permit best expression of each personality.

V. Principle of Creative Leadership

The best supervision is that which is not apparent to the employee.

A. Stimulate, don't drive employees to creative action.
B. Emphasize doing good things.
C. Encourage employees to do what they do best.
D. Do not be too greatly concerned with details of subject or method.
E. Do not be concerned exclusively with immediate problems and activities.
F. Reveal higher activities and make them both desired and maximally possible.
G. Determine procedures in the light of each situation but see that these are derived from a sound basic philosophy.
H. Aid, inspire, and lead so as to liberate the creative spirit latent in all good employees.

VI. Principle of Success and Failure

There are no unsuccessful employees, only unsuccessful supervisors who have failed to give proper leadership.

A. Adapt suggestions to the capacities, attitudes, and prejudices of employees.
B. Be gradual, be progressive, be persistent.
C. Help the employee find the general principle; have the employee apply his own problem to the general principle.
D. Give adequate appreciation for good work and honest effort.
E. Anticipate employee difficulties and help to prevent them.
F. Encourage employees to do the desirable things they will do anyway.
G. Judge your supervision by the results it secures.

VII. Principle of Science

Successful supervision is scientific, objective, and experimental. It is based on facts, not on prejudices.

A. Be cumulative in results.
B. Never divorce your suggestions from the goals of training.
C. Don't be impatient of results.
D. Keep all matters on a professional, not a personal, level.
E. Do not be concerned exclusively with immediate problems and activities.
F. Use objective means of determining achievement and rating where possible.

VIII. Principle of Cooperation

Supervision is a cooperative enterprise between supervisor and employee.

A. Begin with conditions as they are.
B. Ask opinions of all involved when formulating policies.
C. Organization is as good as its weakest link.
D. Let employees help to determine policies and department programs.
E. Be approachable and accessible—physically and mentally.
F. Develop pleasant social relationships.

## WHAT IS ADMINISTRATION

Administration is concerned with providing the environment, the material facilities, and the operational procedures that will promote the maximum growth and development of supervisors and employees. (Organization is an aspect and a concomitant of administration.)

There is no sharp line of demarcation between supervision and administration; these functions are intimately interrelated and, often, overlapping. They are complementary activities.

I. Practices Commonly Classed as "Supervisory"

A. Conducting employees' conferences
B. Visiting sections, units, offices, divisions, departments
C. Arranging for demonstrations
D. Examining plans
E. Suggesting professional reading
F. Interpreting bulletins
G. Recommending in-service training courses
H. Encouraging experimentation
I. Appraising employee morale
J. Providing for intervisitation

II. Practices Commonly Classified as "Administrative"

A. Management of the office
B. Arrangement of schedules for extra duties
C. Assignment of rooms or areas
D. Distribution of supplies
E. Keeping records and reports
F. Care of audio-visual materials
G. Keeping inventory records
H. Checking record cards and books

I. Programming special activities
J. Checking on the attendance and punctuality of employees

III. Practices Commonly Classified as Both "Supervisory" and "Administrative"
A. Program construction
B. Testing or evaluating outcomes
C. Personnel accounting
D. Ordering instructional materials

## RESPONSIBILITIES OF THE SUPERVISOR

A person employed in a supervisory capacity must constantly be able to improve his own efficiency and ability. He represent the employer to the employees and only continuous self-examination can make him a capable supervisor.

Leadership and training are the supervisor's responsibility. An efficient working unit is one in which the employees work with the supervisor. It is his job to bring out the best in his employees. He must always be relaxed, courteous, and calm in his association with his employees. Their feelings are important, and a harsh attitude does not develop the most efficient employees.

## COMPETENCES OF THE SUPERVISOR

I. Complete knowledge of the duties and responsibilities of his position.
II. To be able to organize a job, plan ahead, and carry through.
III. To have self-confidence and initiative.
IV. To be able to handle the unexpected situation and make quick decisions.
V. To be able to properly train subordinates in the positions they are best suited for.
VI. To be able to keep good human relations among his subordinates.
VII. To be able to keep good human relations between his subordinates and himself and to earn their respect and trust.

## THE PROFESSIONAL SUPERVISOR-EMPLOYEE RELATIONSHIP

There are two kinds of efficiency: one kind is only apparent and is produced in organizations through the exercise of mere discipline; this is but a simulation of the second, or true, efficiency which springs from spontaneous cooperation. If you are a manager, no matter how great or small your responsibility, it is your job, in the final analysis, to create and develop this involuntary cooperation among the people whom you supervise. For, no matter how powerful a combination of money, machines, and materials a company may have, this is a dead and sterile thing without a team of willing, thinking, and articulate people to guide it.

The following 21 points are presented as indicative of the exemplary basic relationship that should exist between supervisor and employee:

1. Each person wants to be liked and respected by his fellow employee and wants to be treated with consideration and respect by his superior.
2. The most competent employee will make an error. However, in a unit where good relations exist between the supervisor and his employees, tenseness and fear do not exist. Thus, errors are not hidden or covered up, and the efficiency of a unit is not impaired.

3. Subordinates resent rules, regulations, or orders that are unreasonable or unexplained.
4. Subordinates are quick to resent unfairness, harshness, injustices, and favoritism.
5. An employee will accept responsibility if he knows that he will be complimented for a job well done, and not too harshly chastised for failure; that his supervisor will check the cause of the failure, and, if it was the supervisor's fault, he will assume the blame therefore. If it was the employee's fault, his supervisor will explain the correct method or means of handling the responsibility.
6. An employee wants to receive credit for a suggestion he has made, that is used. If a suggestion cannot be used, the employee is entitled to an explanation. The supervisor should not say "no" and close the subject.
7. Fear and worry slow up a worker's ability. Poor working environment can impair his physical and mental health. A good supervisor avoids forceful methods, threats, and arguments to get a job done.
8. A forceful supervisor is able to train his employees individually and as a team, and is able to motivate them in the proper channels.
9. A mature supervisor is able to properly evaluate his subordinates and to keep them happy and satisfied.
10. A sensitive supervisor will never patronize his subordinates.
11. A worthy supervisor will respect his employees' confidences.
12. Definite and clear-cut responsibilities should be assigned to each executive.
13. Responsibility should always be coupled with corresponding authority.
14. No change should be made in the scope or responsibilities of a position without a definite understanding to that effect on the part of all persons concerned.
15. No executive or employee, occupying a single position in the organization, should be subject to definite orders from more than one source.
16. Orders should never be given to subordinates over the head of a responsible executive. Rather than do this, the officer in question should be supplanted.
17. Criticisms of subordinates should, whoever possible, be made privately, and in no case should a subordinate be criticized in the presence of executives or employees of equal or lower rank.
18. No dispute or difference between executives or employees as to authority or responsibilities should be considered too trivial for prompt and careful adjudication.
19. Promotions, wage changes, and disciplinary action should always be approved by the executive immediately superior to the one directly responsible.
20. No executive or employee should ever be required, or expected, to be at the same time an assistant to, and critic of, another.
21. Any executive whose work is subject to regular inspection should, wherever practicable, be given the assistance and facilities necessary to enable him to maintain an independent check of the quality of his work.

## MINI-TEXT IN SUPERVISION, ADMINISTRATION, MANAGEMENT, AND ORGANIZATION

I. Brief Highlights

Listed concisely and sequentially are major headings and important data in the field for quick recall and review.

A. Levels of Management

Any organization of some size has several levels of management. In terms of a ladder, the levels are:

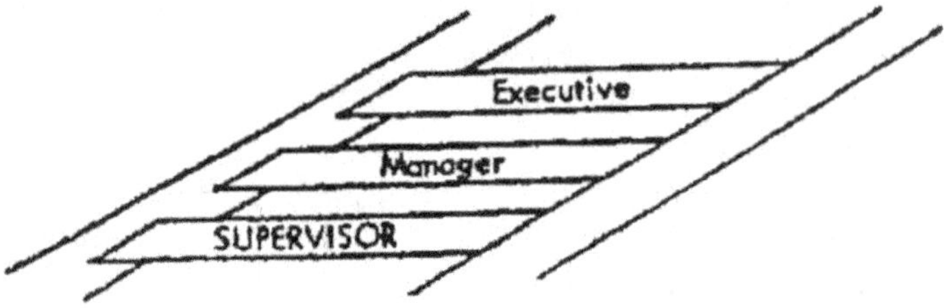


The first level is very important because it is the beginning point of management leadership.

B. What the Supervisor Must Learn

A supervisor must learn to:

1. Deal with people and their differences
2. Get the job done through people
3. Recognize the problems when they exist
4. Overcome obstacles to good performance
5. Evaluate the performance of people
6. Check his own performance in terms of accomplishment

C. A Definition of Supervisor

The term supervisor means any individual having authority, in the interests of the employer, to hire, transfer, suspend, lay-off, recall, promote, discharge, assign, reward, or discipline other employees or responsibility to direct them, or to adjust their grievances, or effectively to recommend such action, if, in connection with the foregoing, exercise of such authority is not of a merely routine or clerical nature but requires the use of independent judgment.

D. Elements of the Team Concept

What is involved in teamwork? The component parts are:

1. Members
2. A leader
3. Goals
4. Plans
5. Cooperation
6. Spirit

E. Principles of Organization

1. A team member must know what his job is.
2. Be sure that the nature and scope of a job are understood.
3. Authority and responsibility should be carefully spelled out.
4. A supervisor should be permitted to make the maximum number of decisions affecting his employees.
5. Employees should report to only one supervisor.
6. A supervisor should direct only as many employees as he can handle effectively.
7. An organization plan should be flexible.

8. Inspection and performance of work should be separate.
9. Organizational problems should receive immediate attention.
10. Assign work in line with ability and experience.

F. The Four Important Parts of Every Job
1. Inherent in every job is the *accountability* for results.
2. A second set of factors in every job is *responsibilities*.
3. Along with duties and responsibilities one must have the *authority* to act within certain limits without obtaining permission to proceed.
4. No job exists in a vacuum. The supervisor is surrounded by key *relationships*.

G. Principles of Delegation
Where work is delegated for the first time, the supervisor should think in terms of these questions:
1. Who is best qualified to do this?
2. Can an employee improve his abilities by doing this?
3. How long should an employee spend on this?
4. Are there any special problems for which he will need guidance?
5. How broad a delegation can I make?

H. Principles of Effective Communications
1. Determine the media.
2. To whom directed?
3. Identification and source authority.
4. Is communication understood?

I. Principles of Work Improvement
1. Most people usually do only the work which is assigned to them.
2. Workers are likely to fit assigned work into the time available to perform it.
3. A good workload usually stimulates output.
4. People usually do their best work when they know that results will be reviewed or inspected.
5. Employees usually feel that someone else is responsible for conditions of work, workplace layout, job methods, type of tools/equipment, and other such factors.
6. Employees are usually defensive about their job security.
7. Employees have natural resistance to change.
8. Employees can support or destroy a supervisor.
9. A supervisor usually earns the respect of his people through his personal example of diligence and efficiency.

J. Areas of Job Improvement
The areas of job improvement are quite numerous, but the most common ones which a supervisor can identify and utilize are:
1. Departmental layout
2. Flow of work
3. Workplace layout
4. Utilization of manpower
5. Work methods
6. Materials handling

7. Utilization
8. Motion economy

K. Seven Key Points in Making Improvements
1. Select the job to be improved
2. Study how it is being done now
3. Question the present method
4. Determine actions to be taken
5. Chart proposed method
6. Get approval and apply
7. Solicit worker participation

I. Corrective Techniques of Job Improvement

Specific Problems
1. Size of workload
2. Inability to meet schedules
3. Strain and fatigue
4. Improper use of men and skills
5. Waste, poor quality, unsafe conditions
6. Bottleneck conditions that hinder output
7. Poor utilization of equipment and machine
8. Efficiency and productivity of labor

General Improvement
1. Departmental layout
2. Flow of work
3. Work plan layout
4. Utilization of manpower
5. Work methods
6. Materials handling
7. Utilization of equipment
8. Motion economy

Corrective Techniques
1. Study with scale model
2. Flow chart study
3. Motion analysis
4. Comparison of units produced to standard allowance
5. Methods analysis
6. Flow chart and equipment study
7. Down time vs. running time
8. Motion analysis

M. A Planning Checklist
1. Objectives
2. Controls
3. Delegations
4. Communications
5. Resources
6. Manpower

7. Equipment
8. Supplies and materials
9. Utilization of time
10. Safety
11. Money
12. Work
13. Timing of improvements

N. Five Characteristics of Good Directions

In order to get results, directions must be:

1. Possible of accomplishment
2. Agreeable with worker interests
3. Related to mission
4. Planned and complete
5. Unmistakably clear

O. Types of Directions

1. Demands or direct orders
2. Requests
3. Suggestion or implication
4. volunteering

P. Controls

A typical listing of the overall areas in which the supervisor should establish controls might be:

1. Manpower
2. Materials
3. Quality of work
4. Quantity of work
5. Time
6. Space
7. Money
8. Methods

Q. Orienting the New Employee

1. Prepare for him
2. Welcome the new employee
3. Orientation for the job
4. Follow-up

R. Checklist for Orienting New Employees

| | Yes | No |
|---|---|---|
| 1. Do you appreciate the feelings of new employees when they first report for work? | ___ | ___ |
| 2. Are you aware of the fact that the new employee must make a big adjustment to his job? | ___ | ___ |
| 3. Have you given him good reasons for liking the job and the organization? | ___ | ___ |
| 4. Have you prepared for his first day on the job? | ___ | ___ |
| 5. Did you welcome him cordially and make him feel needed? | ___ | ___ |

| | Yes | No |
|---|---|---|
| 6. Did you establish rapport with him so that he feels free to talk and discuss matters with you? | ___ | ___ |
| 7. Did you explain his job to him and his relationship to you? | ___ | ___ |
| 8. Does he know that his work will be evaluated periodically on a basis that is fair and objective? | ___ | ___ |
| 9. Did you introduce him to his fellow workers in such a way that they are likely to accept him? | ___ | ___ |
| 10. Does he know what employee benefits he will receive? | ___ | ___ |
| 11. Does he understand the importance of being on the job and what to do if he must leave his duty station? | ___ | ___ |
| 12. Has he been impressed with the importance of accident prevention and safe practice? | ___ | ___ |
| 13. Does he generally know his way around the department? | ___ | ___ |
| 14. Is he under the guidance of a sponsor who will teach the right way of doing things? | ___ | ___ |
| 15. Do you plan to follow-up so that he will continue to adjust successfully to his job? | ___ | ___ |

S. Principles of Learning
1. Motivation
2. Demonstration or explanation
3. Practice

T. Causes of Poor Performance
1. Improper training for job
2. Wrong tools
3. Inadequate directions
4. Lack of supervisory follow-up
5. Poor communications
6. Lack of standards of performance
7. Wrong work habits
8. Low morale
9. Other

U. Four Major Steps in On-The-Job Instruction
1. Prepare the worker
2. Present the operation
3. Tryout performance
4. Follow-up

V. Employees Want Five Things
1. Security
2. Opportunity
3. Recognition
4. Inclusion
5. Expression

W. Some Don'ts in Regard to Praise
1. Don't praise a person for something he hasn't done.
2. Don't praise a person unless you can be sincere.
3. Don't be sparing in praise just because your superior withholds it from you.
4. Don't let too much time elapse between good performance and recognition of it

X. How to Gain Your Workers' Confidence

Methods of developing confidence include such things as:
1. Knowing the interests, habits, hobbies of employees
2. Admitting your own inadequacies
3. Sharing and telling of confidence in others
4. Supporting people when they are in trouble
5. Delegating matters that can be well handled
6. Being frank and straightforward about problems and working conditions
7. Encouraging others to bring their problems to you
8. Taking action on problems which impede worker progress

Y. Sources of Employee Problems

On-the-job causes might be such things as:
1. A feeling that favoritism is exercised in assignments
2. Assignment of overtime
3. An undue amount of supervision
4. Changing methods or systems
5. Stealing of ideas or trade secrets
6. Lack of interest in job
7. Threat of reduction in force
8. Ignorance or lack of communications
9. Poor equipment
10. Lack of knowing how supervisor feels toward employee
11. Shift assignments

Off-the-job problems might have to do with:
1. Health
2. Finances
3. Housing
4. Family

Z. The Supervisor's Key to Discipline

There are several key points about discipline which the supervisor should keep in mind:
1. Job discipline is one of the disciplines of life and is directed by the supervisor.
2. It is more important to correct an employee fault than to fix blame for it.
3. Employee performance is affected by problems both on the job and off.
4. Sudden or abrupt changes in behavior can be indications of important employee problems.
5. Problems should be dealt with as soon as possible after they are identified.
6. The attitude of the supervisor may have more to do with solving problems than the techniques of problem solving.
7. Correction of employee behavior should be resorted to only after the supervisor is sure that training or counseling will not be helpful.

8. Be sure to document your disciplinary actions.
9. Make sure that you are disciplining on the basis of facts rather than personal feelings.
10. Take each disciplinary step in order, being careful not to make snap judgments, or decisions based on impatience.

AA. Five Important Processes of Management

1. Planning
2. Organizing
3. Scheduling
4. Controlling
5. Motivating

BB. When the Supervisor Fails to Plan

1. Supervisor creates impression of not knowing his job
2. May lead to excessive overtime
3. Job runs itself—supervisor lacks control
4. Deadlines and appointments missed
5. Parts of the work go undone
6. Work interrupted by emergencies
7. Sets a bad example
8. Uneven workload creates peaks and valleys
9. Too much time on minor details at expense of more important tasks

CC. Fourteen General Principles of Management

1. Division of work
2. Authority and responsibility
3. Discipline
4. Unity of command
5. Unity of direction
6. Subordination of individual interest to general interest
7. Remuneration of personnel
8. Centralization
9. Scalar chain
10. Order
11. Equity
12. Stability of tenure of personnel
13. Initiative
14. Esprit de corps

DD. Change

Bringing about change is perhaps attempted more often, and yet less well understood, than anything else the supervisor does. How do people generally react to change? (People tend to resist change that is imposed upon them by other individuals or circumstances.

Change is characteristic of every situation. It is a part of every real endeavor where the efforts of people are concerned.

1. Why do people resist change?
   People may resist change because of:
   a. Fear of the unknown
   b. Implied criticism
   c. Unpleasant experiences in the past
   d. Fear of loss of status
   e. Threat to the ego
   f. Fear of loss of economic stability

2. How can we best overcome the resistance to change?
   In initiating change, take these steps:
   a. Get ready to sell
   b. Identify sources of help
   c. Anticipate objections
   d. Sell benefits
   e. Listen in depth
   f. Follow up

II. Brief Topical Summaries

A. Who/What is the Supervisor?
   1. The supervisor is often called the "highest level employee and the lowest level manager."
   2. A supervisor is a member of both management and the work group. He acts as a bridge between the two.
   3. Most problems in supervision are in the area of human relations, or people problems.
   4. Employees expect: Respect, opportunity to learn and to advance, and a sense of belonging, and so forth.
   5. Supervisors are responsible for directing people and organizing work. Planning is of paramount importance.
   6. A position description is a set of duties and responsibilities inherent to a given position.
   7. It is important to keep the position description up-to-date and to provide each employee with his own copy.

B. The Sociology of Work
   1. People are alike in many ways; however, each individual is unique.
   2. The supervisor is challenged in getting to know employee differences. Acquiring skills in evaluating individuals is an asset.
   3. Maintaining meaningful working relationships in the organization is of great importance.
   4. The supervisor has an obligation to help individuals to develop to their fullest potential.
   5. Job rotation on a planned basis helps to build versatility and to maintain interest and enthusiasm in work groups.
   6. Cross training (job rotation) provides backup skills.

7. The supervisor can help reduce tension by maintaining a sense of humor, providing guidance to employees, and by making reasonable and timely decisions. Employees respond favorably to working under reasonably predictable circumstances.
8. Change is characteristic of all managerial behavior. The supervisor must adjust to changes in procedures, new methods, technological changes, and to a number of new and sometimes challenging situations.
9. To overcome the natural tendency for people to resist change, the supervisor should become more skillful in initiating change.

C. Principles and Practices of Supervision
1. Employees should be required to answer to only one superior.
2. A supervisor can effectively direct only a limited number of employees, depending upon the complexity, variety, and proximity of the jobs involved.
3. The organizational chart presents the organization in graphic form. It reflects lines of authority and responsibility as well as interrelationships of units within the organization.
4. Distribution of work can be improved through an analysis using the "Work Distribution Chart."
5. The "Work Distribution Chart" reflects the division of work within a unit in understandable form.
6. When related tasks are given to an employee, he has a better chance of increasing his skills through training.
7. The individual who is given the responsibility for tasks must also be given the appropriate authority to insure adequate results.
8. The supervisor should delegate repetitive, routine work. Preparation of recurring reports, maintaining leave and attendance records are some examples.
9. Good discipline is essential to good task performance. Discipline is reflected in the actions of employees on the job in the absence of supervision.
10. Disciplinary action may have to be taken when the positive aspects of discipline have failed. Reprimand, warning, and suspension are examples of disciplinary action.
11. If a situation calls for a reprimand, be sure it is deserved and remember it is to be done in private.

D. Dynamic Leadership
1. A style is a personal method or manner of exerting influence.
2. Authoritarian leaders often see themselves as the source of power and authority.
3. The democratic leader often perceives the group as the source of authority and power.
4. Supervisors tend to do better when using the pattern of leadership that is most natural for them.
5. Social scientists suggest that the effective supervisor use the leadership style that best fits the problem or circumstances involved.
6. All four styles—telling, selling, consulting, joining—have their place. Using one does not preclude using the other at another time.

7. The theory X point of view assumes that the average person dislikes work, will avoid it whenever possible, and must be coerced to achieve organizational objectives.
8. The theory Y point of view assumes that the average person considers work to be a natural as play, and, when the individual is committed, he requires little supervision or direction to accomplish desired objectives.
9. The leader's basic assumptions concerning human behavior and human nature affect his actions, decisions, and other managerial practices.
10. Dissatisfaction among employees is often present, but difficult to isolate. The supervisor should seek to weaken dissatisfaction by keeping promises, being sincere and considerate, keeping employees informed, and so forth.
11. Constructive suggestions should be encouraged during the natural progress of the work.

E. Processes for Solving Problems

1. People find their daily tasks more meaningful and satisfying when they can improve them.
2. The causes of problems, or the key factors, are often hidden in the background. Ability to solve problems often involves the ability to isolate them from their backgrounds. There is some substance to the cliché that some persons "can't see the forest for the trees."
3. New procedures are often developed from old ones. Problems should be broken down into manageable parts. New ideas can be adapted from old one.
4. People think differently in problem-solving situations. Using a logical, patterned approach is often useful. One approach found to be useful includes these steps:
   a. Define the problem
   b. Establish objectives
   c. Get the facts
   d. Weigh and decide
   e. Take action
   f. Evaluate action

F. Training for Results

1. Participants respond best when they feel training is important to them.
2. The supervisor has responsibility for the training and development of those who report to him.
3. When training is delegated to others, great care must be exercised to insure the trainer has knowledge, aptitude, and interest for his work as a trainer.
4. Training (learning) of some type goes on continually. The most successful supervisor makes certain the learning contributes in a productive manner to operational goals.
5. New employees are particularly susceptible to training. Older employees facing new job situations require specific training, as well as having need for development and growth opportunities.
6. Training needs require continuous monitoring.
7. The training officer of an agency is a professional with a responsibility to assist supervisors in solving training problems.

8. Many of the self-development steps important to the supervisor's own growth are equally important to the development of peers and subordinates. Knowledge of these is important when the supervisor consults with others on development and growth opportunities.

G. Health, Safety, and Accident Prevention
   1. Management-minded supervisors take appropriate measures to assist employees in maintaining health and in assuring safe practices in the work environment.
   2. Effective safety training and practices help to avoid injury and accidents.
   3. Safety should be a management goal. All infractions of safety which are observed should be corrected without exception.
   4. Employees' safety attitude, training and instruction, provision of safe tools and equipment, supervision, and leadership are considered highly important factors which contribute to safety and which can be influenced directly by supervisors.
   5. When accidents do occur, they should be investigated promptly for very important reasons, including the fact that information which is gained can be used to prevent accidents in the future.

H. Equal Employment Opportunity
   1. The supervisor should endeavor to treat all employees fairly, without regard to religion, race, sex, or national origin.
   2. Groups tend to reflect the attitude of the leader. Prejudice can be detected even in very subtle form. Supervisors must strive to create a feeling of mutual respect and confidence in every employee.
   3. Complete utilization of all human resources is a national goal. Equitable consideration should be accorded women in the work force, minority-group members, the physically and mentally handicapped, and the older employee. The important question is: "Who can do the job?"
   4. Training opportunities, recognition for performance, overtime assignments, promotional opportunities, and all other personnel actions are to be handled on an equitable basis.

I. Improving Communications
   1. Communications is achieving understanding between the sender and the receiver of a message. It also means sharing information—the creation of understanding.
   2. Communication is basic to all human activity. Words are means of conveying meanings; however, real meanings are in people.
   3. There are very practical differences in the effectiveness of one-way, impersonal, and two-way communications. Words spoken face-to-face are better understood. Telephone conversations are effective, but lack the rapport of person-to-person exchanges. The whole person communicates.
   4. Cooperation and communication in an organization go hand in hand. When there is a mutual respect between people, spelling out rules and procedures for communicating is unnecessary.
   5. There are several barriers to effective communications. These include failure to listen with respect and understanding, lack of skill in feedback, and misinterpreting the meanings of words used by the speaker. It is also common

practice to listen to what we want to hear, and tune out things we do not want to hear.

6. Communication is management's chief problem. The supervisor should accept the challenge to communicate more effectively and to improve interagency and intra-agency communications.
7. The supervisor may often plan for and conduct meetings. The planning phase is critical and may determine the success or the failure of a meeting.
8. Speaking before groups usually requires extra effort. Stage fright may never disappear completely, but it can be controlled.

J. Self-Development

1. Every employee is responsible for his own self-development.
2. Toastmaster and toastmistress clubs offer opportunities to improve skills in oral communications.
3. Planning for one's own self-development is of vital importance. Supervisors know their own strengths and limitations better than anyone else.
4. Many opportunities are open to aid the supervisor in his developmental efforts, including job assignments; training opportunities, both governmental and non-governmental—to include universities and professional conferences and seminars.
5. Programmed instruction offers a means of studying at one's own rate.
6. Where difficulties may arise from a supervisor's being away from his work for training, he may participate in televised home study or correspondence courses to meet his self-development needs.

K. Teaching and Training

1. The Teaching Process

Teaching is encouraging and guiding the learning activities of students toward established goals. In most cases this process consists of five steps: preparation, presentation, summarization, evaluation, and application.

a. Preparation

Preparation is two-fold in nature; that of the supervisor and the employee. Preparation by the supervisor is absolutely essential to success. He must know what, when, where, how, and whom he will teach. Some of the factors that should be considered are:

1) The objectives
2) The materials needed
3) The methods to be used
4) Employee participation
5) Employee interest
6) Training aids
7) Evaluation
8) Summarization

Employee preparation consists in preparing the employee to receive the material. Probably the most important single factor in the preparation of the employee is arousing and maintaining his interest. He must know the objectives of the training, why he is there, how the material can be used, and its importance to him.

b. Presentation

In presentation, have a carefully designed plan and follow it. The plan should be accurate and complete, yet flexible enough to meet situations as they arise. The method of presentation will be determined by the particular situation and objectives.

c. Summary

A summary should be made at the end of every training unit and program. In addition, there may be internal summaries depending on the nature of the material being taught. The important thing is that the trainee must always be able to understand how each part of the new material relates to the whole.

d. Application

The supervisor must arrange work so the employee will be given a chance to apply new knowledge or skills while the material is still clear in his mind and interest is high. The trainee does not really know whether he has learned the material until he has been given a chance to apply it. If the material is not applied, it loses most of its value.

e. Evaluation

The purpose of all training is to promote learning. To determine whether the training has been a success or failure, the supervisor must evaluate this learning.

In the broadest sense, evaluation includes all the devices, methods, skills, and techniques used by the supervisor to keep himself and the employees informed as to their progress toward the objectives they are pursuing. The extent to which the employee has mastered the knowledge, skills, and abilities, or changed his attitudes, as determined by the program objectives, is the extent to which instruction has succeeded or failed.

Evaluation should not be confined to the end of the lesson, day, or program but should be used continuously. We shall note later the way this relates to the rest of the teaching process.

2. Teaching Methods

A teaching method is a pattern of identifiable student and instructor activity used in presenting training material.

All supervisors are faced with the problem of deciding which method should be used at a given time.

a. Lecture

The lecture is direct oral presentation of material by the supervisor. The present trend is to place less emphasis on the trainer's activity and more on that of the trainee.

b. Discussion

Teaching by discussion or conference involves using questions and other techniques to arouse interest and focus attention upon certain areas, and by doing so creating a learning situation. This can be one of the most valuable methods because it gives the employees an opportunity to express their ideas and pool their knowledge.

c. Demonstration
The demonstration is used to teach how something works or how to do something. It can be used to show a principle or what the results of a series of actions will be. A well-staged demonstration is particularly effective because it shows proper methods of performance in a realistic manner.

d. Performance
Performance is one of the most fundamental of all learning techniques or teaching methods. The trainee may be able to tell how a specific operation should be performed but he cannot be sure he knows how to perform the operation until he has done so.
As with all methods, there are certain advantages and disadvantages to each method.

e. Which Method to Use
Moreover, there are other methods and techniques of teaching. It is difficult to use any method without other methods entering into it. In any learning situation, a combination of methods is usually more effective than any one method alone.

Finally, evaluation must be integrated into the other aspects of the teaching-learning process.

It must be used in the motivation of the trainees; it must be used to assist in developing understanding during the training; and it must be related to employee application of the results of training.

This is distinctly the role of the supervisor.

www.ingramcontent.com/pod-product-compliance
Lightning Source LLC
Chambersburg PA
CBHW081812300426
44116CB00014B/2330
*9781799310402*